THE

MILITARY WIVES'

COOKBOOK

THE
MILITARY WIVES' COOKBOOK

200 YEARS OF TRADITIONS, RECIPES, AND REMEMBRANCES

CAROLYN QUICK TILLERY

CUMBERLAND HOUSE
NASHVILLE, TENNESSEE

THE MILITARY WIVES' COOKBOOK
PUBLISHED BY CUMBERLAND HOUSE PUBLISHING
431 Harding Industrial Drive
Nashville, Tennessee 37211

Cover design: Roy Roper, wideyedesign
Text design: Mary Sanford

Library of Congress Cataloging-in-Publication Data
Tillery, Carolyn Quick.
  The military wives' cookbook : 200 years of traditions, recipes, and remembrances / Carolyn Quick Tillery.
      p. cm.
  Previously published under title: At freedom's table.
  Includes bibliographical references and index.
  ISBN-13: 978-1-58182-672-2 (hardcover : alk. paper)
  ISBN-10: 1-58182-672-9 (hardcover : alk. paper)
  1. Cookery, American. 2. Cookery. 3. Military spouses—United States—History. I. Tillery, Carolyn Quick. At freedom's table. II. Title.
  TX715.T568255 2008
  641.5973—dc22

                                                                    2008031274

Printed in the United States of America
1 2 3 4 5 6 7—14 13 12 11 10 09 08

CONTENTS
★★★★★

OVER THERE:
AN INTERNATIONAL AFFAIR

HOME FOR THE HOLIDAYS
AND OTHER CELEBRATIONS

UNITED IN SPIRIT

We are sisters—bound, not by blood but by unity of spirit. We share many of the same experiences, hopes and fears. You carry some of my thoughts and I some of yours.

You understand the chest I have labeled "Special Memories" that grows heavier and heavier as it is moved from assignment to assignment.

I understand your box marked "Curtains" which contains several different sets, each of which fit one window in all of the U.S. and Europe.

You know what it is like to plant a tree, knowing that someone else will sample its fruit and enjoy its shade.

I know how you paused while hanging a picture in base housing to hear for a moment . . . the echoing footsteps of the families who preceded you.

I also know that you never write in your address book in ink.

To us, home is not so much a geographic location as it is a place in our hearts.

The evening news is more than a 30-minute blitz of information; it is often the compass that directs our lives.

I have stood in your shoes and you in mine on docks, piers, flight lines, and terminals of every description around the world, waving goodbye and whispering a silent prayer.

To us the words "support our troops" are more than a bumper sticker logo.

We wear yellow ribbons around our hearts every day; because we know that every day a military family is separated by time and distance while that military member stands watch at freedom's door.

We come from all walks of life.

We are homemakers, workers, professionals; and in our number are those who also serve our country on active duty or in the reserves.

We are different and yet we are the same.

Sometimes I see your face in my mirror.

Sometimes you dream my dreams.

So, we come together today to celebrate our similarities and explore our differences in the spirit of friendship and unity. I am honored to count myself among you.

—AUTHOR UNKNOWN

THANKS FOR THE MEMORIES: THE AIR WAR COLLEGE 50TH ANNIVERSARY COOKBOOK

FOREWORD

"The modern [military] wife derives her heritage from the past. She carries with her a trunk-load of memories. . . .She is given this inheritance from those who have gone before, along the wagontrails of the American West and the jet contrails of the contemporary world. From the earliest camp followers of the Revolutionary War, through the companionship of the frontier and the constabulary forces, and the waiting wives of the Vietnam era [and Gulf War and Iraq]—each generation has experienced the trials and joys of service life and added to the contents of the trunk" [*The Air Force Wife Handbook: A Complete Social Guide* by Ann Crossley and Carol A. Keller]

My mother is among those military wives who have gone before, leaving behind a rich and loving legacy. My father was a career Noncommissioned Officer (NCO) in the United States Air Force. He first joined the Army Air Corps at age eighteen and was part of the famous Red Ball Express. When the Air Corps became a separate service, he was on the very cusp of this extremely exciting transition. Wherever his assignments took him, there we were. However, due to my mother's influence, each duty station was more than "just another assignment," it was home.

Among my most cherished childhood memories is that of my mother's home cooking. It was the one constant in our lives as we traveled the world. The aroma of her home cooking greeted my brother and me as we came in from play. It marked every special occasion such as birthdays and anniversaries. It made me feel safe, warm, and loved. The kitchen was, and remains, in my own home, the most important room in the house. It is the last room packed on moving day and the first unpacked. Meals were part of the routine regulating our lives, even when the household goods had not arrived. My mother quickly adapted, learning to cook in tin cans and aluminum foil.

Sometimes she and the international friends she made could be found huddled in the kitchen. Through their exchange of recipes, they shared a bit of themselves and their respective cultures. To this day, my mother maintains close contact with the friends she made in Great Britain and other parts of the world. Over the years they exchanged cards, letters, photographs, and yes, even a recipe or two. Many of those recipes remain family favorites and, like the loving attitude found in a close-knit family, there was always room for one more. They are among my most treasured family heirlooms which I will pass down to my daughter, and hopefully she to her daughter.

Today, I am a military wife and sometimes in retrospect, I have wondered how my mother managed with all of the years of travel so far from family and home. I now know that she was blessed with the support of friends, family, and very special military wives who shared her love of country and military life.

ACKNOWLEDGMENTS

First, giving all honor to God and Jesus Christ, my Lord and Savior, I wish to express appreciation to my husband, J. R. Tillery, Colonel, USAF, and daughter, Ashley Elizabeth. My father, John Gordon Quick, grandmother, Mrs. Mable Gordon and the affable "Missy" are no longer in our presence; however, their memory will always be a part of our lives. Thanks to Ronald and Julia Pitkin for believing in and embracing this project. Thanks to Dixie Paronto, Vandenberg AFB librarian for her invaluable research support. A very special thanks to those women who have gone before me, blazing trails and offering words of encouragement along the way: my mother, Mrs. Delores Quick, Mrs. Marty Kelley, Mrs. Suzanne Smith, Mrs. Betty Karle, Mrs. Candace Lanning, and a host of other women. I thank you for your exemplary lives and commitment to service life.

INTRODUCTION

My experience as an Air Force spouse has been forged and shaped by those who went before me, countless, sometimes faceless, and often nameless women of amazing strength, courage, and vision. Committed to God, country, and family, they too gave their last measure of strength as they fought with the courage of their convictions.

AMERICAN REVOLUTION

If the first shots of the American Revolution were heard around the world, it is almost certain that they reverberated in the hearts of Colonial women, preparing to send sons, husbands, and sweethearts into battle. Sometimes following their loved ones, and seeking to provide something more than moral support, they cooked, washed, mended clothing, and tended to the sick and wounded. Some also served in battle. They carried cartridges in their pinned-up aprons and stood ready to retrieve the colors from the ground or from an incapacitated color bearer, should the need arise. They also were alert to the opportunity to seize and ably use an unattended musket as well.

"Even the weamin [women] had firelocks," wrote a British soldier following a sniping on the road from Lexington to Concord. And, it was reported to the British General, Lord Cornwallis, that, "if we destroyed all the men in North America, we should have enough to do to conquer the weamin."

"The Heroine of Groton," Anna Warner, was the wife of Captain Elija Bailey. Her fearless efforts to aid the wounded after the massacre of Fort Griswold earned her this title. Without concern for personal safety, she ventured forth from the relative security of her home to collect material for soldier's bandages. Courageous women, such as Anna, also provided front-line combat support by loading guns, without hesitation, and taking up arms when necessary.

Mary Ludwig Hayes McCauley (Molly Pitcher) served with her husband, John Hayes, in the Pennsylvania State Regiment of Artillery for seven years. All women camp followers were addressed as "Molly" followed by their last name. However, during the Battle of Monmouth on June 28, 1778, Mary so distinguished herself on the field of battle by carrying pitchers of water to quench the thirst of her husband and other soldiers, they nicknamed her "Molly Pitcher." During the course of battle, "Molly Pitcher" used the water to cool down the red hot cannons. In addition, she swabbed cannon bores and loaded shot. And when her husband was seriously wounded and unable to attend his position, she ignored her own wounds to operate the cannon until the battle ended. Replacements eventually took her position but she remained as a rammer until an artilleryman relieved her. According to legend, she was later presented to George Washington, who praised her courage. In the decades following her unselfish acts of heroism, American artillerymen have remembered her in the following toast:

> . . . *Drunk in a beverage richer and stronger than was poured that day from Molly Pitcher's pitcher.*

Despite the evidence supporting her existence, the true identity or actual existence of "Molly Pitcher" continues to be debated. I prefer to believe that she did exist, if only in the indomitable spirit of the women fighting and contributing to the great cause of freedom.

Margaret Cocharan Corbin stepped up to the artillery on November 16, 1776, when her husband fell by her side during a British Hessian attack on Fort Washington. She took his place and performed his duties at the cannon. Her heroic actions were appreciated by the officers of the army and noted by Congress by passage in July 1779 of the following resolution:

> *Resolved, that Margaret Corbin, wounded and disabled at the battle of Fort Washington while she heroically filled the post of her husband, who was killed by her side, serving a piece of artillery, do receive during her natural life . . . one half of the monthly pay drawn by a soldier in the service of these States; and that she now receive out of public store one suit of clothes, or value thereof in money.*

During the heat of yet another battle, Angelica Vrooman sat in a tent with a bullet mold, some lead, and an iron spoon calmly making bullets. Mary Haigidorn, in refusing an order for women and children to retreat to the long cellar during an attack, said, "Captain, I shall not go to the cellar should the enemy come. I will take up a spear, which I can use, as well as any man and help defend the fort." Yielding to her determination, the captain replied, "then take a spear, Mary, and be ready at the pickets to repel an attack." Mary held her position at the pickets until a wild explosion of hurrahs for the American flag brought reassurances of security and well being. This first generation of courageous military wives followed the Continental Army and became known as "Camp Followers."

When Martha Washington, wife of our first Commander-in-Chief, joined the general at his winter quarters, she always arrived in a carriage bulging with food and medicine. Martha was with her husband in Morristown, Valley Forge, and Newburgh. In later years, she recounted hearing the opening and closing sounds of every campaign.

Mrs. Washington also hosted small dinners and held bi-weekly open houses for her husband's officers. Other officer's wives soon followed her example. On occasion, Martha would gather only the officer's wives and they would knit, sew, share recipes, and in this manner entertain one another in this first and informal officer's wives club.

THE WAR OF 1812

Lucy Brewer, who served as "George Baker" on the *U.S.S. Constitution* during its grand first battle in the War of 1812, was the first woman marine. However, it would be more than 200 years before the Marine Corps seriously recruited women.

Not all wives fought in battle; some women simply sought to marry, establish a frontier home, and raise a family with the man she loved. Even this simple ambition was often fraught with difficulty and danger. Obtaining a plentiful and well-balanced supply of food was a challenge, giving birth and raising children was difficult in remote areas, where housing was crude at best, and the specter of death and early widowhood a constant companion.

In one sad tale, Captain Burdett Terrett was dismounting from his horse when his gun accidentally discharged. As his wife rushed to his side, he declared, "I know you, I'm not much hurt." And as she recited the Lord's Prayer over him, he died in her arms. Two weeks earlier, their one-month-old son had died within three hours of the onset of illness. It is not surprising that parents often discouraged and even prohibited their daughters from marrying soldiers. Abandoning amenities, they joined their husbands on the new frontier and brought with them what they could of the small comforts of their eastern homes. Like the design on the dinner plates that often accompanied them, the pattern of their actions would be repeated for generations to come.

Sarah Knox Taylor married a young lieutenant by the name of Jefferson Davis. The marriage took place over the stringent objection of her father, General Zachary Taylor. The general, who knew firsthand the hardships facing a frontier wife, was fearful for his second daughter's health and safety. Within three months of the wedding, the general's worst fears were realized when Sarah died of malaria. Taylor and Davis did not reconcile until they fought together in Mexico.

MEXICAN-AMERICAN WAR

> *We are in our own house now and almost settled. When one has only a few pieces of furniture it does not take long to get them in place. . . . The house is of logs . . . and was built originally for an officer's mess. [Frances Roe, Camp Supply Indian Territory, 1872]*

By the 1830s an officer's quarters consisted of a one-room cabin with a dirt floor.

> *Our dining room has a sand floor, and almost every night little white toadstools grow up all along the base of the long walls. [Frances Roe, Letters from an Officer's Wife]*

If an officer's wife was lucky, she would find quarters with a wood plank floor and walls consisting of rough, unhewn logs.

All of the logs are of cottonwood and have the bark on, and the army of bugs that hide underneath the bark during the day and march upon us at night is to be dreaded. . . .

The roof often involved no more than a framework of logs over which a sheet of canvas was stretched. Cooking was done on small sheet or cast-iron stoves and boards laid on sawhorses, covered with a white and crisply starched linen tablecloth, served as an elegant table. One wife proudly wrote of serving a five-course meal in her tented quarters—borrowing linen and serving pieces from other garrison wives.

Due to the high cost of transportation, furniture was limited to makeshift pieces—readily sold or left behind. An easy chair was quickly crafted by stuffing a cutout camp barrel with moss and covering it with calico. "Cupboards" were constructed by lining packing crates with calico and nailing them to the wall. The cupboards were then used to display a few cherished pieces of china, silver, or crystal.

However, wives often hesitated to make their homes too attractive or comfortable because of an army practice known as "ranking." When a senior ranking officer arrived on post he could take the quarters of any soldier he outranked. Ranking then had a domino effect because the dispossessed soldier could then do likewise to any soldier he outranked.

Camp Supply Indian Territory
June 1872

It seems as if I have to write constantly of unpleasant experiences, but what else can I do since unpleasant experiences are ever coming along? This time I must tell you that Faye has been turned out of quarters—"ranked out," as it is spoke of in the Army. But it amounts to the same thing, and means we have been driven out of our house and home, bag and baggage, because a captain wanted that one set of quarters. . . . We had been in the house only three weeks and worked so hard during that time to make it comfortable. . . .

One morning at ten o'clock I received a note from Faye, written at the guard house, saying that his set of quarters had been selected by a cavalry officer who had just arrived on post, and every article of ours must be out by one o'clock! Also that, as he was officer of the guard, it would be impossible for him to assist me.

I was dazed. . . . All that was possible . . . was almost to throw things out in a side yard. . . . All things big and small were out . . . and just in time to avoid collision with . . . soldiers of the incoming cavalry officer, who commenced taking furniture and boxes in the house at precisely that hour. . . . I sat down on a chair in the yard with the little dog by me, thinking, I remember that the chair was our own property and no one had a right to object to me being there. . . .

Just as I reached the very lowest depths of my misery and woe, Mrs. Vincent appeared, and Faye almost immediately after. We three went to Mrs. Vincent's house for luncheon, and I in fact remained there until we came to this house. There came a ludicrous turn of all this unpleasantness. . . . It was great fun the next day to see moving up and down the officer's line all sorts of household goods. But no one took our house from Captain Park, much to my disappointment, and he still has it.

The house that we are in now is built of cedar logs, and was the commanding officer's house at one time. It has a long hall running through the center, and on the left side Major Hunt and his family have the four rooms, and we have the two on the right side. Our kitchen is across the yard and was a chicken house not very long ago. It has no floor, of course, so we had loads of dirt dug out and filled in again with clean white sand, and now after the log walls have been scraped and whitened, and a number of shelves put up, it is really quite nice. [Frances Roe]

Ten years later:

Fort Shaw Montana Territory,
November, 1882

You will be shocked, I know, when you hear that we are houseless—homeless—that for the second time Faye has been ranked out of quarters! At Camp Supply the turnout was swift, but this time it has been long and drawn out. . . . Major Bagley came here from Fort Maginnis, and as we had rather expected that he would select our house, we made no preparations for winter previous to his coming. But as soon as he reached the post, and many times, he assured that nothing could possibly induce him to disturb us. Having faith in Major Bagley's word, the house was cleaned from top to bottom, much painting and calcimining having been done. All the floors were painted and hard-oiled, and everyone knows what a discomfort that always brings about, and we were about to settle down to the enjoyment of a tidy, cheerful little home when Major Bagley appeared, . . . and within two hours Faye was notified that his quarters had been selected by him! . . . We are at present in two rooms and a shed that hap-

pens to be unoccupied. . . . I can assure you that I am more than cross. . . . I have made up my mind unalterably to one thing—the nice little dinner I had expected to give Major and Mrs. Bagley later on, will be for the other people, friends who have less honey to dispose of. [Frances Roe]

Enlisted wives, faced with fewer options, often worked to help make ends meet. Often occupying the position of company laundress, they received pay and drew an extra daily ration, better enabling the family to survive on the soldier's low pay. Other wives served as cooks.

Other women such as Cathay Williams, born into slavery, were pressed into service during the Civil War. Eventually sent to Washington to be a cook and laundress for Gen. Phil Sheridan and his staff, Cathay accompanied them when the general made his raids in the Shenandoah Valley. Following the Civil War, Congress authorized six all-black units of the military. Collectively, the 9th and 10th Cavalry and the 38th, 39th, 40th, and 41st Infantry became known as "Buffalo Soldiers." It is thought that this name was given them by Native American warriors who admired the soldiers' fierce fighting spirit and courage, which they thought to be like that of the buffalo. Following the Civil War, Cathay joined the 38th United States Infantry under the name William Cathay. Cathay enlisted because she wanted to make her own living and not be dependent on relations and friends. By enlisting she became the first and perhaps only woman Buffalo Soldier. She continued to serve until she became ill and a physical examination revealed her to be a woman. Following her discharge, she would eventually marry. However, she continued to make her own living, including running a boarding house in Raton, New Mexico, where she died at age eighty-two in 1924.

CIVIL WAR

During the Civil War, women served in much the same capacity as in previous wars. Lucy Ware Webb Hayes, wife of future president Rutherford B. Hayes, won the name "Mother Lucy" from the men of the 23rd Ohio Volunteer Infantry who served under her husband's command. She is fondly remembered for camp visits during which she ministered to the sick and dying and comforted the homesick.

Marie "French Mary" Tebe followed her husband, Bernardo, into battle. When he enlisted in the 27th Pennsylvania Volunteer Infantry Company I, she enlisted as a Vivandiere, providing supplies to the soldiers. And on occasion, she cooked, washed, and mended soldier's clothing. However, she also was under fire thirteen times. She was in the Battle of Bull Run, witnessed the carnage at Fair Oaks, was present during McClellan's campaign, and finally was wounded at Fredericksburg. For her efforts in assisting the wounded, she was awarded the Kearny Cross. She survived Chancellorsville and Gettys-

MARY E. WALKER   MARY BOWSER

burg. And following the Battle of Spotsylvania's Bloody Angle an officer of the 8th Ohio Infantry would recount:

> I looked around. Sure enough there was a woman! She was about 25 years of age. . . dressed in a Zouave uniform of the Vivandiere style. She was wonderfully courageous or else she did not understand the danger . . . the shower of musket balls, shrapnel and every sort of projectile falling in the midst of us was trying to the nerves of our coolest.

During this period, the number of paid positions available to women expanded and their contributions were officially recognized. President Andrew Johnson awarded Dr. Mary E. Walker the nation's highest honor—the Congressional Medal of Honor. The accompanying citation reads in part: "She faithfully served as a contract surgeon in the services of the United States, and devoted herself with much patriotic zeal to the sick and wounded, both in the field and hospitals, to the detriment of her own health, and endured hardships as a prisoner of war four months in a southern prison while acting as a contract surgeon."

From medicine to espionage, women fearlessly served their country. Mary Elizabeth Bowser, a freed slave, was one of the Union's highest placed and most productive espionage agents of the Civil War. As a servant in the Confederate White House in Richmond, Virginia, she gathered critical information by reading war dispatches and listening to conversations relating to strategy and Confederate movements as she cleaned house and waited on Confederate soldiers. Mary Bowser then relayed the information to the Union's Richmond spymaster, Thomas McNiven. McNiven, who also operated a bakery, credited Bowser with being one of the best sources of wartime information. "She had a photographic mind . . . everything she saw on the rebel president's desk, she could repeat word for word. She made a point of coming out to my wagon when I made deliveries at the Davis's home to drop information."

Susie King Taylor married a sergeant in the First South Carolina Volunteers, a U.S. black regiment, and served as a nurse and laundress. According to Taylor, "I enrolled as company laundress, but did very little of it because I was busy doing other things through the camp. . . . I learned to handle a musket very well while in the regiment, and I learned to shoot straight and often hit the target. . . . I was able to take a gun apart and put it back together again."

POST-CIVIL WAR ERA

In the post–Civil War era, the army went West to help open and secure the new frontier.

> *Life in the Army is certainly full of surprises! . . . for three weeks we lived en famille and intimately, with Jefferson Davis! . . . You probably can remember a little of what I wrote you at the time—how we were boarding with his niece in her splendid home when he came to visit her. I remember so well the day he arrived. . . . When we went down to dinner that night I was almost shivering from nervousness, although the air was excessively warm. And then as we went into the large dining room, Faye in his very bluest, shiniest uniform, looked as if he might be Uncle Sam himself. I was afraid of something unpleasant coming up, for although Mrs. Porterfield and her daughter were women of culture and refinement, they were also rebels to the very quick and never failed at any given time to remind one that their uncle was "President" Davis! . . . But there was nothing to fear whatever. A tall, thin old man came forward with Mrs. Porterfield to meet us—a courtly gentleman of the old Southern school—who, apparently had never heard of the Civil War, and who, if he noticed the blue uniform at all, did not take the slightest interest in what it represented. After greeting me with grave dignity, he turned to Faye and grasped his hand firmly and cordially, the whole expression of his face softening just a little. I have always thought that he was deeply moved*

> *to see the Federal blue under such cordial circumstances. . . . [E]very warm evening after dinner, during the time he was at the house, Jefferson Davis and Faye would sit on the grand marble porch and smoke and tell of little incidents that had occurred at West Point when each had been a cadet there. At sometimes they would almost touch what was left of a massive pillar . . . that had been shattered and racked by pieces of shell from the U.S. gunboats, one piece still imbedded in the white marble. [Frances Roe]*

Also following her husband, General George Armstrong Custer, was Elizabeth "Libbie" Bacon Custer. Libbie, who was with her husband during the Civil War, claimed to be the "only officer's wife who always followed the regiment." From letters, journals, and books, she gives a firsthand account of frontier life as a military wife. She and her husband lived at Fort Riley, in Kansas, from 1866 until 1871 as the U.S. Seventh Cavalry protected settlers and railroad workers on the western plains. During those years, she survived prairie fires, an earthquake, mutiny by Fort Riley soldiers, and a cholera epidemic. Yet, according to Libbie, "there was never a suggestion of returning to a well-regulated climate." In 1871, the U.S. Seventh Cavalry was reassigned to Kentucky for a brief period, but Libbie observed, "A true cavalryman feels that a life in the saddle on the free open plain is his legitimate existence." In the spring of 1873, the U.S. Seventh Cavalry was ordered to Fort Lincoln in the Dakota Territory. Just three years later in May of 1876, Libbie Custer last saw her husband and his regiment as they marched toward Montana and the Little Bighorn River while the regimental band played "The Girl I Left Behind Me."

From the very first days of their Civil War marriage, Libbie followed her husband to every military encampment. She became the first military wife to do so. Moreover, as an early military wife, she helped establish precedence for "accompanied tours of duty." Not only did she follow the general to every camp, but she often set up housekeeping in a tent. Tents were quite commonly used to house military members and their families when a regiment was relocating.

> *Once again we have our trunks packed for the long trip to Montana. . . . We are almost one week coming out, but finally got here yesterday morning. As soon as possible after we arrived, the tents were unpacked and put up. . . . This morning the camp looks like a little white city—streets and all. [Frances Roe, Corinne, Utah Territory, 1877]*

> *Our camp mess has been started, and we will be very comfortable, I think. . . . I am making covers for the bed, trunk and folding table, of dark blue cretonne with white figures, which carries out the color scheme of the folding chairs and will give a little air of cheeriness to the tent, and of the same material I am*

> *making pockets that can be pinned to the side walls of the tent, in which various things can be tucked at night. These covers and big pockets will be folded and put in a roll of bedding every morning. [Frances Roe]*

Tenting on the plains could be particularly challenging during storms, which blew down tents and drenched their occupants' belongings.

> *The day was so cold and our tents were closed tight to keep the heat in, so we knew nothing of the storm until it struck us with such fierceness it seemed as if the tents must go down. . . . The wind seemed to get worse every minute, and once in a while there would be a loud "boom" when a big Sibley tent would be ripped open, and then would come the yells from the men as they scrambled for their belongings. [Frances Roe]*

After one such incident, Libbie was forced to wear her husband's dry underclothes beneath her dress, and his cavalry boots while her own shoes dried. Undaunted by the inconvenience, Libbie would write,

> *The tent might go down nightly for all I cared. . . . Every thought of separation departed, and I gave myself up to the happiest hours, clamping about the tent in those old troop boots, indifferent whether my shoes ever dried.*

On each expedition she rode alongside him, nearly to the line of battle, before returning to camp and awaiting his return from battle.

In Libbie's own words, "I was not in the least prepared for the seriousness or importance of my husband's command. I was completely overwhelmed with intense anxiety for my husband, bewilderment over the strange situation, and terror of the desolate place. The wives of the officers in the regular Army were kind but unconsciously a trifle condescending to the wives, who, through no fault of their own, were "new-comer brides." I confess that I was awed, but after having been thoroughly disciplined by these women, I received some excellent hints as to my future military life."

It is likely that some of those hints involved preparing for a permanent change of station, or "moving day" in civilian lingo. Leaving a post was often as challenging as arriving.

Fort Shaw, Montana Territory
May 1888

> *There can be only two more days at this dear old post, where we have been so happy, and I want them to pass as quickly as possible, and have some of the misery over. . . . These moves are of the greatest importance to army officers, and many times the change of station is a mere nothing in comparison to the fit-*

ting of a house, something that is never taken into consideration when the pay of the army is under discussion.

Our house is perfectly forlorn, with just a few absolute necessaries in it for our use while here. Everything has been sold or given away, and all that is left to us are our trunks and army chests.

Some fine china and a few pieces of cut glass I kept, and even those are packed in small boxes and in the chests. The general selling-out business has been funny. No one in the regiment possessed many things that they cared to move East with them, and as we did not desire to turn our houses into second-hand shops . . . it was decided that everything to be sold could be moved to the large hall. Our only purchasers were people from Sun River Crossing, and a few ranches that are some distance from the post, and it was soon discovered that anything at all nice was passed by them, so we became sharp—bunching the worthless with the good—and that worked beautifully and things sold fast. [Frances Roe]

One family's loss was often another's gain.

There was in the family a mania for auctions. A red flag out in front of a house . . . set us in a perfect flutter, and was a sad disquieter of domestic peace, so hard did it *seem to pass it by. While stationed at Fort Leavenworth there was a wide scope for the exercise of this family predilection. Sometimes the queerest imaginable articles came home, and if one of the family of two had not had a hand in the excitement of the bidding and purchasing, there was very likely to follow an inquiry common in domestic circles—"What on earth do you ever suppose one can ever do with that?"—some scorn underlying the emphasized "that." [Libbie Custer]*

The selling out tradition continues at military thrift shops and weekend yard sales in the military housing area. And this writer has received a similar greeting upon returning from one of these outings with a "great find!"

Once a huge bowl—too big for any ordinary occasion—made its entrée with just such a welcome. But a great "find" it proved eventually; there came to be no festive occasion complete without it. My dish was the belle; it was invited to more dinners than anyone in the garrison. [Libbie Custer, Following the Guidon*]*

Despite the challenges of arriving, departing, and living on the frontier, more wives followed—as did the Korean War and World War I. And the women—they followed and even more began leading the way!

With the modern era and World War II came introduction of the airplane into military strategy and doctrine. One of the era's legends, Major General H. H. "Hap" Arnold, commanded the flying unit at Fairfield Depot, Wright Field, Ohio. (The very place where, almost a decade earlier, Hap was taught to fly by none other than the Wright brothers!) The Arnolds' two-story farmhouse, complete with a large eat-in, country-style kitchen and glassed-in porches, was ideal for entertaining. Early aviation luminaries such as Carl "Tooey" Spaatz and Ira C. Eaker visited the couple there. And on Sundays, Orville Wright would occasionally drop by for dinner, just as Arnold had dined at the Wrights' home when the brothers were teaching him to fly. During the Christmas holidays, when the farmhouse was aglow with holiday festivities, Hap, in accordance with his German family tradition, would bake cookies in the shapes of the Christmas Nativity scene. Family and friends took part in the festivity by decorating and, of course, devouring the cookies.

In the late afternoon and on weekends Hap and his wife, Eleanor, or "Bee" as she was known, extended an open house invitation to young officers. After Hap became Chief of the Army Corps, Bee implemented a service organization that helped young wives through the war years. Soon more than forty thousand wives nationwide were volunteering. Today, the Air Force Aid Society continues to assist millions of U.S. service members and their families.

Blacks, however, were forbidden from serving in the U.S. Air Service, an elite officer flying corps. Despite this ban, the War Department began training African-American pilots at the legendary Tuskegee Institute in 1941. The 99th Pursuit Squadron and the 332 Fighter Group served with distinction as part of the segregated service, flying over 15,553 sorties and completing 1,578 bomber escort missions over Europe with the 12th Tactical U.S. Army Air Force. Known in later years as the Tuskegee Airmen, they destroyed 409 enemy aircraft and did not lose a single bomber to enemy fighters in 200 escort bombing missions. Because of their reputation, bomber crews reverently referred to them as Red Tail Angels.

Following the war, the military led the way as they integrated the Air Corps with Executive Order 9981. During this period of dramatic social change, military spouses began to seriously question their traditional roles while demanding support and recognition of their own needs. In 1980, Barbara Allen, wife of General Lew Allen Jr., Air Force Chief of Staff, founded the Spouses Issues Group. This group of women came together to share information, voice concerns, and make recommendations. Today's Family Support and Military Spouse Employment Centers are a direct result of their efforts.

These women and their contributions are part of the legacy and tradition of the life of a military wife. Like those who went before them, they often balanced maintaining home and hearth, raising a family, managing a business, and supporting a great cause. Whether participating in the birth of a nation or making recommendations that influence decisions at the national level, they also found time to extend themselves in friendship and hospitality.

MILITARY FAMILIES: THEIR SERVICE AND SACRIFICE

My heartfelt thanks to the families who sacrifice so much—you are patriots in a quiet, strong way and you make all the difference. You support us, even though we work long hours that often interrupt your plans. When we are away, you hold our families together. When we get tired, you remind us how important our jobs are. When we receive recognition, you stand in the background. You define us and sustain us. You promise us the tomorrows for which we strive. [Chairman of the Joint Chiefs of Staff Gen. Peter Pace]

My earliest family memory involves my father coming home in uniform from his office at Ramstein Air Force Base, Germany, where he was a senior enlisted member, and my mom preparing meals or reviewing homework in the kitchen of our stairwell housing. I also remember dressing up and sitting on my mom's lap to take a photograph for the passport necessary for us to sail back to the United States. We would travel on many more boats, planes, trains, and automobiles to various locations around the world during the course of my dad's military career. It was a transient and mobile lifestyle that I would eventually learn to love and adopt as my own.

Since that time, a life of service is all I have known—first as an officer on active duty, then as the spouse of an active duty member, and now as a DoD civilian serving the families of our active duty members fighting the Global War on Terrorism (GWOT), perhaps the most important defense of democracy in the free world since our fathers and mothers defended against totalitarianism and fascism during World War II. Tom Brokaw referred to them as the "Greatest Generation," and for good reason—their courage and sacrifice brought the world back from the brink and set captive peoples and nations free. In so doing, they ably modeled the ideals, the nobility of character, and the indomitable American fighting spirit that has kept our American flag flying free for more than 225 years. Because of their service and sacrifice, not only has the flag flown free over our own nation, but it was first in combat to defend the freedom of our allies and others for whom self-determination was denied. That generation has now passed the baton to their sons and daughters, whom I am blessed to serve.

Since the initial publication of this book, I was much honored to be selected to serve as the Chief of the Family Readiness Program, Headquarters, United States Central Command, which enhances the quality of life for service members and their families by giving them access to services and programs supportive of the mobile military lifestyle and prepares them for all phases of deployment. I have a unique opportunity to give back even as it was given to me and my family while my dad served on active duty. Back then the Airmen and Family Readiness Center was an all-volunteer force of friends and neighbors looking out for each other because it was and remains the military way. As you will see throughout this book, the importance of military families to service life is far from a new phenomenon. The historic and steadfast support of military families in times of peace, crisis, and war has always been a source of inspiration.

Today's modern military families face the special challenges associated with long deployments, family separations, and frequent relocations with great courage and steadfast resolve. The military downsizing of the last decade has increased the likelihood that each soldier will eventually be sent on an extended deployment. As a result, the emotional trauma of sending a loved one to war is experienced by military families on an unprecedented scale since the end of the Gulf War. Yet they can be seen at ports, railway stations, and air fields around the country proudly waving an American flag and brushing away a tear as they kiss a loved one goodbye.

As a result of the selfless dedication of these families we are mission ready and able to take the fight to the enemy. And according to Representative Thelma Drake, (R-Virginia) "Certainly, the military spouse is the backbone, the moral support for our military men and women. . . . They can't do their best fighting for our freedom and defending us if they have to worry about what's going on at home." As a family readiness professional, I am keenly aware of the service and sacrifice of our military families. Ruth Ellen Patton Totten, widow of Major General James W. Totten and daughter of the late General George S. Patton, perhaps expressed it best when she wrote,

> *You ladies have had your inconveniences and troubles and, to put it mildly, the ladies of the old Army had theirs. They faced for their time, what you face in yours.*
>
> *It is hard to be a good army wife because you do share so much in your husband's life. It's hard to be a young lieutenant's wife, living in a strange place with no money, no family closeby, and no old friends to lean on. It's hard to be an in-between wife, sweating out orders, the children's schooling, hardship tours, promotion, and always—separation. It's hard to be a senior officer's wife, watching your loved one growing older, greyer, and wearier while putting more and more of himself into the service . . . knowing that the final acknowledgment of a lifetime of service is, for all, a flag-draped coffin, the volley, and the bugle's lonely farewell.*
>
> *But the rewards are very great. You are living in the company of heroes and heroines who have chosen to practice a life of service to their country. You belong to a select group of Americans . . . and their daughters and granddaughters are among you today.*

Those daughters and granddaughters are likely to move, on average, every two years, and as a result be unable to work consistently for one employer or build a conventional résumé. Their uniformed spouse will deploy anywhere from one to six times. And in one of the most dramatic shifts, our citizen-soldiers, once largely considered a strategic reserve, now deploy regularly in support of our efforts in Afghanistan and Iraq. And currently nearly 1.3 million Guard and Reserve personnel serve. Half of the children of

CAROLYN QUICK TILLERY (FRONT RIGHT): FIRST GRADE STUDENT AT RAMSTEIN AIR FORCE BASE

OUR STUDENT "CAMPUS" AT RAMSTEIN CONSISTED OF A SERIES OF QUONSET HUTS, DESIGNED IN 1941 WHEN THE UNITED STATES NAVY NEEDED AN ALL-PURPOSE, LIGHT-WEIGHT BUILDING THAT COULD BE SHIPPED ANY-WHERE AND ASSEMBLED WITHOUT SKILLED LABOR.

these personnel, or 1.2 million children—the vast majority of whom are under the age of seven—have one or both parents deployed at any given time. Yet despite the frequent stressors of deployment and or frequent moves they continue to test ahead of the national norm.

My experiences as a military spouse were forged and shaped by those who went before me, countless, sometimes faceless, often nameless women of amazing strength, grace, courage, and vision. Committed to God, country, and family, they too gave their last measure of strength to this great experiment in self-government—a democracy known and respected throughout the world as the United States of America. So as an old guard former military spouse who stood tall on their shoulders, I take off my hat and my gloves to salute those who went before me. In seeking to honor our military children, spouses, and families, I have developed three distinct table settings inspired by the table setting and ceremony performed at dining-outs and other special occasions that recognizes the sacrifice of fallen service members.

MILITARY CHILDREN: THEY SERVE TOO

I'm a military child; I stay strong when my dad goes away. . . . My family's support helps me carry on. . . . Whenever we move, I start over again, I have to go to a new school, and make new friends. [From "I Serve Too" by Kiara, a sixth grade student in Louisiana, 2004]

United States military members answer the call to service every day as they defend freedom around the world. That service often comes at a great personal sacrifice—not only for the service member, but also for his or her family. As a family readiness professional, a retired military spouse, and a former military brat, I am keenly aware of and can readily identify with the sacrifices made by the spouses and children of our uniformed service members.

The mobile military lifestyle inherent to military service and increased deployments as we continue to fight the Global War on Terrorism are among the many challenges that confront our military families. In recognizing the service and sacrifice of our military families First Lady Laura Bush noted,

> *All of those who serve in our military deserve our utmost respect—and so do those who serve behind the front lines—their families and children. As I've traveled to military bases, I've become aware of the special challenges that face military families. Like many families and like some of you, President Bush and I have moved a lot—five times—and we've lived in six different homes. Moving, packing, and hoping our children will be happy in a new home is something many of us can relate to. And so is change. For us and for military families, change means moving and starting over; but it also means new friends, and new challenges. A military family's determination to make a home wherever they are matches their loved ones' devotion to duty. Separation and transition are part of a military child's life, and they accept their duty with brave hearts.*
>
> *There are more than one million military children around the world, and eight hundred thousand children go to public and Department of Defense (DoD) schools in your neighborhoods. A military child may move as many as six to nine times from kindergarten to high school. By her senior year, a child will have attended six elementary and middle schools and two or more high schools—often in different states. This constant change has a huge impact— both academically and socially—on children. Many school districts are not prepared to help military children transition from one school to another. There is no systematic process that ensures that records, grades, and accomplishments transfer with a military child. And this is a problem for many children, not just military children, in our highly mobile society. Many students lose their class rank after transferring, and many fall behind in class requirements because their new school will not grant credits for their previous coursework. Many children who were athletes at their old school miss the opportunity to play sports because they miss tryouts.*
>
> *When an Air Force officer was asked what he needed in Iraq, he said, "Please don't send cookies, care packages, or socks. Just help take care of our children." Our country has always supported its military—in times of war there were community efforts to roll bandages and knit socks. We have a great capacity to care for the home front. Now is the time for a new Victory garden.*

In this garden, we can tend to the needs of military children. [Mrs. Bush's Remarks at the Congressional Club First Lady's Luncheon, April 22, 2004]

TABLE SETTING FOR A MILITARY CHILD

In 1986, Secretary of Defense Caspar Weinberger recognized the importance of military-connected children and their role in military families when he established April as the "Month of the Military Child," underscoring the important role military children play in the armed forces community. This is a time to applaud children for their daily sacrifices and the challenges they overcome.

The Military Child's Table Setting, inspired by the ceremony performed at dining-outs for fallen service members, honors the sacrifices and contribution of our military children. The potted flowering plant symbolizes that they flower and flourish where planted. The hand spade inserted in the pot recognizes that they may be transplanted to a new location any place in the world at a moment's notice, where they become fully immersed in the culture, make new friends, and acclimate themselves to a new school. The birthday cake and unlit candles and baseball and ballet slippers represent the fact that sometimes special occasions are missed by one or both parents while serving their country. The family photo depicting a child or children with their uniformed parent(s) represents the foundation of our country's strength—families united in their commitment to national service and willing to make any sacrifice, both at home and abroad, to ensure that our flag continues to fly free.

CHILD OF A SOLDIER

My hometown is nowhere,
my friends are everywhere.
I grew up with knowledge
that home is where the heart is
and the family with no independence
on the dwelling.
Mobility is my way of life.
Some would wonder about my roots,
yet they are as deep and strong
as the mighty oak.
I sink them quickly absorbing all an area offers
and hopefully giving enrichment in retrospect.
Friendships are formed in hours
and kept for decades.
I will never grow up with someone,
but I will mature with many.

Be it inevitable that paths part,
there is constant hope that they will meet again.
Love of country . . .
respect and pride fill my being
when Old Glory passes in review.
As I stand to honor that flag,
so I also stand in honor of all soldiers and,
most especially,
to the parents whose life created mine.
Because of this . . .
I have shared in the rich heritage of Army life.

AUTHOR UNKNOWN

A SPOUSE'S THANKS AND DADDY'S DEPLOYMENT KISSES

The following is a letter received from one of our CENTCOM spouses detailing a charming and effective method of helping kids deal with deployment.

Mrs. Tillery, Thank you so much for all the information you provided! I am glad there are so many helpful, supportive programs for spouses and families of deployed soldiers! I will definitely try and make use of them as often as possible! A friend of mine at Fort Campbell gave me a tip that has helped my three-year-old tremendously. I have filled a mason jar with Hershey kisses equal to the number of days left in Daddy's deployment. Each morning she gets a kiss from Daddy and when all his kisses are gone, she knows Daddy will be home. Granted . . . I will be able to add some kisses should he be extended! This is my husband's first deployment since Desert Storm. I am a little rusty with the whole thing, but needless to say, I have managed to get the brakes and tires fixed on my vehicle and even jump-started my son's car! I would be happy to help with FRG-related activities if I can. . . . Anyway, thank you for the information and keep me in mind for any mild volunteer opportunities or if I can provide a meal to a family who has just had a baby or similar circumstance, I would love to help! Thanks again for your hard work!

Victoria Glynn

THE MILITARY SPOUSE'S TABLE SETTING

This table setting is the manner in which we say, "Welcome, you are one of us now; we stand by you—through good times and bad." It is also a way of bidding a fond farewell to old friends. Always at its center is a circle of friendship and sense of community.

The hand-woven basket represents the sometimes sparse simplicity of service life and the strength and useful service created when our patriotic pride, sacrifice, and commitment is interwoven with that of our spouses, family, and other military families. It represents an interwoven pattern of service that has been our tradition for more than two hundred years.

The American wildflowers contained in the basket represent the military spouse—strong and resilient. Found in the most unlikely of places such as craggy mountainous areas with barely enough soil to sustain them, or dry, sandy, barren areas where nothing else worthwhile seems to grow, the military wife, like an American wildflower, takes root, flourishes, and brings beauty to her surroundings. The strand of pearls represents our ability to produce beauty and comfort from discomfort. The coffeepot or teapot represents our heritage of hospitality, begun when early wives, far from home in desolate places, came together to share a cup of coffee or tea, a favorite recipe, and the burdens of their commitment to service life. The tradition, dating back to those turn-of-the-century army posts where a shared cup of coffee brought a welcome respite, continues to this day.

The single lit taper represents the vigilant hope of a waiting family. The cup represents our common cup of shared experience. What one drinks, we all in a sense share. It contains a slice of lemon representing the bitterness of the sacrifice we, on occasion, are called upon to make. Finally, the sterling teaspoon represents the purity of love for God, family, and country. The sugar contained in it represents the sweetness of the love and friendships that helps in removing the bitterness from our shared cup.

THE MILITARY FAMILY TABLE SETTING

Any place where love abides is home sweet home. For military families who seem to thrive under circumstances that would severely challenge others, love remains the family tie that sustains and binds them. Their love of God, country, and family, as exemplified by a life of selfless service, are values most consistent with the service life. This table setting honors our American military families and their commitment to the service of our country.

At the center of the table is a three-ply rope, tied with three square knots, or binding knots. The square knot, which is used for strength when securing objects of importance, represents the strength of our families, which is found in their unity of purpose. Two are better than one and three together is better than two together. Regardless of family size, demographics, or situation, our strength is in our commitment to each other and the service life. It is a force multiplier, providing additional strength and courage to endure the difficulties associated with the mobile military lifestyle and frequent deployments that often place a loved one in harm's way. It forms a circle at the center of the table to demonstrate that, at their very heart, families are an eternal and unbroken circle.

And at their very foundation is an anchor that represents their reliance and personal faith in God.

While these families have the same aspirations, dreams, hopes, and goals as any other American family, they differ from their civilian counterparts because they have chosen a life of service. For them home is not so much a geographic location, as represented by the compass and map, as it is a place in their hearts. They share the pride and sometimes the pain of supporting their military member(s) service to our nation during times of peace, crisis, or war. The single taper, when lit, reminds us of a waiting family. God bless America and these American military families.

THE RECIPES AND STORIES IN THIS BOOK

Whether you are a military spouse, of whom there are approximately 2.5 million (active, retired, reserve), or simply a patriot, you will love hearing these stories of courage, commitment, and sacrifice. Presented in menu format style, each set of recipes is accompanied by a story that relates to it and is evocative of the period. Some menus recreate recipes from a historic account, such as "A Colonial Thanksgiving" and "Christmas in a Confederate White House," both of which describe holidays celebrated during wartime conditions.

Today's modern military wife continues to enjoy a well-deserved reputation for hospitality. Her entertaining ideas and recipes are highly prized. Reflecting a variety of styles, the recipes are well-seasoned by the flavors of regional and international travel. Each individual leaves his or her mark on a recipe. And as these recipes filter through many creative, innovative hands, they change and evolve, culminating in truly memorable meals and social occasions. When combined in a recipe and remembrance book, the recipes, narratives, and photographs provide a unique story in American history: *her* story!

THE
MILITARY
WIVES'
COOKBOOK

TEAS AND COFFEES

After setting their table with the fine linen, sterling silver, and china, our great-great-grandmothers would serve either tea or coffee to their invited guests.

From colonial times, tea played an important role in our social, cultural, and political history. Following the costly French-Indian War, Britain imposed a burdensome series of taxes on the colonies, including an unpopular tax on tea. Colonists, already seething with rebellion, openly imported tea from the Dutch; in 1773, the Continental Congress declared coffee the national beverage.

In a move calculated to punish, the crown permitted the John Company to bypass merchants and sell directly to the colonies. The success of this strategy depended on the well-known passion of colonial women for tea to force its sale.

An Independence Tea Party

★ ★ ★ ★ ★

On October 25, 1774, fifty-one ladies of Edenton, North Carolina, were called together by Penelope Barker and met in the home of Elizabeth King to express their indignation over the newly imposed British tax on tea. The ladies vowed (while sipping tea made from raspberry leaves) that: "We, the ladies of Edenton, do hereby solemnly engage not to conform to the Pernicious Custom of Drinking Tea."

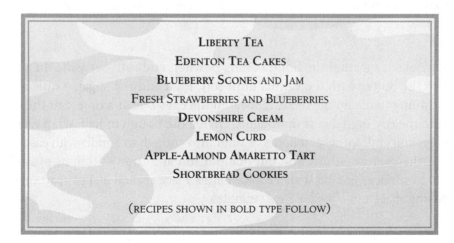

LIBERTY TEA

EDENTON TEA CAKES

BLUEBERRY SCONES AND JAM

FRESH STRAWBERRIES AND BLUEBERRIES

DEVONSHIRE CREAM

LEMON CURD

APPLE-ALMOND AMARETTO TART

SHORTBREAD COOKIES

(RECIPES SHOWN IN BOLD TYPE FOLLOW)

"LIBERTY TEA"
(RED RASPBERRY TEA)

★ ★ ★ ★ ★

Beverages brewed from the leaves of raspberry, sage, or strawberry plants replaced the use of British tea. One of the earliest of herbal teas, women used red raspberry tea for many years to ease labor contractions. And it was this tea that they politely sipped while assisting in the birth of this new nation.

| 6 | OUNCES RED RASPBERRY LEAVES, UNSPRAYED | ¼ | OUNCE PEPPERMINT LEAVES, UNSPRAYED |

Mix the leaves together and store in an airtight opaque container. To prepare tea, pour 1 cup of boiling water over 1 teaspoon of the herbal tea mixture. Steep 10 minutes. Strain and add honey or lemon, if desired.

YIELDS 1 SERVING.

EDENTON TEA CAKES
★ ★ ★ ★ ★

A colonial teapot mounted on a revolutionary cannon marks the site of the Edenton Tea Party and reminds us of the earliest organized political activity among colonial women, some of whom became military wives when revolution ensued. The tastiest reminder however, is these tea cakes, served at the meeting and made according to Penelope Barker's recipe.

3½	CUPS ALL-PURPOSE FLOUR, SIFTED	1	TEASPOON VANILLA EXTRACT
1	TEASPOON BAKING POWDER	2	CUPS FIRMLY PACKED BROWN SUGAR
½	TEASPOON SALT	3	EGGS
¾	CUP BUTTER		

In a large bowl sift together the flour, baking powder, and salt. Set aside. In a medium bowl cream the butter with the vanilla until soft, then add the sugar, a little at a time, while continuing to cream the mixture. Beat in the eggs one at a time. Stir the creamed mixture into the dry ingredients thoroughly. Divide the dough in half, wrap each half in waxed paper, and chill for several hours or until firm enough to handle with ease.

Preheat the oven to 400°F. Roll out one portion at a time as thin as possible on a lightly floured surface, and cut with a cookie cutter. Place several inches apart on a lightly greased baking sheet and bake for 7 to 9 minutes.

YIELDS APPROXIMATELY 6 DOZEN TEA CAKES.

BLUEBERRY SCONES
★ ★ ★ ★ ★

On August 18, 1776, Abigail Adams, while traveling to a church service of thanksgiving for independence, heard the Declaration of Independence read from the State House balcony. . . . The first shots of the Revolution were heard at Lexington and Concord on April 19, 1775. The Declaration, however, was also a declaration of war, and women known as Camp Followers or Mollies "followed" loved ones into war, caring for the wounded, cooking meals, washing clothes, and, when time permitted, coming together to encourage one another and renew their commitment to the cause.

2	CUPS ALL-PURPOSE FLOUR	1	CUP FRESH BLUEBERRIES
1	TABLESPOON BAKING POWDER	1	EGG
¼	TEASPOON SALT	¾	CUP HALF AND HALF
¼	CUP FIRMLY PACKED BROWN SUGAR	½	TEASPOON VANILLA EXTRACT
¼	CUP UNSALTED BUTTER, CHILLED		

Preheat the oven to 375°F. In a large mixing bowl combine the flour, baking powder, salt, and sugar. Mix well and then cut the butter into the flour mixture. Add the blueberries and toss to mix.

In a separate bowl mix together the egg, half and half, and vanilla extract. Slowly pour the liquid mixture into the flour mixture. Gently stir with a rubber spatula, taking care not to over-mix. Turn the dough out onto a floured board and lightly knead 3 or 4 times, just until the dough comes together. Divide the dough in half and shape each half into a 6-inch round. Cut each round into 6 wedges and place on an ungreased cookie sheet. Bake for approximately 20 minutes. Serve warm with Faux Devonshire Cream and Lemon Curd (see recipes on the following pages).

YIELDS 12 SCONES.

FAUX DEVONSHIRE CREAM
★★★★★

These revolutionary women would also share a cup of tea, coffee, or a favorite recipe and thus the strong bonds of friendship were forged. The tradition continues to this day.

½	CUP CREAM CHEESE (4 OUNCES)	1	CUP SOUR CREAM
½	CUP HEAVY WHIPPING CREAM	¼	CUP CONFECTIONERS' SUGAR

Freeze a small-sized mixing bowl and beaters for 10 minutes before proceeding. Remove the bowl and beaters from the freezer and combine all of the above ingredients in the mixing bowl. Beat on medium-high speed until stiff peaks form. Serve immediately or refrigerate. If you must refrigerate, just rewhip the cream before serving.

Faux Devonshire Cream is an excellent and quick substitute for clotted cream. However, if you have the time, the more traditional clotted cream may be made in the following manner: Preheat the oven to warm. Pour 2 cups of pasteurized heavy cream in a shallow pan such as a 9-inch pie plate. Cover the pan with foil; place it into the warm oven and allow it to sit, untouched, for at least 8 hours. (It may be left overnight.) At the end of the selected period, carefully remove the cream from the oven, taking care not to shake it and allow to completely cool. After the cream has cooled, skim the thick cream from the surface. A thin residue will be left behind. Either discard the residue or save it for use in soup. The cream will be lumpy with a yellow skin. Stir it with a spoon to blend and smooth it. Store it in the refrigerator, but serve at room temperature.

YIELDS APPROXIMATELY 2 CUPS.

APPLE-ALMOND AMARETTO TART

★ ★ ★ ★ ★

On the homefront other colonial women formed ladies' patriotic societies. Also seeking to provide something more than moral support, they knitted, quilted, dipped candles, and very likely shared an invigorating cup of raspberry tea and a home-baked dessert.

1	REFRIGERATED PIE CRUST		6	TABLESPOONS BUTTER, ROOM TEMPERATURE, DIVIDED
1	CUP BLANCHED SLIVERED ALMONDS		3	TART GREEN APPLES, PEELED, QUARTERED, CORED, CUT INTO ⅛-INCH THICK WEDGES
¾	CUP SUGAR			
2	LARGE EGGS		2	TABLESPOONS FIRMLY PACKED BROWN SUGAR, DIVIDED
¼	CUP AMARETTO, DIVIDED			
¼	TEASPOON LEMON EXTRACT		¾	TEASPOON GROUND CINNAMON
1	TEASPOON VANILLA EXTRACT			PINCH GROUND ALLSPICE
¼	TEASPOON SALT		¼	CUP APPLE JELLY

Preheat the oven to 450°F. Place the pie crust in a 10-inch tart pan; lightly press the crust into the pan and trim the excess pastry from edges. Line the pastry shell with aluminum foil, and fill with aluminum pie weights, which can be purchased at any specialty shop. Dried beans may be substituted. Bake at 450°F for approximately 8 minutes. Remove the weights and foil; bake another 2 minutes, and set aside while preparing the tart filling. Reduce the oven temperature to 400°F.

In a food processor combine the almonds, sugar, eggs, 1 tablespoon Amaretto, extracts, and salt. Process to form a soft paste. Add 4 tablespoons of butter and process 10 seconds. Spread across the bottom of the crust and chill until firm, approximately 45 minutes.

In a large bowl combine the apples, 2 tablespoons of Amaretto, 1 tablespoon of brown sugar, cinnamon, and allspice. Allow the apple mixture to stand for 1 hour.

Preheat the oven to 400°F. Drain the apples and arrange in the tart shell. Beginning at the outer edge of the pie, arrange the apples in a spiraling and overlapping circle, ending in the center of the tart. Melt 2 tablespoons of butter and brush the apples with melted butter. Sprinkle with the remaining tablespoon of brown sugar. Bake for 15 minutes. Reduce the heat to 350°F and bake until the apples are fork-tender, approximately 45 minutes. Transfer to a rack. Stir the jelly and remaining tablespoon of the Amaretto in a small saucepan over low heat until the jelly melts. Brush the apples with the mixture. Allow the tart to cool before serving.

YIELDS 8 SERVINGS.

LEMON CURD
★ ★ ★ ★ ★

Many colonial women shipped countless socks, sweaters, scarves, and bandages, while still others raised money to purchase boots and gunpowder. And perhaps in their busy day, they found time for a cup of herbal tea and a scone spread with lemon curd or raspberry jam.

JUICE FROM 3 MEDIUM-SIZE LEMONS (DO NOT USE BOTTLED)	1	CUP SUGAR
	½	CUP UNSALTED BUTTER
GRATED RIND FROM 3 LEMONS	4	SMALL EGG YOLKS

Wash the lemons and grate the rinds. Place the grated rind, lemon juice, sugar, and butter in a small saucepan; set over medium-low heat and stir until the butter melts and the sugar dissolves.

In a small bowl beat the egg yolks until they are thick and bright yellow. Slowly add the eggs to the lemon mixture, stirring constantly with a wooden spoon, and cook approximately 6 or 7 minutes. At this point the curd should thickly coat the back of the wooden spoon and change from transparent to opaque. Make certain the mixture does not boil or it will curdle. Increase the heat to medium and continue to stir until well blended. Should the curd begin to steam or boil, immediately remove it from the heat and stir constantly while it cools. When the curd thickens, pour it immediately into a strainer placed over a warm, sterilized jar and press with the back of a spoon until only the residue remains in the strainer. Discard the residue. Cover the curd and refrigerate, but serve at room temperature.

YIELDS APPROXIMATELY 1 CUP AND MAY BE KEPT REFRIGERATED FOR UP TO 2 WEEKS.

SHORTBREAD COOKIES
★ ★ ★ ★ ★

In Philadelphia, Ester Reed and Sarah Bache organized 39 women who raised money to purchase linen for shirts. These women made more than 2,000 shirts and delivered them to General Washington's troops.

½	CUP CONFECTIONERS' SUGAR	2	CUPS ALL-PURPOSE FLOUR
2	TABLESPOONS SUPERFINE SUGAR		PINCH GRATED NUTMEG
1	CUP UNSALTED BUTTER, SOFTENED		

Preheat the oven to 275°F. In a medium bowl whisk together the sugars and set aside. In a large bowl cream the butter. Slowly add the sugars and continue to cream until light and fluffy.

Measure the flour into a separate bowl; add the nutmeg and mix well. Add the flour to the butter mixture and, using your fingers, blend it into the flour until well incorporated. Divide the dough into 2 equal parts. Pat each half into an ungreased 8-inch round cake pan. Use the flat tines of a fork to press lines around the outer edges of the dough. According to lore, this traditional design represents the rays of the sun. Next, using the tine points, lightly prick the dough evenly. Bake for 60 to 70 minutes or until golden but not brown. Place the pan on a wire rack and cool for 10 minutes.

YIELDS 12 WEDGES.

Midwinter Tea with Friends

★ ★ ★ ★ ★

Strongly united by their commitment, these colonial women supported a revolutionary cause with simple domestic tools. And they shared the burden of their concerns as well. Perhaps a maternal concern was expressed for sixteen-year-old Sybil Ludington, the teenage daughter of Colonel Henry Ludington. On April 26, 1777, Sybil rode forty miles through the moonless countryside to summon her father's regiment to arms after a British attack on a Danbury, Connecticut, supply depot.

SPICED PUMPKIN RAISIN BREAD

CRANBERRY ORANGE MUFFINS

SALLY LUNN

ASSORTED CHEESES AND BUTTER SPREADS

ORANGE MARMALADE

HOT SPICED ORANGE PEKOE TEA

HOT MULLED CIDER

SPICED PUMPKIN RAISIN BREAD

★ ★ ★ ★ ★

It is conceivable that a sister or aunt expressed her concern when an intrepid Deborah Champion galloped for two days through enemy lines to deliver intelligence information to General Washington.

1	CUP SUGAR		¾	TEASPOON SALT
⅓	CUP FIRMLY PACKED LIGHT BROWN SUGAR		¼	TEASPOON GRATED NUTMEG
⅓	CUP SHORTENING		¼	TEASPOON GROUND CLOVES
1	CUP PUMPKIN PIE FILLING		½	CUP GOLDEN RAISINS, CHOPPED
1⅓	CUPS ALL-PURPOSE FLOUR		½	TEASPOON VANILLA EXTRACT
1	TEASPOON BAKING SODA		⅓	CUP WATER
¼	TEASPOON BAKING POWDER		½	CUP CHOPPED PECANS
¾	TEASPOON GROUND CINNAMON			

Preheat the oven to 350°F. Butter and flour a 9 x 5 x 3-inch loaf pan and set aside. In a large mixing bowl combine all of the above ingredients in the order given and mix well. Spoon into the prepared loaf pan. Bake for 45 to 50 minutes. Cool.

Turn out onto a plate. Wrap in aluminum foil and store until the next day.

YIELDS 1 LOAF OR 18 HALF-INCH-WIDE SLICES.

During the siege of Valley Forge, half famished, ill-equipped soldiers endured the darkest days of the revolution. As flickering hope faded to despair, ten women in ten ox-drawn carts arrived with tons of meal and other desperately needed supplies.

CRANBERRY ORANGE MUFFINS

★ ★ ★ ★ ★

Perhaps these Revolutionary War wives discussed Prudence Wright, the commander of a troop of women who dressed as men to defend the town of Pepperell, Massachusetts. And then lifted their cups in approval upon learning that these dauntless women captured a British courier and forwarded the plans he carried to the leaders of the Massachusetts militia. Here! Here! Or perhaps like Abigail Adams they gave voice to the cause of revolution. "Is it not better to die the last of British Freemen than live the first of British Slaves."

FOR THE TOPPING:

½	CUP FIRMLY PACKED LIGHT BROWN SUGAR
¼	CUP ALL-PURPOSE FLOUR
¼	CUP BUTTER, CUT INTO SMALL PIECES
1	TEASPOON GROUND CINNAMON
⅛	TEASPOON GROUND ALLSPICE

FOR THE MUFFIN MIX:

2 ⅓	CUPS ALL-PURPOSE FLOUR
4	TEASPOONS BAKING POWDER
¼	TEASPOON BAKING SODA
½	TEASPOON SALT

¼	TEASPOON GROUND ALLSPICE
¼	TEASPOON GROUND CINNAMON
¼	CUP BUTTER, SOFTENED
⅓	CUP SUGAR
¼	TEASPOON LEMON EXTRACT
1	EGG, BEATEN
1	TEASPOON GRATED ZEST FROM 1 LARGE ORANGE
1	CUP HALF AND HALF
	JUICE FROM 1 LARGE ORANGE (½ CUP)
1	CUP FRESH OR FROZEN CRANBERRIES, HALVED

In a small mixing bowl combine the ingredients for the topping and cut with a pastry blender until crumbly. Refrigerate until ready for use.

Preheat the oven to 375°F. Line 12 muffin cups with paper liners. In a medium bowl combine the flour, baking powder, baking soda, salt, allspice, and cinnamon. In a large bowl use an electric mixer to cream together the butter and sugar for approximately 2 minutes or until fluffy. Add the lemon extract. Beat in egg and zest.

> *The die is caste. . . . Heaven only knows what is next to take place but it seems to me the Sword is now our only, yet dreadful alternative. [Abigail Adams]*

Add the flour mixture to the butter mixture alternately with the half and half and orange juice. Fold in the cranberries. The batter should be thick at this point. Spoon 3 heaping teaspoons of batter into each cup. Fill all cups in this manner and sprinkle each muffin with 1 tablespoon of the topping mixture. Spoon the remaining batter on top of each muffin. Sprinkle the remaining topping over the muffin batter. Bake for 26 minutes or until a tester inserted into the center of a muffin comes out clean.

Allow to cool in the pan for 5 minutes before removing to a rack to cool.

YIELDS 12 MUFFINS.

SALLY LUNN
★★★★★

Perhaps these colonial women wrapped their hopes in the red, white, and blue of an original American flag that lay draped across their laps as they sewed a "new constellation" of thirteen stars upon a field of blue.

1	CUP WHOLE MILK		2½	TABLESPOONS SUGAR
¼	CAKE YEAST		2	TABLESPOONS MELTED BUTTER
1	CUP HALF AND HALF		4	CUPS ALL-PURPOSE FLOUR
2	EGGS, WELL BEATEN			SALT TO TASTE (OPTIONAL)

In a small saucepan scald ¼ cup of milk. Cool to lukewarm, transfer to a large mixing bowl, and dissolve the yeast into it. Add the remaining milk and half and half. Add the eggs, sugar, and melted butter to the yeast mixture. Sift in the flour and salt, and beat well. Set aside and allow to rise until almost doubled.

Punch down the dough; place in a well-buttered 8½-inch Sally Lunn, turban mold, 9-inch ring mold, or tube pan. Cover and allow the dough to rise in a warm place (80°F to 85°F). until almost double in bulk.

Preheat the oven to 350°F. Place the pan in the oven and bake for approximately 1 hour. Serve hot with butter or cheese, if desired.

YIELDS 6 TO 8 SERVINGS.

TRULY ORANGE ORANGE PEKOE TEA
★★★★★

Several patriots, including Cornelia Bridges, Rebecca Young, and Elizabeth "Betsy" Ross have been credited with making the first American flag.

	BOILING WATER		9	TEASPOONS LOOSE ORANGE PEKOE TEA
8	CUPS WATER		2	TO 4 ORANGE SLICES, TO GARNISH
4	TO 8 3-INCH STRIPS ORANGE PEEL, BITTER PITH REMOVED		4	3-INCH CINNAMON STICKS
				HONEY TO TASTE
12	WHOLE CLOVES			

Heat a serving teapot with boiling water. While the serving pot is warming, boil 8 cups of water for making tea. Stud the orange peels with cloves. Place a clove-studded orange peel at the bottom of each teacup. When the serving pot is thoroughly warmed, discard the warming water and place 1 teaspoon of loose tea per cup into the teapot. Add 1 additional teaspoon for the pot. Pour the boiling water over the tea. Allow the tea to steep for 3 to 5 minutes. Pour the tea through a wire mesh strainer into cups garnished with an orange slice and serve with cinnamon stick on the side. Sweeten if desired.

YIELDS 8 1-CUP SERVINGS OR 4 2-CUP SERVINGS.

HOT MULLED CIDER
★★★★★

"Resolved, that the flag of the United States be thirteen stripes, alternate red and white; that the union be thirteen stars, white in a blue field representing a new constellation." [The Marine Committee of the Second Continental Congress at Philadelphia on June 14, 1777]

½	GALLON APPLE CIDER		1	SMALL BAY LEAF
1	CUP ORANGE JUICE		1	TEASPOON WHOLE CLOVES
¼	CUP LEMON JUICE		½	TEASPOON GROUND ALLSPICE
2	TABLESPOONS LIME JUICE		1	TEASPOON GRATED NUTMEG
½	CUP FIRMLY PACKED BROWN SUGAR		1	CUP DARK RUM (OPTIONAL)
4	3-INCH CINNAMON STICKS			

In a large saucepan combine all of the ingredients except the rum and bring to a simmer over medium heat. Allow the cider to simmer for 20 minutes. Strain into a crockpot and reheat. Add rum, if desired, just before serving. Cider may be made several days ahead, if refrigerated.

YIELDS 12 CUPS.

Following the American Victory in Yorktown, General Washington moved his troops to establish his final winter quarters in New Windsor. Accompanying the troops were 500 women and children camp followers. This army followed an American flag.

The first flag flown by the colonies to bear any resemblance to our present-day stars and stripes was the Grand Union Flag. Coincidentally, it was the standard of the British East India Company. While its design included the familiar thirteen stripes, representing the Thirteen Colonies, its canton contained the British Union.

It remained our unofficial national flag until June 14, 1777, when the Continental Congress, "[r]esolved that the flag of the United States be thirteen stripes, alternate red and white; that the union be thirteen stars. White in a blue field representing a new constellation." The field of blue replaced the union jack; however, the resolution provided no further instruction, nor written record of the design and making of the very first flag.

BETSY ROSS WITH GEORGE WASHINGTON

One of those credited with making the first American flag was Betsy Ross, a military wife, who eventually would lose two husbands to the war effort. Betsy was also a businesswoman who owned an upholstery shop that provided a variety of services, including flag making. In addition, she made the pouches in which the militia carried their gunpowder.

According to her grandson, William J. Canby, "Colonel Ross (Ross's nephew by marriage) with Robert Morris and General Washington called on Mrs. Ross and told her they were a committee of Congress and wanted her to make a flag from a drawing which upon her suggestions was redrawn by General Washington in her back parlor." [William J. Canby, in a paper read before the meeting of the Pennsylvania Historical Society 1870]

However, in an 1876 letter Caroline Pickersgill Purdy claimed, "My grandmother, Rebecca Young made the first flag of the Revolution under General Washington's directions. "Purdy's further claim to fame was that she and her mother Mary Young Pickersgill made the original star-spangled flag, which flew over Fort McHenry, inspiring Francis Scott Key to write "The Star Spangled Banner."

Regardless of which military wife made the first American flag, it is clear, "This flag, which we honor . . . is the emblem of our unity, our power, our thought and purpose as a nation. . . . It speaks to us . . . of the past, of the men and women who went before us, and of the records they wrote upon it." [President Woodrow Wilson, Flag Day 1917]

With the end of the Revolutionary War, these women returned home to resume their lives. In 1784, when the U.S. Congress met in the Maryland State House in Annapolis to ratify the treaty of Paris, marking the official end of hostilities, the flag which flew over the state house to mark the occasion was made by Annapolis cabinetmaker John Shaw. Despite Martha Washington's reluctance, when duty called she again left her beloved Mount Vernon to become First Lady of a fledgling nation that would grow to become one of the greatest superpowers on earth.

"Lady Washington," as she was called by an adoring public, arrived in Washington on a presidential barge with thirteen oarsmen—one for each of the new American states.

In the Capitol City, Martha met and greeted visitors, and again served tea.

Afternoon tea should be provided, fresh supplies, with thin bread-and-butter sandwiches, fancy pastries, cakes etc., being brought in as guests arrive. [Mrs. Beeton, The Book of Household Management]

Lady's Afternoon Delight: A Garden Tea Party

✷　✷　✷　✷　✷

Steeped in rich tradition and elegant custom, after-noon tea is designed for casual conversation and refreshment. Like so many of our American tradi-tions, this one originated in England, courtesy of Anna the Duchess of Bedford. As Henry James said, "There are few hours in life more agreeable than the hour dedicated to the ceremony known as afternoon tea."

MRS. POWERS'S TABLE

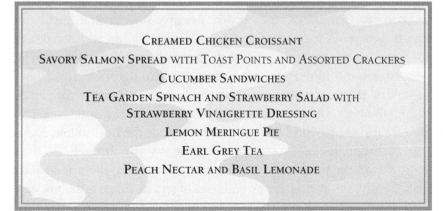

CREAMED CHICKEN CROISSANT

SAVORY SALMON SPREAD WITH TOAST POINTS AND ASSORTED CRACKERS

CUCUMBER SANDWICHES

TEA GARDEN SPINACH AND STRAWBERRY SALAD WITH
STRAWBERRY VINAIGRETTE DRESSING

LEMON MERINGUE PIE

EARL GREY TEA

PEACH NECTAR AND BASIL LEMONADE

19

CREAMED CHICKEN CROISSANT
★★★★★

Prior to the innovation of afternoon tea, the English served only two main meals, breakfast, in early morning, and late night dinners. Therefore, it is not surprising that Anna complained of a "sinking feeling in the late afternoon. As a remedy, she invited friends to her boudoir in Belvoir Castle for an additional meal at five o'clock.

5	BONELESS, SKINLESS CHICKEN BREAST FILLETS	1	MEDIUM CLOVE GARLIC, MINCED
½	TEASPOON ONION POWDER	1	TABLESPOON MINCED SHALLOT
¼	TEASPOON GARLIC POWDER	3	TABLESPOONS ALL-PURPOSE FLOUR
¼	TEASPOON CUMIN	5	CUPS UNSALTED CHICKEN BROTH
¼	TEASPOON GROUND GINGER	7	GREEN ONIONS, SLICED THINLY
1	TEASPOON SEASONED SALT	1	CUP HALF AND HALF
¼	TEASPOON DRY MUSTARD	⅓	CUP COOKING SHERRY
1	PACKAGE UNCLE BEN'S WILD RICE, COOKED ACCORDING TO PACKAGE DIRECTIONS	8	DINNER CROISSANTS
½	POUND MEDIUM SHRIMP	2	TEASPOONS SOUR CREAM
¼	CUP UNSALTED BUTTER	1	TABLESPOON DIJON MUSTARD

Wash the chicken breasts and place in a colander to drain. In a small bowl combine the onion powder, garlic powder, cumin, ginger, salt, and mustard. Use to season the chicken breasts. Prior to seasoning, remove excess moisture from the chicken but ensure that they are still damp. Season the chicken breasts on both sides and refrigerate. Meanwhile, begin cooking the wild rice. Peel, devein, and wash the shrimp; refrigerate until needed.

In a large pan melt the butter over medium heat and sauté the garlic and shallot. Add the chicken; cook for 3 minutes on each side. Remove the chicken, garlic, and shallots from the pan to a plate. Dice the chicken and set aside. Add an additional tablespoon of butter to the pan if necessary, and sauté the shrimp just until they turn pink. Remove the shrimp from the pan. Add flour to the pan, and stir until lightly brown. Slowly add the broth and continue to stir, scraping any sediment from the bottom of the pan. Reduce the heat to low and allow the sauce to thicken. Add the green onions and simmer for an additional minute. Stir in the half and half and sherry; reduce the heat to low, and cover. Add the chicken and shrimp just before serving and allow to warm through.

Form a pocket in the top of the croissant by cutting along the upper, outer curve of the croissant. Gently pull the flap back and use fingers to shape a flat pocket inside the croissant. In a cup combine the sour cream and mustard and lightly brush the bottom of each croissant with a small amount of mustard mixture. Place approximately 2 to 3 tablespoons of rice on the bottom of each croissant. Spoon the chicken and shrimp mixture

THE MILITARY WIVES' COOKBOOK

into the warmed croissants. (Rice may be made a day ahead, stored in a microwave-proof container, and reheated. Chicken and shrimp may be prepared, sautéed a day in advance, and stored. Also, you should deglaze the pan and prepare the sauce, but do not return the chicken and shrimp to it until ready to serve.)

YIELDS 8 SERVINGS.

SAVORY SALMON SPREAD
✮ ✮ ✮ ✮ ✮

Ladies accepting a tea invitation from the duchess delighted in dining on an assortment of foods.

½	CUP BUTTER, SOFTENED	¼	TEASPOON CHOPPED PARSLEY
1	8-OUNCE PACKAGE CREAM CHEESE, SOFTENED	¼	TEASPOON SALT
1	14¾-OUNCE CAN PINK SALMON, DRAINED, SKIN AND BONES REMOVED		BIBB OR OTHER SOFT LETTUCE LEAVES
		2	FINELY SHREDDED BOILED EGGS TO GARNISH
3	TABLESPOONS CHOPPED GREEN ONIONS		FRESH PARSLEY CHOPPED FINE TO GARNISH
2	TEASPOONS LEMON JUICE		TOAST POINTS AND ASSORTED CRACKERS

In the bowl of an electric mixer blend the butter and cream cheese at medium speed until creamy. Flake the salmon and add to the mixture. Add the green onions, lemon juice, parsley, and salt. Mix well, and chill until firm, approximately 1 hour.

Shape into a 7-inch round and flatten the top slightly. Place on a lettuce-lined serving plate and garnish with egg and parsley. Serve with toast points and assorted crackers.

(To make toast points, trim crusts from whole wheat bread, toast and cut on the diagonal line to form four triangles.)

YIELDS 6 SERVINGS.

*W*hen brewing tea, loose tea and pure water are best. Today as in the bygone era, the setting should be gracious and elegant. White teacloths, sparkling china, crystal, and silver all set the mood for an afternoon delight.

CUCUMBER SANDWICHES

★ ★ ★ ★ ★

While sitting in the duchess's boudoir, genteel ladies ate small cakes and bread and butter sandwiches.

1	8-OUNCE PACKAGE CREAM CHEESE, SOFTENED	¼	TEASPOON SALT
2½	TABLESPOONS MAYONNAISE	1	TEASPOON MINCED FRESH DILLWEED
1½	TABLESPOONS SOUR CREAM	¼	TEASPOON MINCED FRESH PARSLEY
1	MEDIUM ENGLISH CUCUMBER, PEELED AND FINELY CHOPPED	20	THIN SANDWICH BREAD SLICES
		20	THIN WHEAT BREAD SLICES
⅛	TEASPOON ONION POWDER		

In a blender process the cream cheese, mayonnaise, and sour cream. Scrape down once during processing. In a bowl combine the cream cheese mixture, cucumber, seasonings, and herbs, and set aside. Using a rolling pin, lightly flatten the bread (2 or 3 quick, light rolls should be sufficient). Spread the cucumber mixture onto the white bread slices and top with wheat bread. Using a 2- to 3-inch round cutter, cut sandwiches; discard the trimmings. Store in an airtight container up to 1 hour before serving.

Serve on a bed of iceberg lettuce. The high water content of the lettuce will help keep the sandwiches soft and fresh.

YIELDS 20 ROUNDS.

WOLHURST FETE

Took a moonlight walk after tea. We had tea at the Halcott Greens, and all of the company did honor to the beautiful night by walking home with me. [Mary Chestnut, 1862]

THE MILITARY WIVES' COOKBOOK

A TEA GARDEN SALAD

WITH STRAWBERRY VINAIGRETTE DRESSING

✭ ✭ ✭ ✭ ✭

Another English tea custom quickly adopted by colonial Americans was that of the tea garden. Tea gardens permitted the taking of tea out of doors in the presence of an orchestra, often accompanied by other forms of entertainment such as hidden arbors, bowling greens, and nighttime fireworks.

8	CUPS TORN FRESH SPINACH		STRAWBERRY VINAIGRETTE DRESSING (RECIPE BELOW)
1	11-OUNCE CAN MANDARIN ORANGES, DRAINED		
1½	QUARTS FRESH STRAWBERRIES, HULLED AND QUARTERED (SET ASIDE 4 WHOLE STRAWBERRIES FOR LATER USE)	1	CUP CHOPPED WALNUTS, TOASTED (SEE NOTE BELOW)
2	GREEN ONIONS, THINLY SLICED		
5	KIWIFRUIT, PEELED AND SLICED		

In a salad bowl gently toss together the spinach, oranges, strawberries, onions, and kiwifruit. Refrigerate while preparing the dressing.

STRAWBERRY VINAIGRETTE DRESSING

When tea became available for public sale in America in the 1690s, tea gardens opened in New York City, centered on the natural springs.

4	MEDIUM STRAWBERRIES	1	TEASPOON DRY MUSTARD
¼	CUP WATER	¾	CUP VEGETABLE OIL
⅓	CUP RED WINE VINEGAR	½	TEASPOON FRESH MINT
1	TABLESPOON FRESH LEMON JUICE	1	TABLESPOON POPPY SEEDS
¼	CUP SUGAR		

In a blender or food processor place the strawberries and water and purée. Press the liquid from the pulp and strain into a small bowl. Discard the pulp. Clean the blender or processor and return the liquid to it. Add the red wine vinegar, lemon juice, sugar, and dry mustard. Process until smooth, stopping once to scrape down the sides. Turn the blender on high; add the vegetable oil in a slow, steady stream. Pour mixture into a serving dish, stir in the mint and poppy seeds, and refrigerate. Just before serving, gently toss the salad and walnuts together. Dress with salad dressing and serve immediately.

Note: Toast the walnuts by baking in a shallow baking pan at 350°F while stirring occasionally. Continue to bake for 5 to 10 minutes or until toasted.

LEMON MERINGUE PIE
★ ★ ★ ★ ★

The afternoon garden tea party is a combination of the tradition of the afternoon tea and, of course, tea gardens.

PIE SHELL

The quintessential afternoon tea, Earl Grey was originally blended by R. Twining for Charles, the Second Earl Grey. According to legend, Grey was presented the recipe by an envoy on his return from China. The custom and culture of teas was adopted by well-to-do eastern women who made it uniquely their own.

1 ¼	CUPS ALL-PURPOSE FLOUR		2½	TABLESPOONS CHILLED, UNSALTED BUTTER, CUT INTO PIECES
1 ¼	TEASPOONS SUGAR		2¼	TABLESPOONS CHILLED VEGETABLE SHORTENING
¾	TEASPOON SALT		9	TABLESPOONS ICE WATER

Preheat the oven to 350°F. In a medium bowl sift together the flour, sugar, and salt. Cut in the butter and shortening until the mixture resembles coarse meal. Stir in just enough water for the mixture to come together. Form the dough into a ball and flatten into a thin disk. Wrap in plastic wrap and chill at least 30 minutes.

Roll out onto a lightly floured surface. Starting at the center, roll toward the edge, using light strokes. When the dough is approximately ⅛-inch thick press it into a 9-inch pie pan and trim the edges. Line the shell with aluminum foil. Place pie weights, which can be purchased at most kitchen or culinary stores, on the bottom of the shell. Dried beans may be substituted. Bake for 5 to 7 minutes. Remove from the oven and allow to cool slightly before removing the foil and weights. Bake the pie crust an additional 5 to 7 minutes or until lightly browned; remove from the oven and set aside.

FILLING

1¼	CUPS SUGAR		5	LARGE EGG YOLKS
¼	CUP CORNSTARCH		½	CUP FRESH LEMON JUICE
3	TABLESPOONS ALL-PURPOSE FLOUR		2	TABLESPOONS UNSALTED BUTTER
¼	TEASPOON SALT		1¼	TEASPOONS GRATED LEMON PEEL
1½	CUPS COLD WATER			

In a medium saucepan combine the sugar, cornstarch, flour, and salt. Gradually whisk the water into the flour mixture 1 tablespoon at a time. Bring the mixture to a boil over medium heat and continue to boil for approximately 1 minute, stirring constantly. Remove the pan from the heat, and set aside. In a separate bowl whisk the egg yolks. Gradually whisk in some of the hot cornstarch mixture. Return the warmed yolks to the saucepan and boil until very thick. Gradually stir in the remainder of the mixture. Continue to stir as the mixture cooks, approximately 5 minutes.

Remove from the heat and whisk in the juice, butter, and lemon peel. Cool completely. Spoon the filling into the crust, cover, and chill while making the meringue. If the filling is not sufficiently cool, your pie will weep and cause the crust to be soggy.

MERINGUE

3	EGG WHITES	6	TABLESPOONS SUGAR
¼	TEASPOON CREAM OF TARTAR	1	TEASPOON LEMON PEEL, FINELY GRATED

Preheat the oven to 425°F. In a glass bowl beat the egg whites until frothy but not stiff. Add the cream of tartar and continue beating until stiff enough to hold a peak. Gradually beat in the sugar; then add the grated lemon peel. At this point the egg whites should be stiff and glossy. Spoon the meringue on top of the cool pie filling and spread to the outer crust, to prevent shrinkage, while mounding high in the middle. Bake for 5 to 7 minutes until delicately browned. Check often as oven temperatures vary. Allow to cool at room temperature before serving.

This pie may be frozen by first placing it in freezer without any wrapping. Once frozen, place in a zippered freezer bag and return to the freezer. The pie may be kept in this manner for up to 1 year. Remove from the freezer and thaw at room temperature for 2 to 3 hours before serving.

YIELDS 6 TO 8 SERVINGS.

When service academies were established and military service recognized as an honorable profession, these well-to-do genteel women began marrying military officers and took their traditions to the western frontier. The Afternoon Garden Tea presented here honors the highest ideal of that tradition.

EARL GREY TEA

★ ★ ★ ★ ★

One eastern woman, "following her husband to the western frontier, brought with her a one-year supply of tea. When the tired couple stopped at a roadside inn for the night, the woman asked the innkeeper's wife to prepare her a much needed cup of tea from her precious supply. Imagine her horror when half an hour later the innkeeper reported that after boiling and boiling those 'greens' and even changing the water three times, she found [them] too bitter for anyone in this territory to eat."

EARL GREY TEA	CREAM
BOTTLED SPRING WATER	LEMON
SUGAR	

Bring spring water to a boil and use it to fill the pot from which you will serve tea. Next, boil additional spring water for tea, one cup of water for each guest. Discard the water from the serving pot. As a rule of thumb use 1 heaping teaspoonful of tea for each cup of water, plus one teaspoon "for the pot."

When the water boils, pour it over the tea and let it steep for 3 to 5 minutes. Stir once and then strain the tea directly into the teacups or into a serving teapot. Loose tea and pure water are key to a perfect pot of tea!

MISS ARNOLD'S TABLE

AT FOUR O'CLOCK, EVERYTHING STOPS.

PEACH NECTAR AND BASIL LEMONADE
★★★★★

The military wives' tradition of teas continued on the frontier where they served delightful confections with coffee and tea.

3½ CUPS WATER	3 12-OUNCE CANS APRICOT NECTAR
1 CUP FRESH BASIL LEAVES, PLUS ADDITIONAL FOR GARNISH	½ CUP FRESH LEMON JUICE
½ CUP SUGAR, OR TO TASTE	FRESH SPEARMINT

In a small saucepan stir together 2 cups of the water, the cup of basil, and the sugar. Bring this mixture to a boil, stirring until the sugar dissolves, and simmer for 5 minutes. Let the mixture cool and strain through a fine sieve set over a pitcher. Discard the basil from the strainer. Stir in the remaining ingredients and pour into tall, ice-filled, frosted glasses. Garnish with fresh basil leaves and a sprig of fresh spearmint.

YIELDS 4 TO 6 SERVINGS.

White Gloves and Hats: A Silver and Crystal Tea

✫ ✫ ✫ ✫ ✫

Enter a genteel world where a freshly brewed cup of tea is shared in the quiet intimacy of friendship and sweetened with laughter delicate and true.

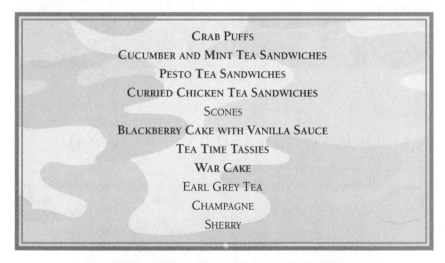

CRAB PUFFS
CUCUMBER AND MINT TEA SANDWICHES
PESTO TEA SANDWICHES
CURRIED CHICKEN TEA SANDWICHES
SCONES
BLACKBERRY CAKE WITH VANILLA SAUCE
TEA TIME TASSIES
WAR CAKE
EARL GREY TEA
CHAMPAGNE
SHERRY

TEA TABLE

CRAB PUFFS
★★★★★

The traditional elegance of formal teas was reserved for special occasions. These social affairs were patterned after those of a bygone era.

1	POUND FRESH BACKFIN CRABMEAT, DRAINED AND FLAKED
¼	CUP MAYONNAISE
1	TABLESPOON SOUR CREAM
1	LARGE EGG
½	TEASPOON TABASCO SAUCE
3	TABLESPOONS FINELY CHOPPED ONION
2	TABLESPOONS FINELY CHOPPED RED BELL PEPPER
2	TABLESPOONS FINELY CHOPPED CELERY (INCLUDE A FEW LEAVES)
¼	TEASPOON OLD BAY SEASONING
¼	TEASPOON PAPRIKA
⅛	TEASPOON CAYENNE
½	TEASPOON DRY MUSTARD
¼	TEASPOON GARLIC POWDER
½	TEASPOON ONION POWDER
¼	TEASPOON SALT
	UP TO ⅓ CUP FINE DRY BREADCRUMBS
⅔	CUP CRACKER MEAL

In a large bowl combine the crabmeat and remaining ingredients except the breadcrumbs and cracker meal. Mix well. Add breadcrumbs until the mixture holds its shape. Using about 1 tablespoon of the mixture for each serving, shape into a ball; coat evenly with cracker crumbs and place on a wax-paper-lined baking sheet. Repeat until all the mixture is used and refrigerate until chilled, approximately 1 hour. In a Dutch oven, pour the oil to a depth of about 3 inches and heat to 375°F. Fry the crabmeat balls a few at a time until golden. Drain on a paper towel. Reheat just prior to serving, either in a microwave or conventional oven.

YIELDS 3 DOZEN.

MISS CARMEN MOUZON AT TEA

CUCUMBER MINT TEA SANDWICHES
★★★★★

In later years Libbie Custer would recall, "We fished out from the little finery at the bottom of our trunks some frivolities in the way of ribbons or flowers or trimmings that had served their time, and were ready for retirement even before coming West."

5	OUNCES CREAM CHEESE, SOFTENED	⅛	TEASPOON ONION SALT
1	TABLESPOON MAYONNAISE	3½	TEASPOONS MINCED FRESH MINT
1	TABLESPOON SOUR CREAM	15	THIN WHEAT BREAD SLICES
1	MEDIUM ENGLISH CUCUMBER, PEELED, FINELY CHOPPED, AND DRAINED (APPROXIMATELY 1 CUP)		

In a blender process the cream cheese, mayonnaise, and sour cream. Scrape down once during processing. In a bowl combine the cream cheese mixture, cucumber, salt, and mint, and refrigerate.

Using a rolling pin, lightly roll the bread (2 or 3 quick, light rolls should be sufficient). Use a 3-inch round cookie or biscuit cutter to cut sandwiches. Discard the trimmings. Lightly toast the rounds and allow to cool completely before placing a mound of cucumber mixture in the middle of each. Garnish with a light sprinkle of paprika. Store in an airtight container up to 1 hour before serving.

YIELDS 30 ROUNDS.

READY FOR A PARTY

THE MILITARY WIVES' COOKBOOK

PESTO TEA SANDWICHES
★★★★★

"But in our efforts to emphasize the occasion a white or black gown was decorated with trimmings." [Libbie Custer, Following the Guidon]

1	8-OUNCE PACKAGE CREAM CHEESE	10	THIN WHEAT BREAD SLICES
1	TABLESPOON SOUR CREAM	10	WHITE BREAD SLICES
2½	TEASPOONS PESTO, OR TO TASTE (STORE BOUGHT OR SEE RECIPE ON PAGE 198)	10	THIN SLICES OF UNPEELED CUCUMBER

In a blender process the cream cheese, sour cream, and pesto. Scrape down once during processing. Transfer to a bowl. Refrigerate the pesto mixture for 15 minutes.

For proper tea sandwiches, the bread must be very thin. When slicing from a whole loaf of bread, you should partially freeze the bread. Freezing the bread allows for an easier job of slicing. If you are using pre-sliced bread, using a rolling pin, lightly roll the bread (2 or 3 quick light rolls should be sufficient). While the pesto mixture is chilling, use a 3-inch biscuit cutter to cut rounds from the whole wheat and white bread slices. Discard the trimmings, including crusts.

Halve the cucumber slices. Slice each half down the middle and to the rind, but do not slice through the rind. Next, spread a ¼-inch thickness of pesto mixture onto the rounds. Take each end of the cucumber, gently twist each end in the opposite direction, and press the "cucumber twist" into the spread on each round. Arrange the rounds in a single layer on the bottom of an airtight container. Keep flat and refrigerate for up to 1 hour before serving. Serve on a bed of iceberg lettuce. The high water content of the lettuce will help keep the sandwiches soft and fresh.

YIELDS 20 SANDWICHES.

CURRIED CHICKEN TEA SANDWICHES

★★★★★

"Fortunately we had no city [finery] to compete with, and it took a great deal to disfigure fresh healthful, happy women." [Libbie Custer]

4	OUNCES CREAM CHEESE, SOFTENED		1	CUP FINELY CHOPPED CHICKEN (WHITE MEAT)
¼	CUP MAYONNAISE		1	MEDIUM APPLE, PARED, CORED, AND COARSELY CHOPPED
2	TABLESPOONS SOUR CREAM			
⅛	TEASPOON ONION POWDER		¼	CUP COARSELY CHOPPED WALNUTS
¼	TEASPOON CURRY POWDER		2	TABLESPOONS CHOPPED GOLDEN RAISINS
	PINCH CUMIN		20	THIN SANDWICH BREAD SLICES

In a blender process the cream cheese, mayonnaise, sour cream, and spices. Scrape down once during processing. Transfer to a bowl. Add the remaining ingredients and set aside.

Spread a ¼-inch thickness of the spread onto half the bread slices and top with another bread slice. Use a 3-inch cookie or biscuit cutter to cut sandwiches into the desired shape, discarding the trimmings. Store in an airtight container up to 1 hour before serving. Serve on a bed of iceberg lettuce. The high water content of the lettuce will help keep the sandwiches soft and fresh.

YIELDS 10 SANDWICHES.

WOMEN AT TEA

BLACKBERRY CAKE WITH VANILLA SAUCE
⭐⭐⭐⭐⭐

Our great-great-grandmothers would take from their trunks carefully packed heirloom linens and lace. They would then set their table, or perhaps the top of the trunk itself, depending upon circumstances, with their very best sterling and china. Having set the table, they would serve either tea or coffee to their invited guests.

½	CUP BUTTER	¼	TEASPOON ALMOND EXTRACT
1	CUP SUGAR	½	TEASPOON VANILLA EXTRACT
1	CUP ALL-PURPOSE FLOUR	1	TABLESPOON BLACKBERRY JAM
1	TEASPOON BAKING POWDER	1	CUP FRESH OR FROZEN SUGAR-FREE BLACKBERRIES
2	LARGE EGGS		

Preheat the oven to 350°F. Butter and flour a 9-inch cake pan with a removable rim, and set aside. In a medium bowl combine the butter and sugar. Cream together until well blended and fluffy. In a separate bowl sift together the flour and baking powder. Add the dry ingredients to the butter mixture. Add the eggs, extracts, and jam, and mix until well blended, approximately 2 minutes. The batter should be stiff. Scrape the batter into the prepared cake pan and spread the top smooth. Scatter berries evenly over the batter and sprinkle the fruit with 1 tablespoon of sugar. Bake on the center rack of a preheated oven for 55 to 60 minutes or until the cake begins to pull away from the rim of the pan. Run a thin-bladed knife between the cake and the rim. Allow the cake to cool for 10 minutes before removing from the pan. Place on a serving plate while making vanilla sauce.

Yields 8 servings.

VANILLA SAUCE

⅔	CUP BUTTER	1	CUP LIGHT CORN SYRUP
2	CUPS FIRMLY PACKED SUGAR	3	TABLESPOONS VANILLA EXTRACT
1½	CUPS HALF AND HALF		

In a saucepan melt the butter over medium-low heat. Stir in the sugar and mix well. Add the half and half and corn syrup, and bring to a quick boil, stirring until the sugar dissolves. Remove from the heat and cool to warm while stirring constantly. Stir in the vanilla. Serve warm with blackberry cake.

TEA TIME TASSIES
★★★★★

Separated from family, home, and friends, frontier army wives endured many hardships. The tradition of military wives' coffees dates back to those turn-of-the-century frontier army posts, where a shared cup of coffee brought welcome respite.

CRUST

½	CUP SIFTED ALL-PURPOSE FLOUR	3	OUNCES CREAM CHEESE, SOFTENED
⅛	TEASPOON GRATED NUTMEG	¼	CUP BUTTER, SOFTENED

In a large bowl combine the flour and nutmeg. Blend in the cream cheese and butter. Wrap in plastic wrap and chill overnight.

The next day preheat the oven to 350°F. Take marble sized pieces of the chilled dough and mold to the inside of ungreased 1¾-inch tartlet tins. Place the tartlet pans on a baking sheet and refrigerate while mixing the filling ingredients.

FILLING

⅓	CUP FIRMLY PACKED LIGHT BROWN SUGAR	1	TABLESPOON BUTTER, MELTED
½	CUP DARK CORN SYRUP	½	CUP CHOPPED PECANS
¼	TEASPOON GROUND CINNAMON	1	TEASPOON VANILLA EXTRACT
1	EGG		DASH SALT

In a medium bowl combine the filling ingredients and spoon approximately 1 heaping teaspoon into each cup. Bake at 350°F for 20 to 25 minutes or until filling sets. Allow the tassies to cool and remove from tartlet pans.

YIELDS 24 TASSIES.

WAR CAKE
(LIBBIE'S DREAM CAKE)

★ ★ ★ ★ ★

On June 17, John Quincy's mother, Abigail Adams, took him to the top of Penn's Hill, near their home, to witness the Battle of Bunker Hill. Although she faced food shortages and battles that threatened to cross her threshold, she would write to her husband, John, "very brave upon the whole." Every generation of American wives faced war with this courage and a dash of creativity.

2	CUPS FIRMLY PACKED BROWN SUGAR	1	TEASPOON GROUND CINNAMON
2	CUPS HOT WATER	1	TEASPOON CLOVES
2	TEASPOONS SHORTENING	3	CUPS ALL-PURPOSE FLOUR
½	TO ¾ CUP RAISINS	1	TEASPOON BAKING SODA DISSOLVED IN 2 TEASPOONS OF HOT WATER
1	TEASPOON SALT		

Grease and flour a Bundt or tube pan. In a medium saucepan combine the brown sugar, hot water, shortening, raisins, salt, and spices. Bring to a boil and continue to boil for 5 minutes. Remove the mixture from the heat and allow it to cool completely. Add the flour and dissolved soda. Pour into the prepared pan and bake at 325° for approximately 1 hour.

> *"The cookbooks were maddening to us, for a casual glance at any of them proves how necessary eggs, butter, and cream are to every recipe." [Libbie Custer] It was Libbie's hope that an enterprising wife would write a cookbook that met the needs of the frontier military wife. Many years later, Alice Kirk Grierson's personal recipes were published in* The Army Wife's Cookbook. *During the shortages of World War I and II this recipe was devised. "War Cake" did not call for rationed milk, eggs, or butter.*

Many traditions of nineteenth-century military wives have survived to be handed down to each generation. Coffee is no exception. Perhaps coffee's popularity is rooted in America's revolt against King George's tea tax. Following the Boston and Edenton Tea Parties, coffee eclipsed tea as the most popular American beverage. In 1773 the Continental Congress declared coffee the official national beverage.

Following the establishment of the United States Military Academy at West Point in 1802 and the Naval Academy at Annapolis in the 1840s, officers were considered professionals. These now "eligible" bachelors began marrying the socially prominent daughters of well-to-do families.

Because military service was, by its very nature, a mobile profession, daughters who once remained near home after marriage now found themselves on the outer boundaries of the new frontier, far from the comforts of home.

MARY CODY

Morning Bridal Shower Coffee for Twenty-Five

✶ ✶ ✶ ✶ ✶

Wake up to a steaming cup of coffee, buttery croissants, ruby red strawberries, and sweet cream. Morning has broken!

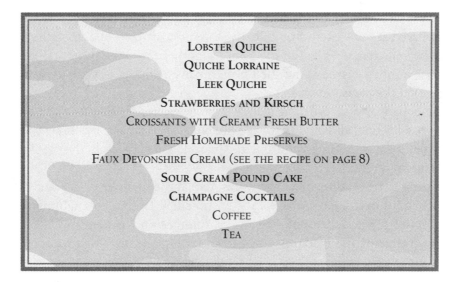

LOBSTER QUICHE

QUICHE LORRAINE

LEEK QUICHE

STRAWBERRIES AND KIRSCH

CROISSANTS WITH CREAMY FRESH BUTTER

FRESH HOMEMADE PRESERVES

FAUX DEVONSHIRE CREAM (SEE THE RECIPE ON PAGE 8)

SOUR CREAM POUND CAKE

CHAMPAGNE COCKTAILS

COFFEE

TEA

LOBSTER QUICHE
★★★★★

"When I think of Andrew I am happy, but when I think of leaving my father, my mother, my home people, I feel a deep sinking heart. I am going so far away and for such an indefinite time." [Eveline Alexander]

1	9-INCH DEEP-DISH PIE SHELL		PINCH NUTMEG
3	TABLESPOONS BUTTER, DIVIDED	¼	TEASPOON SALT
2	GREEN ONIONS, THINLY SLICED	¼	TEASPOON WHITE PEPPER
2	TEASPOONS FINELY CHOPPED PARSLEY	½	CUP GRATED GRUYERE CHEESE
1½	CUPS COOKED LOBSTER MEAT, CUT INTO ½-INCH CUBES	2	EGGS
		3	EGG YOLKS
⅛	TEASPOON GARLIC POWDER	1½	CUPS HALF AND HALF
	PINCH CURRY POWDER	1	TABLESPOON ALL-PURPOSE FLOUR
	PINCH PAPRIKA	2	OUNCES BRANDY

Preheat the oven to 375°F. Line the pie shell with aluminum foil. Place pie weights, which can be purchased at most kitchen or culinary stores, on the bottom of the pie shell. Dried beans may be substituted. Bake the shell until slightly browned, but not done, approximately 5 to 7 minutes. Remove the shell from the oven and set it aside to cool. Remove the weights after the pie has cooled.

In a saucepan over medium heat melt 2 tablespoons of the butter and sauté the onions and parsley until all liquid is cooked off, but do not brown. In a bowl combine the onions, lobster meat, seasonings, and spices. Mix well and spoon into the pie shell. Sprinkle the mixture with cheese.

In a mixing bowl combine the eggs, yolks, half and half, flour, and brandy. Mix well and carefully pour over the contents of the pastry shell. Dot with remaining butter and place on a baking sheet in the oven. Bake for 30 minutes until golden and firmly set. Test doneness by inserting the blade of a butter knife into the middle of the quiche. The quiche is done when a knife inserted in its center comes out clean.

YIELDS 8 SMALL SLICES.

QUICHE LORRAINE
★ ★ ★ ★ ★

For some women the choice was clear and they could not be deterred. When Miss Mary Hughes was courted by Dragoon Lieutenant Thomas Clark, her father, Judge M. M. Hughes, had already lost two daughters to dragoon officers. He did not want to lose a third daughter. Despite opposition by the bride's father, the clever couple arranged to be married at a place called Pilot Knob. Perhaps anticipating the need for a rapid retreat, the ceremony was performed by the minister while the bride and groom sat astride their horses.

1	9-INCH DEEP-DISH PASTRY SHELL		¼	TEASPOON DIJON MUSTARD
9	SLICES BACON		1	CUP HALF AND HALF
8	THIN SLICES ONION		½	TEASPOON SALT
¾	CUP SHREDDED SWISS CHEESE		¼	TEASPOON WHITE PEPPER
¼	CUP GRATED PARMESAN CHEESE			PINCH GRATED NUTMEG
3	EGGS			

Preheat the oven to 375°F. Line the pie shell with aluminum foil. Place pie weights, which can be purchased at most kitchen or culinary stores, on the bottom of the pie shell. Dried beans may be substituted. Bake the shell until slightly browned, but not done, approximately 5 to 7 minutes. Remove the weights after the pie has cooled.

In a skillet fry the bacon or cook in the microwave, drain, and allow to cool before crumbling. Reserve the drippings. In the skillet sauté the onion slices in the reserved bacon drippings over medium heat until soft but not browned. Sprinkle the bacon and onion over the bottom of the pie crust. Sprinkle cheeses on top of the bacon and onion mixture. In a medium bowl beat together the eggs, mustard, half and half, and seasonings. Pour over the pie shell contents and allow to stand for 10 minutes.

Place on a baking sheet in the oven. Bake for 30 minutes until golden and firmly set. Test by inserting the blade of a butter knife in the middle of the quiche. The quiche is done when a knife inserted in the center comes out clean.

YIELDS 8 SMALL SERVINGS.

LEEK QUICHE
★★★★★

In 1846, a double wedding at Fort Gibson united Miss Catherine Mix with Lieutenant Ralph Kirkman and Miss Donna Mullen with Lieutenant Franklin F. Flint. The brides, wearing muslin dresses and veils, rode in a two-person carriage called a Victoria.

1	9-INCH DEEP-DISH PASTRY SHELL	2	EGGS
8	MEDIUM-SIZED LEEKS, SLICED THIN (WHITE PART ONLY)	2	CUPS HALF AND HALF
¼	CUP BUTTER	1	TABLESPOON ALL-PURPOSE FLOUR
1	TEASPOON SALT	1	TEASPOON PAPRIKA
¼	TEASPOON GARLIC POWDER	½	CUP GRATED PARMESAN CHEESE
¼	TEASPOON WHITE PEPPER	¼	CUP GRATED GRUYERE CHEESE
3	EGG YOLKS	¼	CUP GRATED SWISS CHEESE

Preheat the oven to 375°F. Place weights at the bottom of the pie shell, and bake until slightly browned, but not done. Remove the shell from the oven and set aside to cool. Remove the weights after the pie shell has cooled.

In a saucepan sauté the leeks in butter over medium heat. Reduce the heat to low and add the salt, garlic powder, and white pepper; continue to sauté until the leeks are tender and the liquid has cooked off. Do not brown. If the leeks are not sufficiently tender, add a small amount of water and allow it to cook off. In a large mixing bowl beat together the yolks, eggs, half and half, flour, and paprika. Distribute the leeks over the bottom of the pie shell; add the cheeses. Carefully pour the egg mixture over the pie shell contents, so as not to disturb. Place the quiche on a baking sheet in the oven. Bake for 30 minutes until golden and firmly set. The quiche is done when a butter knife inserted in the middle of the quiche comes out clean.

YIELDS 8 SMALL SLICES.

STRAWBERRIES AND KIRSCH
★★★★★

As the Victoria was the only carriage on the post, the bridegrooms, in full uniform, walked beside it while the band assembled outside the chapel played "Come Haste to the Wedding!" A wedding reception for the two couples was held in the quarters of the commanding officer.

2	PINTS FRESH STRAWBERRIES, HULLED		2	TABLESPOONS GRAND MARNIER
3	TABLESPOONS CONFECTIONERS' SUGAR		1	CUP HEAVY CREAM, WHIPPED
4	OUNCES KIRSCH			

Wash strawberries; drain well; and sprinkle with sugar. Cover tightly and refrigerate. One hour before serving, mix in Kirsch and Grand Marnier. Return to the refrigerator until just before serving. Serve with whipped cream.

For a marriage made in heaven, serve with Sour Cream Pound Cake (see recipe on the next page).

AN AFTERNOON OF CROQUET

SOUR CREAM POUND CAKE
★★★★★

No longer considered "Camp Followers," these socially prominent military wives continued the tradition of carrying with them into the untamed frontier the picnics, dances, and the afternoon calls of home. They hosted teas and coffees to welcome "newcomer brides." The tradition of welcome teas, coffees, and showers continues to this day. It is a way of saying, "Welcome, you are one of us now and we stand by you."

1	CUP BUTTER
1 ½	CUPS SUGAR
6	EGGS SEPARATED (RESERVE WHITES)
2	CUPS ALL-PURPOSE FLOUR, SIFTED
¼	TEASPOON BAKING SODA
1¾	CUPS SOUR CREAM

½	CUP LEMON-FLAVORED CONFECTIONERS' SUGAR (IF NOT AVAILABLE, USE PLAIN)
1	TABLESPOON VANILLA EXTRACT
2	TEASPOONS LEMON EXTRACT
	ADDITIONAL SUGAR SUFFICIENT TO DUST CAKE

Preheat the oven to 350°F. Grease and flour a Bundt cake pan and set aside. In a large mixing bowl cream together the butter and sugar. Add the egg yolks one at a time. In a separate bowl sift together the flour and baking soda, and add to butter mixture. Alternate with additions of sour cream and confectioners' sugar. Add the extracts and beat well.

Beat the egg whites until stiff peaks form and fold into the batter. Spoon the batter into the prepared Bundt pan; place in the oven and bake for 1 to 1½ hours or until golden brown. When a tester inserted in the cake's center comes out clean, the cake is done. Sprinkle a layer of confectioners' sugar on each serving plate. Allow the cake to cool for 15 minutes and turn out onto the serving plate. Dust the cake with additional confectioners' sugar.

YIELDS 8 TO 12 SERVINGS.

"Of all our happy days, the happiest had now come to us at Fort Lincoln. I never knew more happily united married people than those of our regiment. The wife had the privilege of becoming the comrade of her husband in that isolated existence and the officers seemed to feel that every amusement was heightened if shared by the other sex. Life grew more enjoyable every day as we realized the blessings of our home." [Libbie Custer]

CHAMPAGNE COCKTAILS
★ ★ ★ ★ ★

"The pretty reception was in the quarters of Major and Mrs. Stokes, and there was a delicious supper served. Some of the presents were elegant. . . . A superb silver pitcher by the men of Major Stokes Company, and an exquisite silver after-dinner coffee set by the company in which the groom is a lieutenant." [Frances Roe]

	CHAMBORD (BLACK RASPBERRY LIQUEUR)	6	BOTTLES CHILLED CHAMPAGNE
25	SUGAR CUBES	25	LEMON TWISTS

Place 1 teaspoon of raspberry liqueur in each glass; add a sugar cube, gently pour the champagne into the glass. Top with a twist of lemon and serve.

YIELDS 25 GLASSES.

"The bride is petite and very young, and looked almost a child as she and her father slowly passed us, her gown of heavy ivory satin trailing far back of her. The orchestra played several numbers previous to the ceremony—the Mendelssohn March for processional, and Lohengrin for recessional, but the really exquisite music was during the ceremony, when there came to us softly, as if floating from afar over gold lace and perfumed silks and satins, the enchanting strains of Moszowski's serenade. . . . The excitement is about over. Our guests have returned to their homes, and now we are settling down to everyday garrison life." [Frances Roe]

Sunrise Coffee

★　★　★　★　★

According to Private Samuel Chamberlain, 1st Dragoons, "Dut Mary," a well-known laundress of the Second Illinois Regiment, came onto the field with two camp kettles of coffee. Observing her bravery, Captain George Lincoln cried out to rally the troops, "Hurrah boys, be of good cheer, for the ladies are on our side!"

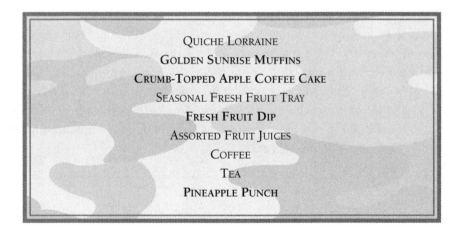

QUICHE LORRAINE
GOLDEN SUNRISE MUFFINS
CRUMB-TOPPED APPLE COFFEE CAKE
SEASONAL FRESH FRUIT TRAY
FRESH FRUIT DIP
ASSORTED FRUIT JUICES
COFFEE
TEA
PINEAPPLE PUNCH

GOLDEN SUNRISE MUFFINS
★★★★★

Indeed, then as always the ladies were on their side, often over their family's objections. Nineteen-year-old Anna Symmes was a young lady boasting a fine eastern boarding school education, pretty clothes, and dainty manners. As such, she quickly attracted the courtly attentions of a young lieutenant from one of Virginia's best families. Despite the young man's sterling credentials, Judge Symmes objected to the union because it would expose his daughter to the dangers and harshness of frontier fort life.

½	CUP ALL-PURPOSE FLOUR	¼	CUP BUTTER, MELTED
¾	CUP WHOLE WHEAT FLOUR	½	CUP FIRMLY PACKED BROWN SUGAR
2	TEASPOONS BAKING POWDER	½	CUP HALF AND HALF
½	TEASPOON SALT	9	SUGAR CUBES, DIVIDED
¼	TEASPOON GROUND CINNAMON	1	TABLESPOON APRICOT BRANDY
⅛	TEASPOON GRATED NUTMEG	9	TEASPOONS APRICOT JAM, DIVIDED
1	EGG		

Preheat the oven to 350°F. In a large bowl combine all-purpose flour and whole wheat flour, baking powder, salt, and spices. Make a well in the center of the flour mixture and set aside. In a smaller bowl, lightly beat egg; mix in melted butter, sugar, and half and half. Pour into flour well and stir just enough to moisten ingredients, approximately 12 to 15 circular strokes. Fill greased and floured or paper-lined 2½-inch muffin cups about 2/3 full. Quickly roll sugar-cube in brandy and place on top of muffin; add 1 teaspoon apricot jam to each. Bake for approximately 25 minutes or until golden.

YIELDS 9 MUFFINS.

CRUMB-TOPPED APPLE COFFEE CAKE
★ ★ ★ ★ ★

Love triumphed and on November 25, 1795, Miss Symmes and Lieutenant William Henry Harrison were covertly united in marriage. First distinguishing himself in the War of 1812 and, later, as a territorial delegate from Ohio, the lieutenant was appointed governor of the Indiana Territory. This assignment took the couple further into the wilderness. However, in Vincennes he built for his bride a fortified plantation home. In a landslide victory in 1840, William Henry Harrison became the ninth president of the United States!

1	CUP ALL-PURPOSE FLOUR	1	CUP SUGAR
½	TEASPOON SALT	1	TEASPOON GROUND CINNAMON
1	TEASPOON BAKING SODA	¼	TEASPOON GRATED NUTMEG
2	CUPS CORED, PEELED, AND DICED SWEET APPLES	⅛	TEASPOON GROUND ALLSPICE
1	EGG	½	CUP CHOPPED PECANS
¼	CUP VEGETABLE OIL		

Preheat the oven to 350°F. In a large bowl sift together flour, salt, and soda. Set aside. Place the apples in a medium-sized bowl and break the egg over them. Add the oil, sugar, cinnamon, nutmeg, allspice, and chopped pecans. Blend thoroughly. Stir the apple mixture into the flour mixture just until the flour is moist. (The mixture will appear to be dry and stiff). Spread into an 8-inch square baking pan. Sprinkle the topping (see recipe below) over the cake. Bake for 40 to 45 minutes. Allow to cool. Cut into 9 squares and remove to a serving dish.

TOPPING

½	CUP FIRMLY PACKED LIGHT BROWN SUGAR	¼	CUP BUTTER, CUT INTO SMALL PIECES
¼	CUP ALL-PURPOSE FLOUR	1	TEASPOON GROUND CINNAMON

In a small bowl combine the topping ingredients and sprinkle over the coffeecake.

> *"The vagrant life, the inability to keep household goods, giving up the privileges, . . . the anxiety and suspense of a soldier's wife, might well make the mothers opposed to the life. One said, in trying to persuade me . . . to break my engagement with the General, 'Why, girl, you can't be a poor man's wife.'"* [Libbie Custer]

FRESH FRUIT TRAY AND FRUIT DIP
★★★★★

In the winter of 1876, Libbie Custer finally took up residence in a large, new, stately Victorian home at Fort Lincoln in the Dakota Territory. It is likely that the other military wives gathered at her home for afternoon socials, or to review books, sew, and, undoubtedly, trade a recipe or two. Like cherished heirloom china, the tradition has passed through many hands.

4	CUPS HULLED STRAWBERRIES		1	CUP PEELED AND SLICED KIWI FRUIT
2	CUPS 2-INCH CANTALOUPE CUBES			OTHER FRUIT OF CHOICE
2	CUPS HONEYDEW MELON			

FRUIT DIP

2	EGGS		¼	CUP LEMON JUICE
½	CUP HONEY		½	CUP HEAVY CREAM, WHIPPED

Over a double boiler (with water almost to the boiling point) use a wire whisk to beat the eggs until light. Add the honey and lemon juice; whip an additional 1 to 2 minutes until the mixture is completely foamy. Stir in the whipping cream and continue to whip over the double boiler for approximately 1 minute. Remove to a heatproof serving dish and refrigerate to chill before serving.

YIELDS APPROXIMATELY 1½ CUPS.

Almost without exeption, this new breed of military wife carried with her warm embers from her mother's kitchen in the form of recipes, which she exchanged with other wives . . . the tradition continues.

PINEAPPLE PUNCH
★★★★★

From 1773 onward, the "Pernicious Custom of Drinking Tea" gave way to that of coffee, which remained the favorite social drink of military wives. Katherine Tupper Marshall, wife of General George Marshall, was so shocked to learn that coffee "outranked" tea, she mentioned it in her memoirs years later. The drinks continue to be ranked: coffee, tea, and punch.

1	32-OUNCE CAN PINEAPPLE JUICE	1	32-OUNCE BOTTLE LEMON-LIME SODA
1	6-OUNCE CAN FROZEN LEMONADE, THAWED	1	20-OUNCE CAN PINEAPPLE CHUNKS WITH JUICE
½	CUP CONFECTIONERS' SUGAR		LEMON SLICES TO GARNISH

In a punch bowl combine the pineapple juice, frozen lemonade, and confectioners' sugar. Mix well until the confectioners' sugar is well blended. Add the soda and pineapple chunks with juice. Garnish with lemon slices and add ice just prior to serving. Have additional pineapple juice on hand as ice melts.

YIELDS 3 QUARTS.

"After tea I asked the ladies who assisted me to remain and I unburdened my heart to them. I told them that I knew nothing of Army customs and conventions and asked their help, thereby winning some staunch friends. I recall one of them said, 'At a tea such as this one, you always ask the highest ranking officer's wife to pour coffee, not tea.' Upon asking the reason why, the woman replied, 'Well, coffee outranks tea.' It was not until years later that I found this custom had good reason: With Americans, coffee is more popular than tea and naturally you put the guest of honor at the end of the table where the crowd gathers.

"Later, during World War II, when I had to speak before women's clubs and groups of young Army wives, my advice to them was not to cling to their hometown customs when they were called upon to uproot and follow their husbands and not to be critical of strange customs and ideas; that I had found from living all over this country that if you tried you could always find good reason why these customs had developed.

"At the end of our two years at Fort Benning I was a fair Army wife. At least I had learned many things, among them to be on time, to listen rather than express opinions, that Lieutenants do not dance with Colonel's wives for pleasure, that aquiring a good seat in the saddle takes endurance beyond the power of a man to express." [Katherine Tupper Marshall]

Afternoon Coffee

★ ★ ★ ★ ★

Coffee received its common nickname from U.S. Navy admiral Josephus "Joe" Daniels. The navy tradition-
ally allowed alcoholic beverages on U.S. Navy ships. Ale, grog, and beer were routinely supplied in the gen-
eral canteen. But when Admiral Joe Daniels became chief of naval operations, he outlawed the practice and
ordered coffee to be made the "beverage of service" on U.S. Navy ships. Hence the term "cup of hot joe,"
later shortened to "hot joe" and then to "hojo" or just "joe."

Later, as secretary of the navy, Daniels would, in the 1916 law that created the Naval Reserve,
authorize the enlistment of yeomen "(F)." Referred to as "yeomenettes," they were recruited to "Free a Man
to Fight" and at Daniels's insistence they received the same pay as a yeoman "(M)," $28.75 per month.

HAM AND CHEESE MUFFINS
SOUR CREAM COFFEE CAKE
FRUIT COMPOTE

HAM AND CHEESE MUFFINS

★★★★★

Following World War II, coffee cliques or circles became regularly scheduled events, providing a means for sharing unit and community information.

2	CUPS SIFTED ALL-PURPOSE FLOUR		1	EGG
½	TEASPOON SALT		3	TABLESPOONS BUTTER, MELTED
1	TABLESPOON SUGAR		¾	CUP CHOPPED HAM
4	TEASPOONS BAKING POWDER		½	CUP SHREDDED CHEDDAR CHEESE
1	CUP MILK			

Preheat the oven to 425°F. Butter and flour a 12-muffin tin and set aside. In a medium bowl sift together the flour, salt, sugar, and baking powder. In a separate bowl combine the milk, egg, and butter; add to the dry ingredients. Sprinkle ham and cheese across the surface and stir just until the dry ingredients are moistened. The batter should be lumpy. Fill each muffin cup ⅔ full. Bake for 20 to 25 minutes.

YIELDS 12 MUFFINS.

SKATING PARTY AT FORT KEOGH, MONTANA, 1890

SOUR CREAM COFFEE CAKE
⋆ ⋆ ⋆ ⋆ ⋆

Coffees also served as a forum for welcoming new friends, bidding a fond farewell to old friends, or simply enjoying the common bond of military life.

FOR THE CAKE:

1	CUP BUTTER, SOFTENED
2	CUPS SUGAR
2	TEASPOONS VANILLA EXTRACT
2	TEASPOONS ALMOND EXTRACT
6	EGGS AT ROOM TEMPERATURE
3	CUPS ALL-PURPOSE FLOUR, SIFTED
2½	TEASPOONS BAKING SODA
1	TEASPOON GROUND CINNAMON
1	CUP SOUR CREAM

FOR THE TOPPING:

2	TABLESPOONS BUTTER, SOFTENED
1	CUP FIRMLY PACKED BROWN SUGAR
2½	TEASPOONS GROUND CINNAMON
⅛	TEASPOON GROUND ALLSPICE
1	CUP CHOPPED WALNUTS
½	PINT SOUR CREAM

Preheat the oven to 325°F. Butter and line a 10-inch tube pan with parchment paper. In a large mixing bowl cream together the butter and sugar. Add the vanilla and almond extracts. Add the eggs one at a time, beating well after each addition, and set aside. In a separate bowl sift together the flour, baking soda, and cinnamon. Gradually add to the butter mixture, alternating with additions of sour cream, blending well after each addition.

To make the topping, in a small bowl cream together the butter, brown sugar, cinnamon, and allspice. Blend in the walnuts and sour cream.

Pour half of the batter into the prepared tube cake pan and evenly distribute half of the topping mixture over the batter in the tube pan. Cover with the remaining batter and distribute the remaining topping mixture. Bake for 50 minutes or until golden.

YIELDS 8 TO 12 SERVINGS.

FRUIT COMPOTE
★★★★★

Whenever or wherever they are held, today's coffees remain an integral part of the tradition of military wives. This national drink can be found at the center of almost every special occasion or celebration.

3	TABLESPOONS BUTTER	¼	TEASPOON GROUND ALLSPICE
1	LARGE PEAR, CORED AND THINLY SLICED	⅔	CUP APPLE CIDER
2	LARGE APRICOTS, PITTED AND SLICED	¼	CUP FIRMLY PACKED BROWN SUGAR
2	GREEN APPLES, CORED AND THINLY SLICED	1	TEASPOON ORANGE PEEL (NO WHITE), FINELY GRATED
2	SMALL CINNAMON STICKS, 1 ½ TO 2 INCHES		
¾	CUP YELLOW RAISINS		

In a large saucepan over medium heat melt the butter and sauté the pears, apricots, and apples with cinnamon sticks for 3 to 4 minutes. Add the raisins and allspice. Reduce the heat and add the apple cider, brown sugar, and grated orange peel. Simmer uncovered for 10 to 12 minutes or until the pears and apples are tender and the sauce thickens. Remove and discard the cinnamon sticks. To serve, arrange pound cake slices on individual dessert plates and spoon warm fruit mixture over each slice.

*C*offees are most often the manner in which "new-comer" brides are welcomed into the circle that Ruth Patton Totten described as "the glorious society." The tradition has passed through the welcoming hands of many generations of wives and their mothers.

"Molly's marriage on Christmas Day in Quarters Number One at Fort Myer was the first wedding, I believe ever to take place in that house. She came down on George's arm followed by her maid-of-honor, Mary Winn. They passed through the drawing-room and were met at the altar, which had been constructed at the far end of the oval dining-room. The bride's path was flanked on each side by white chrysanthemums and tall standards holding white candles. Her gown was cream satin with an extremely long train, and her cap and veil were of rose-point lace. She kept her eyes steadily on Captain Winn and his on her. . . . After the ceremony, they walked out beneath the crossed swords of the groomsmen, while the band played Lohengrin's Wedding March. As soon as the reception was over, they left for Panama and I did not see Molly until she came home a year and a half later with her baby son." [Katherine Tupper Marshall]

"I came over to wait while the tents were being pitched. . . . Soon after I came my kind hostess brought in a cup of most delicious coffee and a little pitcher of cream—real cream. . . . And she also brought over a plate piled high with generous pieces of German cinnamon cake. . . ." [Frances Roe, 1877]

"We had a lovely Christmas. I fared beautifully, as some of our staff had been to San Antonio, where the stores have a good many beautiful things from Mexico." On the frontier ". . . we had little opportunity to buy anything, but I managed to get up some trifle for each of our circle." [Libbie Custer]

Holiday Dessert Coffee for Fifty

★ ★ ★ ★ ★

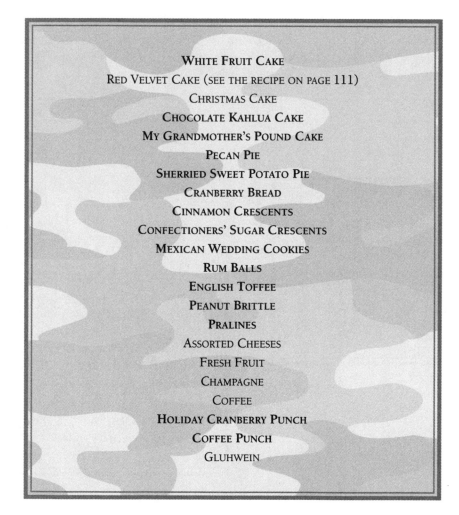

WHITE FRUIT CAKE

RED VELVET CAKE (SEE THE RECIPE ON PAGE 111)

CHRISTMAS CAKE

CHOCOLATE KAHLUA CAKE

MY GRANDMOTHER'S POUND CAKE

PECAN PIE

SHERRIED SWEET POTATO PIE

CRANBERRY BREAD

CINNAMON CRESCENTS

CONFECTIONERS' SUGAR CRESCENTS

MEXICAN WEDDING COOKIES

RUM BALLS

ENGLISH TOFFEE

PEANUT BRITTLE

PRALINES

ASSORTED CHEESES

FRESH FRUIT

CHAMPAGNE

COFFEE

HOLIDAY CRANBERRY PUNCH

COFFEE PUNCH

GLUHWEIN

WHITE FRUIT CAKE
★★★★★

"We had a huge Christmas tree, and Autie was Santa Claus, and handed down the presents, making side-splitting remarks as each person walked up to receive his gift. The tree was well-lighted. I don't know how so many tapers were gotten together." [Libbie Custer]

1	POUND CANDIED CHERRIES	2	TEASPOONS FRESH LEMON JUICE
1	POUND CANDIED PINEAPPLES	2	TEASPOONS GRATED NUTMEG
½	POUND CITRON	12	EGG WHITES, BEATEN
1	CUP WHITE SEEDLESS RAISINS	4	CUPS ALL-PURPOSE FLOUR, SIFTED
½	CUP BRANDY	2	TEASPOONS BAKING POWDER
½	POUND BLANCHED ALMONDS		ZEST OF 1 ORANGE
4	TABLESPOONS ROSE WATER	1 ½	CUP PECANS
1	POUND BUTTER	1 ½	CUPS WALNUTS
2	CUPS SUGAR		

Six weeks in advance: Prepare the fruit by slicing the cherries in half, if necessary, and soaking all of the fruit in brandy for 72 hours.

Soak the blanched almonds in rose water overnight.

Preheat the oven to 275°F. Grease the sides and bottom of a large aluminum pan. In addition, grease brown paper cut to fit the bottom of the pan. In a large bowl cream together the butter and sugar. Add the lemon juice, nutmeg, and egg whites. In a separate bowl sift together the flour and baking powder, saving enough to dust the fruits and nuts. (Dusting prevents them from sticking together.) Combine the flour and butter mixtures well. Add the zest. After dusting, add fruits and nuts to the batter. Spoon into the prepared pan. Bake for 3 to 3¼ hours. Keep a pan of water in the oven to maintain moisture.

Note: The flavor of a fruitcake is enhanced with age. Age for at least thirty days before serving by storing in a cool dry place. Once a week or so, slightly moisten with equal parts brandy and Grand Marnier.

YIELDS 8 SERVINGS.

CHOCOLATE KAHLUA CAKE
★★★★★

"Of course it would not have been us if, with all the substantial gifts, some jokes were not slipped in. No one escapes in such a crowd. Only our own military family was here, and Armstrong gave us a nice supper, all of his own getting up." [Libbie Custer]

FOR THE CAKE:

2	CUPS SUGAR
2	CUPS ALL-PURPOSE FLOUR, SIFTED
	PINCH SALT
½	CUP BUTTER
2	TABLESPOONS COCOA
⅛	TEASPOON GROUND CINNAMON
¼	TEASPOON GRATED NUTMEG
⅓	CUP WATER
⅔	CUP KAHLUA

½	CUP SOUR CREAM
2	EGGS, SLIGHTLY BEATEN
1	TEASPOON BAKING SODA
1	TEASPOON ALMOND EXTRACT

FOR THE GLAZE:

½	CUP SUGAR
⅛	CUP WATER
¼	CUP KAHLUA
¼	CUP BUTTER

Preheat the oven to 300°F. Grease and flour a Bundt cake pan. In a large mixing bowl combine the sugar, flour, and salt; set aside. In a small saucepan bring the butter, cocoa, cinnamon, nutmeg, and water to a boil. Remove from the heat. Add the Kahlua and pour the mixture into the dry ingredients, and mix well. Add the sour cream, eggs, baking soda, and extract, stirring after each addition. Pour into the prepared pan and bake for 50 to 55 minutes or until a toothpick inserted into the center comes out clean. Meanwhile, make the glaze. In a small saucepan combine the sugar, water, Kahlua, and butter over medium-high heat until the butter has melted and the sugar is dissolved. Drizzle over the cake.

YIELDS 10 TO 12 SERVINGS.

"We played games, sang songs, mostly for the chorus [and] danced. The rooms were prettily trimmed with evergreens, and over one door was a great branch of mistletoe, about which the officers sang:

Fair mistletoe!
Loves opportunity!
What tree that grows
Gives such sweet impunity?

MY GRANDMOTHER'S POUND CAKE

★★★★★

1	POUND BUTTER AT ROOM TEMPERATURE	3	TEASPOONS BAKING POWDER
2	CUPS SUGAR	1	CUP EVAPORATED MILK
6	EGGS, AT ROOM TEMPERATURE	1	TABLESPOON VANILLA EXTRACT
3	CUPS ALL-PURPOSE FLOUR		

Preheat the oven to 350°F. Butter and flour a Bundt cake pan or two 9 x 5-inch loaf pans. In a large mixing bowl beat the butter with an electric mixer until creamy. Gradually add the sugar and continue to beat until fluffy. Add the eggs one at a time, beating after each addition. In a separate bowl sift together the flour and baking powder. Add to the butter mixture one cup at a time, beating after each addition. Add the milk, as required, up to 1 cup. Blend in the extract. This thick batter cannot be poured; spoon it into the prepared pan. Bake for 1 hour or until a toothpick inserted into the center comes out clean.

YIELDS 8 TO 12 SERVINGS.

. . . But it is too bad that as pretty as two or three of our women are, they belong to someone else. So kissing begins and ends with every man saluting his own wife. I wish you could see the waxen white berries and the green leaves of the parasites on the naked branches of the trees here, Mother. . . . and oh to have you get one sniff of the December roses, which rival the summer ones in richness of color and perfume would make my pleasure greater, I assure you." [Libbie Custer, Tenting the Plains]

PECAN PIE

★★★★★

1	CUP DARK KARO SYRUP	1	CUP COARSELY CHOPPED PECANS
½	CUP FIRMLY PACKED BROWN SUGAR	1	TEASPOON VANILLA EXTRACT
3	EGGS, SLIGHTLY BEATEN	¼	TEASPOON GROUND CINNAMON
¼	CUP MELTED BUTTER	1	UNBAKED 9-INCH PIE SHELL

Preheat the oven to 350°F. In a medium mixing bowl combine all of the above filling ingredients; mix well and pour into the pie shell. Bake approximately 50 to 60 minutes until firm.

YIELDS 6 TO 8 SERVINGS.

"All the little presents were spread out on a table, and in a way to make them present as fine as possible. . . . They have a charming custom in the Army of going along the line Christmas morning and giving each other pleasant greetings and looking at the pretty things everyone has received. This is a rare treat out here, where we are so far from shops and beautiful Christmas displays." [Frances Roe]

SHERRIED SWEET POTATO PIE

★★★★★

"Our first Christmas on the frontier was ever so pleasant … several women of the garrison sent pretty little gifts to me. It was quite thoughtful of them to remember that I might be a bit homesick just now." [Frances Roe, Fort Lyon Colorado Territory, 1871]

2	UNBAKED 9-INCH PIE SHELLS	¼	TEASPOON LEMON ZEST
4	LARGE SWEET POTATOES	½	CUP SHERRY
½	CUP UNSALTED BUTTER, MELTED	4	EGG WHITES
1½	CUPS SUGAR	⅛	TEASPOON GROUND ALLSPICE
1	CUP HALF AND HALF	1	TEASPOON GRATED NUTMEG
4	EGG YOLKS, WELL BEATEN (RESERVE WHITES)		

Preheat the oven to 450°F. Fill the pastry shell with aluminum pie weights, which can be purchased at any specialty shop, or dried beans. Bake at 450°F for approximately 8 minutes or until lightly browned. When cooled, remove the weights and set the shell aside while preparing the filling. Reset the oven to 425°F.

For the filling: place the potatoes in a large pot with sufficient water to cover. Bring to a boil over high heat and then reduce to medium. Boil until th potatoes are fork-tender. Drain. Allow the potatoes to cool and remove the peels. In a large mixing bowl combine the potatoes, melted butter, sugar, half and half, egg yolks, zest, and sherry. Mix well. In a separate bowl beat the egg whites until stiff peaks form; fold into the potato mixture. Fill 2 prepared pie shells and place in the preheated oven. Bake for 15 minutes at 425°F. Reduce the heat to 350°F and bake an additional 45 minutes until lightly browned.

YIELDS 6 TO 8 SERVINGS.

CRANBERRY-CINNAMON HONEY BREAD

★ ★ ★ ★ ★

"At half past ten yesterday the chaplain held service, and the little chapel was so crowded…. We sang our Christmas music, and received many compliments. Our little choir is really very good." [Frances Roe]

6	CUPS BISQUICK MIX	1½	CUPS HONEY
2	TEASPOONS SALT	1⅓	CUPS MILK
2	TEASPOONS GROUND CINNAMON	2	EGGS, BEATEN
2	TEASPOONS FINELY GRATED ORANGE ZEST	1	CUP CHOPPED PECANS
2	CUPS COARSELY CHOPPED FRESH CRANBERRIES		

Preheat the oven to 375°F. Prepare two 8½ x 4½-inch loaf pans by first greasing the pans and then greasing and cutting 2 pieces of brown paper to fit the bottom of the pans. In a large bowl combine the Bisquick, salt, cinnamon, orange zest, and cranberries and set aside. In a medium bowl combine the honey, milk, and eggs; add to the cranberry mixture and stir until the ingredients are moist. Add the nuts. The mixture should appear lumpy at this point. Spoon the mixture into the 2 prepared loaf pans. Bake for 55 to 60 minutes. Cool and wrap in foil.

YIELDS 2 LOAVES.

CINNAMON CRESCENTS
★★★★★

"From the chapel we—that is the company officers and their wives—went to the company barracks to see the men's dinner tables. When we entered the dining hall we found the entire company standing in two lines, down each side, every man in his best inspection uniform, and every button shining." [Frances Roe]

1	CUP UNSALTED BUTTER	2⅓	CUPS SIFTED ALL-PURPOSE FLOUR
⅔	CUP SIFTED CONFECTIONERS' SUGAR	2	CUPS FINE (BAKER'S) SUGAR
1¼	TEASPOONS VANILLA EXTRACT	3	TABLESPOONS GROUND CINNAMON
½	CUP GROUND ALMONDS		

Preheat the oven to 350°F. Line 2 baking sheets with parchment paper and set aside. In a large mixing bowl cream together the butter and confectioners' sugar until the mixture is light and fluffy. Beat in the vanilla extract and add the ground almonds. Add the flour. Break off approximately 1 tablespoon of dough at a time and form into 2-inch-long cylinders. Place approximately 1 inch apart on baking sheets and form into a crescent. Bake for approximately 15 minutes or until golden brown.

While the cookies are baking, combine the sugar and cinnamon in a small mixing bowl. Mix well and set aside. After the cookies have baked, remove from the oven to cool.

When the cookies are warm but no longer hot to the touch, gently roll them in the cinnamon sugar mixture.

YIELDS 3 DOZEN COOKIES.

CONFECTIONERS' CRESCENTS
★★★★★

Follow the directions for cinnamon crescents and substitute 2 cups of confectioners' sugar for the sugar/cinnamon mixture used to dust the cookies. These cookies look fabulous arranged in alternating rows on a silver tray.

> *"The hall was very prettily decorated with flags and accoutrements, but one missed the greens. There are no evergreens here, only cottonwood."* [Frances Roe]

MEXICAN WEDDING COOKIES
⭐⭐⭐⭐⭐

"It is the custom in the regiment for the wives of officers every Christmas to send the men of their husband's companies large plum cakes rich with fruit and sugar." [Frances Roe]

2	CUPS BUTTER	1	TABLESPOON VANILLA EXTRACT
1	CUP CONFECTIONERS' SUGAR	4	CUPS SIFTED ALL-PURPOSE FLOUR
1	CUP COARSELY CHOPPED PECANS		

Preheat the oven to 325°F. In a large mixing bowl cream together the butter and sugar. Add the nuts and mix well. Stir in the vanilla and sifted flour until just mixed. Taking 1 teaspoon at a time, shape the dough into a ball and place on an ungreased cookie sheet. Bake for approximately 20 minutes. Remove from the pan and cool on wire racks for 7 or 8 minutes before rolling the cookies in the confectioners' sugar.

Note: Placed in tightly sealed containers, they will keep approximately 2 to 3 weeks. These cookies are also delicious when dusted with the cinnamon sugar mixture used on the cinnamon crescents (see page 61).

YIELDS APPROXIMATELY 8 DOZEN COOKIES.

RUM BALLS
⭐⭐⭐⭐⭐

"And in the center of each table, high up, was a huge cake thickly covered with icing. These were the cakes that Mrs. Phillips, Mrs. Barker, and I had sent over that morning." [Frances Roe]

3 ¼	CUPS GROUND VANILLA WAFERS	3	TABLESPOONS LIGHT CORN SYRUP
1	CUP GROUND WALNUTS	1	CUP DARK RUM
1½	CUPS CONFECTIONERS' SUGAR		

In a medium mixing bowl combine the above ingredients and mix thoroughly. The mixture will be very sticky, so dust hands and mixture with confectioners' sugar before attempting to shape. Shape into 1-inch balls and roll in confectioners' sugar. Place on waxed paper for approximately 1 hour before storing in a tightly lidded container.

Make at least two to three days in advance to give rum balls sufficient time to set. Will keep in an air-tight container at room temperature for 2 to 3 weeks.

YIELDS APPROXIMATELY 4 DOZEN.

TOFFEE
★★★★★

"The first sergeant came to meet us, and went around with us. There were three long tables, fairly groaning with the things upon them: buffalo, antelope, boiled ham, several kinds of vegetables, pies, cakes, quantities of pickles, dried 'apple duff,' and coffee." [Frances Roe]

2½	CUPS FINELY CHOPPED ALMONDS	2	CUPS SUGAR
1	POUND BUTTER		

Line a 10 x 15-inch cookie sheet with waxed paper, evenly sprinkle with half of the chopped almonds, and set aside.

In a heavy saucepan melt the butter over medium heat. When the butter is completely melted, gradually add the sugar and stir rapidly to prevent separation. Continue to cook and rapidly stir the mixture until it reaches a temperature of 275°F on a candy thermometer, approximately 8 to 10 minutes. At this point, the mixture should be a rich caramel color. Remove the mixture from the heat source; cool slightly before pouring over the almonds on the cookie sheet. While the toffee is still warm, frost with chocolate frosting and dust with the remaining almonds.

YIELDS 8 SERVINGS.

FROSTING

To frost, melt 1 12-ounce bag of chocolate chips in a pan over hot water. Spread over warm toffee and sprinkle with the remaining nuts. Once the toffee completely cools, break it into pieces and store until ready to serve.

"The time appointed for other people's walnuts and wine was to us the hour for the officer's pipe and coffee." [Libbie Custer]

PEANUT BRITTLE
★ ★ ★ ★ ★

According to legend, coffee was initially discovered by an Abyssinian goat-herder. While observing his goats, he noticed them dancing on their hind legs after eating some red berries. After tasting the berries and becoming noticeably energized, the goatherder took some to the village monastery, where it was well received because it kept everyone awake during their prayers.

4	CUPS SUGAR	1	TEASPOON BAKING SODA
1	CUP LIGHT KARO SYRUP	3	TABLESPOONS BUTTER
1	CUP WATER	3	CUPS RAW PEANUTS
2	TEASPOONS VANILLA EXTRACT		

In a large skillet combine the sugar, syrup, and water. Cook over low heat, stirring constantly, until the mixture reaches 230°F with a candy thermometer. Stir in the vanilla and add the baking soda; continue to cook until the mixture reaches 300°F or until a small dollop becomes hard and brittle when dropped in a bowl of cold water. The mixture should reach a deep caramel color. When drop test is performed, the drop should hold its shape and you will hear it crackle. Remove from the heat and stir in the remaining ingredients. Pour onto a greased cookie sheet and spread thin. When cold, break into serving size pieces.

YIELDS 8 SERVINGS.

PECAN PRALINES
⋆⋆⋆⋆⋆

Sir Francis Bacon noted: "They have in Turkey a drink called coffee . . . which they take, beaten into powder, in water, as hot as they can drink it; and they take it, and sit at it in their coffee houses, which are like our taverns. The Drink comforteth the brain and heart, and helpeth digestion."

1	CUP SUGAR	2	CUPS PECAN HALVES
1	CUP LIGHT BROWN SUGAR	1	TEASPOON VANILLA EXTRACT
½	TEASPOON BAKING SODA	¾	CUP HALF AND HALF
½	CUP BUTTER		

Line a cookie sheet with waxed paper and set aside. In a saucepan combine the sugars, baking soda, and butter, and cook over medium-high heat to a soft ball stage (238°F on a candy thermometer). Add the pecans and vanilla during the last few minutes of cooking time. Remove from the heat, add the half and half, and beat until thick. Drop on the cookie sheet in small patties. Allow to completely cool before storing in a tightly sealed container.

CRANBERRY PUNCH
⋆⋆⋆⋆⋆

8	CUPS CRANBERRY JUICE COCKTAIL	1	TABLESPOON ALMOND EXTRACT
3	CUPS WHITE GRAPE JUICE	1	CUP ORANGE RIND CURLS (NO WHITE PITH)
8	CUPS PINEAPPLE JUICE	2	QUARTS CARBONATED LEMON-LIME SODA, DIVIDED
3	CUPS SUGAR		

Three hours prior to serving, place the orange rind curls on the bottom of 2 Bundt cake pans. In a large bowl combine the cranberry juice, grape juice, pineapple juice, sugar, and almond extract. Fill the pans with cranberry mixture and freeze. Refrigerate any remaining punch and carbonated beverages. Before serving, unmold one frozen ring by quickly placing the mold in warm water and inverting into the punch bowl. Add half of any remaining punch and enough carbonated lemon-lime soda to fill the punch bowl. Reserve the remaining punch ring, punch, and carbonated beverage for refills.

YIELDS 50 SERVINGS.

COFFEE PUNCH
★ ★ ★ ★ ★

In 1672, an Armenian by the name of Pascal came to Paris where he opened the city's first coffeehouse. Pascal made a fortune despite the fact that when first introduced into Europe in the early 1600s, this "modern" coffee drink was denounced as the "hellish black brew" of infidels. Pope Clement VIII enjoyed coffee so much that he promptly baptized it and made it a Christian beverage. As he proclaimed: "Coffee is so delicious it would be a pity to let the infidels have exclusive use of it."

4	QUARTS STRONG COFFEE	¼	CUP VANILLA EXTRACT
2	QUARTS VANILLA ICE CREAM	1	TABLESPOON ALMOND EXTRACT
1	QUART WHIPPING CREAM	2	CUPS KAHLUA (OPTIONAL)
¼	CUP SUGAR		

Prepare the coffee a day before; cover tightly and refrigerate. Just prior to serving, put ice cream scoops into a punch bowl. Whip the cream, adding the sugar and extracts. Add the whipped cream mixture to the punch bowl. Pour the cold coffee over the ice cream mixture; add Kahlua, if desired, and mix well.

YIELDS ABOUT 40 SERVINGS.

It is thought that Captain John Smith, the founder of the Jamestown Colony in Virginia introduced coffee to North America. Following the Boston Tea Party, coffee became the drink of patriots.

GLUHWEIN
★★★★★

"General Phillips said a few pleasant words to the men, wishing them a 'Merry Christmas' for all of us."
[Frances Roe]

FOR THE SYRUP:

4	CUPS WATER
2	CUPS SUGAR
2	TEASPOONS WHOLE CLOVES
2	TEASPOONS WHOLE ALLSPICE
1	SMALL BAY LEAF

FOR THE PUNCH:

4	CINNAMON STICKS
2	LEMONS, SLICED
2	ORANGES, SLICED
¼	TEASPOON GRATED NUTMEG
2	CUPS ORANGE JUICE
4	750-MILLILITER BOTTLES BURGUNDY

In a small saucepan combine all of the syrup ingredients. Cook over medium heat until the mixture comes to a boil, stirring constantly. Reduce the heat to medium-low and simmer for 10 minutes. Strain and cool the mixture. Divide the syrup between two crock-pots; add 2 cinnamon sticks and 2 bottles of wine to each crock-pot. Heat on low for approximately 1½ hours before serving.

YIELDS 50 ½-CUP SERVINGS.

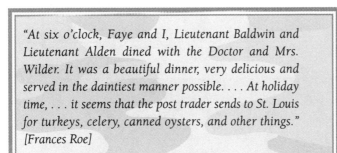

"At six o'clock, Faye and I, Lieutenant Baldwin and Lieutenant Alden dined with the Doctor and Mrs. Wilder. It was a beautiful dinner, very delicious and served in the daintiest manner possible. . . . At holiday time, . . . it seems that the post trader sends to St. Louis for turkeys, celery, canned oysters, and other things."
[Frances Roe]

*O*nly the demands of war would disrupt the supply line, which proved to be a morale booster on the isolated frontier.

Morning After: A Breakfast Coffee

✫ ✫ ✫ ✫ ✫

During the seven-day bombardment of Fort Brown (Fort Texas), Sarah Borginis, who refused to hide, cooked in the open courtyard. Seemingly oblivious to the gunfire, she served breakfast on time and complete with hot coffee.

HAM AND EGG CASSEROLE WITH CHEESE SAUCE
RASPBERRY STREUSEL MUFFINS
BLACK WALNUT BREAD
BUNCH OF BANANAS BREAKFAST PUNCH
FRUIT JUICE

GARRISON HOUSE WITH SOLDIERS AND WIVES

HAM AND EGG CASSEROLE WITH CHEESE SAUCE
★★★★★

"Dear wife, William and myself and four others went to a house near our post and engaged us a supper. . . .
It went so well that we went and took breakfast with them again in the morning." [Edgar Clark, Camp
Upson Hill, October 1, 1862]

½	CUP BUTTER, DIVIDED		⅛	TEASPOON DRY MUSTARD
2	TABLESPOONS ALL-PURPOSE FLOUR		1	CUP GRATED SHARP CHEDDAR CHEESE
2	CUPS WHOLE MILK		1	CUP CUBED HAM, FULLY COOKED
½	TEASPOON SALT		1	4-OUNCE CAN SLICED MUSHROOMS, DRAINED
¼	TEASPOON WHITE PEPPER		¼	CUP SLICED GREEN ONIONS
¼	TEASPOON BAKING POWDER		12	EGG YOLKS, BEATEN (RESERVE WHITES)

Preheat the oven to 325°F. Butter a 12 x 16-inch casserole dish and set aside. In a
saucepan over medium heat melt the butter. Stir in the flour, and gradually add the milk.
Cook and stir until smooth. Add the salt, pepper, baking powder, dry mustard, cheese,
ham, mushrooms, and green onions. Stir until smooth, but do not allow to boil; remove
from heat. In a medium bowl beat the egg yolks lightly. Pour the hot mixture into the egg
yolks, beating well, and allow to cool.

   In a glass bowl beat the egg whites until stiff but not dry and fold into the cheese mixture. Pour the mixture into a buttered casserole dish. Bake for 30 to 35 minutes. Serve
immediately.

YIELDS 6 TO 8 SERVINGS.

RASPBERRY STREUSEL MUFFINS
★★★★★

"We has [sic] a good meal and it cost us 25 cents a meal. There was [sic] sixteen others that took breakfast with us, all soldiers." [Edgar Clark, Camp Upson Hill, October 1, 1862]

FOR THE TOPPING:

½   CUP FIRMLY PACKED LIGHT BROWN SUGAR

¼   CUP ALL-PURPOSE FLOUR

1   TEASPOON GROUND CINNAMON

⅛   TEASPOON GROUND ALLSPICE

¼   CUP BUTTER, CUT INTO SMALL PIECES

FOR THE MUFFINS:

2⅓   CUPS ALL-PURPOSE FLOUR

4   TEASPOONS BAKING POWDER

½   TEASPOON SALT

¼   CUP BUTTER, SOFTENED

⅓   CUP SUGAR

1   EGG, BEATEN

1   TEASPOON GRATED ORANGE ZEST

1   CUP HALF AND HALF

¼   TEASPOON LEMON EXTRACT

¼   TEASPOON GROUND ALLSPICE

¼   TEASPOON GROUND CINNAMON

1   CUP FRESH OR FROZEN RASPBERRIES

First, make the topping. In a small bowl combine the brown sugar, flour, cinnamon, and allspice; mix well. Add the butter and cut in with a pastry blender until crumbly. Refrigerate until ready for use.

Preheat the oven to 375°F. Line twelve 2¾-inch muffin cups with paper liners. In a large bowl combine flour, baking powder, and salt. In a separate bowl use an electric mixer to cream together the butter and sugar for approximately 2 minutes or until fluffy. Beat in the egg and zest. Add the flour mixture to the butter mixture, alternating with the half and half. Stir in the extract and spices. Fold in the raspberries. The batter should be thick at this point. Spoon 1 heaping spoon of batter into each cup. Sprinkle each muffin with 1 tablespoon of the topping mixture. Evenly distribute the remaining batter on top of each muffin. Sprinkle the remaining topping over the muffin batter. Bake for 26 minutes or until a toothpick inserted in the center comes out clean. Allow to cool in the pan 5 minutes before removing to a rack to cool.

YIELDS 12 MUFFINS.

BLACK WALNUT BREAD
★★★★★

For breakfast, "We had good ripe apples and good cider, all we could drink and we had a nice time generally." [Edgar Clark, Camp Upson Hill, October 1, 1862]

3	CUPS ALL-PURPOSE FLOUR	2	EGGS
4½	TEASPOONS BAKING POWDER	1	CUP HALF AND HALF
¼	CUP SUGAR	2	TABLESPOONS HONEY
¼	CUP FIRMLY PACKED BROWN SUGAR	¼	CUP BUTTER, MELTED
¾	TEASPOON SALT	1	CUP CHOPPED BLACK WALNUTS

Preheat the oven to 350°F. In a large mixing bowl combine the flour, baking powder, sugars, and salt. In a separate bowl combine the eggs, half and half, honey, and melted butter. Add the dry ingredients and stir until thoroughly blended but slightly lumpy. Gently mix in the walnuts and spoon into a lightly greased and floured loaf pan. Bake for 1 hour.

YIELDS 1 LOAF.

BUNCH OF BANANAS BREAKFAST PUNCH
★★★★★

"Nearly two months have passed since I took my departure from our much loved home and although I witness many strange sights and there is much . . . to engage my thoughts, yet I assure you my dear wife that I enjoy many fond recollections of your affectionate kindness and love." [Edgar Clark, Camp Upson Hill, October 1, 1862]

6	MEDIUM-SIZE RIPE BANANAS	2	CUPS SUGAR, DIVIDED
1	12-OUNCE CAN FROZEN ORANGE JUICE, THAWED	1	46-OUNCE CAN PINEAPPLE JUICE
1	6-OUNCE CAN FROZEN PINEAPPLE JUICE, THAWED	3	2-LITER BOTTLES LEMON-LIME SODA
1	6-OUNCE CAN FROZEN LEMONADE, THAWED		ORANGE SLICES
4	CUPS WARM WATER, DIVIDED	24	MARASCHINO CHERRIES

In a blender or food processor blend the bananas and frozen juices until smooth. Remove half of the mixture and set aside. Add 2 cups of warm water and 1 cup of sugar to the mixture and blend until smooth. Place in a large freezer container. Repeat with the remaining banana mixture, water, and sugar. Add to the container; cover, and freeze until solid.

An hour before serving, remove the frozen punch base from the freezer. Place in a punch bowl and add the pineapple juice and soda. Garnish with orange slices and cherries.

YIELDS ABOUT 40 SERVINGS.

During the Civil War, or the "War of Northern Aggression" as some termed it, coffee remained the preferred drink of both armies. Northern soldiers ground their beans with the butts of their rifles. However, when they could not build a fire, they found some satisfaction in simply chewing the grounds. Southerners, however, often had to content themselves with substitutes made from peanuts, potatoes, or chicory.

"My dear wife, I will tell you how we work our victuals. Our meals are primarily pork and beef twice a week. We cook them as we would any meat but our coffee we make as you would make tea. We put as much water in our dish as we want and then we put the coffee on at the same time. We put the water over and as soon as it boils we think it is done. We have a loaf of bread a day. It weighs a pound and a half. But I think it will come down to our hardtack and pork and sugar and coffee. I think we will engage in an active campaign." [Camp Bullock, March 25, 1864]

Coffee was the highlight of the Custers' visit when they were briefly detained in New Orleans. Libbie recalled, "The General was enthusiastic over the city. All day we strolled through the streets, visiting the French quarter. . . . We of course spent hours, even matutinal [sic] hours, at the market, and the General drank so much coffee that the old [woman] who served him said many a 'Mon Dieu!' in surprise at his capacity and volubly described in French to her neighbors what marvels a Yankee man could do in coffee-sipping. For years after, when very good coffee was praised, or even Eliza's strongly commended, his ne plus ultra was, 'Almost equal to the French market.'"

Admiral and Mrs. William Fallon:
FAIR WINDS AND FOLLOWING SEAS

It was my privilege to work with Mrs. Mary Fallon and serve as an advisor to her on quality of military family life and readiness issues during Adm. William Fallon's tenure as commander, headquarters, U.S. Central Command (HQ USCENTCOM). I found Mrs. Fallon to be always poised, gracious, and warm, and I greatly admired her dedication and commitment to military families.

On March 11, 2008, President George W. Bush offered the following commendation to Admiral and Mrs. Fallon:

> *Admiral Fallon has served the nation with distinction for forty years. From the Horn of Africa to the streets of Baghdad to the mountains of Afghanistan, the soldiers, sailors, airmen, marines, and Coast Guardsmen of Central Command are vital to the global war on terror. During his tenure at Central Command, Admiral Fallon's job has been to help ensure that America's military forces are ready to meet the threats of an often troubled region of the world, and he deserves considerable credit for progress that has been made there, especially in Iraq and Afghanistan. I thank his wife, Mary, who knows that military service involves the whole family, and I wish them all the best as they begin the next chapter in their lives.*
>
> *In the true tradition of military spouses, Mrs. Mary Elizabeth Fallon served the military and civilian community while supporting her*

husband's service to a nation. Her community involvement included issues of family readiness and numerous board positions dealing with quality of life issues for military families. These issues were and will remain of utmost importance to her, especially those involving housing and education, which heavily impacts military members and their families.

And at CENTCOM she continued in her commitment to service families. During her husband's command, she was instrumental in ensuring families were supported in times of peace, crisis, and war with information that enhanced quality of family life, prepared them for extended deployment separations, sustained them during deployment, and facilitated smooth family reintegration following deployment. In recognition of her numerous contributions, Secretary of Defense Robert Gates presented her with the Distinguished Public Service Award. The Department of Defense Distinguished Public Service Award, the highest DoD award that civilians may receive, recognizes non-career federal employees, private citizens, and foreign nationals who have demonstrated exceptionally distinguished service of significance to the DoD. And the navy previously presented her with its coveted Superior Public Service Award, the second-highest award presented to civilians by the department of the navy.

Mrs. Fallon, born in New York City and raised in Scarsdale, New York, attended Rosemont College in Philadelphia, where she majored in history and political science. She later taught school in Virginia and Georgia. Admiral and Mrs. Fallon have four children and two grandchildren.

BUFFETS, BRUNCHES, AND LUNCHES

*Y*oung wives far from home found great comfort and fellowship in the company of other military wives. By 1898, America had become an empire. It was during this period that the women's club movement was born in the civilian sector of American life. Military wives soon joined the movement. These clubs were both social and service organizations. They raised money for worthy community causes, they joined book clubs and sewing circles, or they came together simply to entertain themselves with popular games. They met in homes for breakfast planning meetings and for business and social luncheon buffets. The tradition continues to this day. A favorite entertainment style was the buffet.

Derived from the French word meaning "sideboard," the term buffet refers to an informal entertainment style where guests serve themselves from a table or countertop. Historically, buffets such as the French *garde manger* were large dramatic productions, with food serving as the artistic medium. Today's buffet, providing for a much simpler style of entertainment, is favored by military families because it is an efficient, cost-effective method of entertaining large groups. Large buffets, such as the Holiday Dessert Party, require volume cooking and advance preparation.

Fortunately most of the recipes that follow can be prepared ahead, either completely and reheated before serving, or partially assembled and finished just before serving.

THEME: The event, season, cuisine, holiday, or other subject around which you organize your buffet. Theme is important because it drives all other decisions, and provides a format for planning and a foundation on which to build. Selecting a theme also provides ideas for making your party unique and special.

MENU SELECTION: A buffet meal should present a beautiful array of choices and a well-balanced blend of flavors, colors, and texture. In addition to considering your appointments, in making a menu choice, you should also consider whether your guests will be seated at a table or using bamboo lap trays (almost a standard item of issue in all military homes). If so, the trays should be outfitted with placemats and matching napkins. Avoid cumbersome foods that require a lot of cutting.

APPOINTMENTS: Appointments selected by a hostess set the mood. Obviously, a table set with fine linen, china, silver, and crystal is much more formal than one set with copper and your favorite set of handmade pottery. One is not better than the other. However, one may be more appropriate on the basis of the theme selected and your own entertainment style.

Additionally, the accessories determine the type of food served. For instance, for years I did not have much flatware for entertaining. Consequently, most of my buffet menus consisted of finger foods. Then I discovered flea markets, antique stores, garage sales, yard sales, and, my all time favorite, the plethora of dollar stores that have sprung up around the country. Over the years, I have collected a unique assortment of flatware and vintage silverware. I also learned that for a buffet, if you wrap your silver in napkins, no one will notice if it does not all match.

My best bargain was a set of twenty-four white restaurant plates I picked up at a flea market for 25 cents apiece. I love them because their oval shape and weight allow guests to balance them in their lap with or without a tray. Additionally, because they are neutral in color, I can use them with any color scheme or theme. I personally do not like to use paper or plastic on a buffet table. I think that freshly starched linen and flatware send the message "I am so glad that you are here and I have made a special effort to ensure that our evening together is special." Like so much about entertaining, however, this is a personal choice for me. Your own entertainment style will dictate your choice and I have been known to use paper dinner napkins in a pinch. The most important rule to remember is that your appointments should contribute to everyone's enjoyment, including your own, and not detract from it.

TABLE ORGANIZATION: Arrange plates, napkins, flatware or silver, and serving dishes in the order in which they will be used. Begin with your plates first. If you have an entrée that is to be served over rice, the rice should then of course precede the entrée. Napkins, silver, and beverages should be last. It is easier for your guests to handle the flatware if it is wrapped. And there is less opportunity for spills if the beverage is the last item selected. If at all possible, have a beverage station separate from your food station. Such an arrangement prevents backups at the buffet table. Choose an area that will allow a guest to safely rest their tray while making their selection. I attended a buffet recently where no such space was available. The host and hostess held a stack of trays which they distributed to their guests after they made their selection from the buffet line. As a result they were able to make their selections without the awkwardness of balancing their trays with one hand.

FOOD PLACEMENT: Place the largest serving dishes at the head and foot of your table. Balance the other dishes around the heaviest dishes, keeping serving order in mind. To the extent possible, balance color, texture, and temperature. It is better to have two small- to medium sized serving dishes of the same item, rather than one large dish. Such an arrangement serves a number of purposes. The buffet looks fuller, the food appears fresher, and if necessary, you can keep one of the two dishes in the oven or refrigerator and rotate it to the table as needed to maintain temperature.

ENTERTAINMENT PATTERNS: An amusing observation about food and libation is that no matter where it is placed, your guests will find it. At a party celebrating my husband's promotion to Lieutenant Colonel, I arranged multiple food and beverage stations throughout the house. A complete Mexican Fiesta was located in the basement. A vegetable crudité landscape covered an oak table in the family room and a more formal spread awaited guests in the dining room. Also included were various appetizer and beverage stations, such as a margarita bar in the kitchen and champagne fountain in the living room. This approach allowed me to experiment with various entertaining styles and my guests to gravitate to the rooms in which they felt most comfortable. Everyone had a great time!

Hearth and Home: A Soup Kitchen Party

★ ★ ★ ★ ★

"In the garrison the head of our household was almost inconsolable without soup. Oxtail soup was, of course, easy to have when the beef was killed daily at the post." However, when there was a shortage, *"like some small boy demanding his supper, he would inquire, 'Where's my soup?' If informed that there was none, he would teasingly demand then, 'go out and get some stones, and boil them up with something; only I want soup.'"* [Libbie Custer]

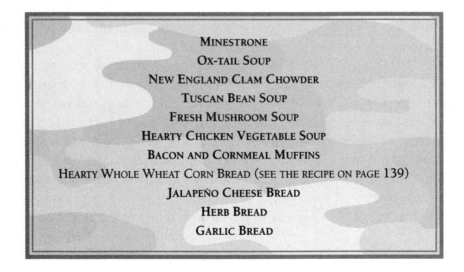

MINESTRONE

OX-TAIL SOUP

NEW ENGLAND CLAM CHOWDER

TUSCAN BEAN SOUP

FRESH MUSHROOM SOUP

HEARTY CHICKEN VEGETABLE SOUP

BACON AND CORNMEAL MUFFINS

HEARTY WHOLE WHEAT CORN BREAD (SEE THE RECIPE ON PAGE 139)

JALAPEÑO CHEESE BREAD

HERB BREAD

GARLIC BREAD

MINESTRONE
★★★★★

Soup was a frontier staple because it was inexpensive and easily prepared from a variety of readily available ingredients.

¼	POUND BACON		½	CUP DICED POTATOES
1	CUP DICED ONION		1	CUP SLICED ZUCCHINI
2	CLOVES GARLIC, MINCED		1	CUP SHREDDED CABBAGE
2	POUNDS SHIN BONES WITH MEAT		3	MEDIUM TOMATOES, PEELED, SEEDED AND DICED
5	QUARTS WATER		¼	CUP PARSLEY, CHOPPED
2	PINTS BEEF STOCK		1	TABLESPOON SALT
½	CUP BIAS SLICED CARROTS		1	TEASPOON BASIL LEAVES
½	CUP DICED CELERY		½	TEASPOON GROUND BLACK PEPPER
½	CUP FRESH SNAP BEANS			GRATED PARMESAN CHEESE

In a skillet or pot cook the bacon until crisp. Remove the bacon and set aside for later use; add the onion and garlic to the drippings and sauté until the onion is transparent. Add the shinbones, water, and stock; bring to a quick boil; reduce the heat and allow to simmer for 3 hours. (This may be accomplished 1 day in advance.) Remove the shinbones from the broth and cut the meat away from them. Return the meat to the broth and discard the bones. Add the carrots, celery, beans, and potatoes. Cover and simmer for 45 minutes.

Add the remaining ingredients except the Parmesan, cover, and cook an additional 20 minutes or until the vegetables are tender. Garnish with crumbled bacon and grated Parmesan cheese.

YIELDS 6 TO 8 SERVINGS.

OXTAIL SOUP
★★★★★

"There was very little hunting about Fort Riley in the winter. The General had shot a great many prairie chickens in the autumn and hung them in the wood-house, and while they lasted, we were not entirely dependent on government beef. As the season advanced, we had only oxtail soup and beef." [Libbie Custer]

5	POUNDS OXTAIL, SECTIONED		7	QUARTS WATER
2	CUPS ALL-PURPOSE FLOUR FOR DREDGING		2	BAY LEAVES
2	TABLESPOONS SEASONED SALT		1	CUP CHOPPED CELERY
2	TEASPOONS ONION POWDER		1	CUP PEELED AND DICED TURNIPS
2	TEASPOONS GROUND BLACK PEPPER		1	CUP DICED CARROTS
1	TEASPOON GARLIC POWDER		1	TABLESPOON WORCESTERSHIRE SAUCE
½	CUP VEGETABLE OIL		½	CUP DRY SHERRY
1	CUP CHOPPED ONIONS		2	TABLESPOONS MINCED PARSLEY

Wash oxtails and place in a colander to drain. In a medium bowl combine the flour, seasoned salt, onion powder, pepper, and garlic powder. Dredge the oxtails in the flour mixture. Heat the vegetable oil in a large soup pot over medium heat. Place the oxtails in the hot oil and brown on all sides. Add the onions; reduce the heat to medium-low and continue to cook until the onions wilt; stir as needed to prevent burning. Add the water and bay leaves; increase the heat to medium-high and bring to a boil. Boil for 10 minutes before reducing the heat to low, skim the excess fat from the broth.

Cover the pot and simmer 2 to 3 hours or until the meat is fork-tender. Remove the meat from the bones. Discard the bones and return meat to the broth. Add all vegetables except the parsley, and simmer until the vegetables are tender to taste. Before serving, stir in the Worcestershire sauce and sherry. Garnish with parsley.

YIELDS 25 SMALL SERVINGS.

NEW ENGLAND CLAM CHOWDER
★★★★★

One day the Custers' "table was crowded with officers, some of whom had just reported for duty." During lunch, "the usual great tureen of soup was disposed of, and the servant brought in an immense platter, on which generally reposed a large roast. But when the dish was placed before the General, to my dismay there appeared in the center of its wide circumference a steak hardly larger than a man's hand." [Libbie Custer]

¾	POUND BACON, DICED	¼	TEASPOON LEAF THYME
1	CUP CHOPPED YELLOW ONIONS	½	TEASPOON FINELY CRUSHED ROSEMARY
½	CUP THINLY SLICED GREEN ONIONS, INCLUDING TOPS	2	CUPS HALF AND HALF
3	CUPS DICED POTATOES, COOKED	2	CUPS WHOLE MILK
4	10½-OUNCE CANS MINCED CLAMS WITH JUICE	2	TABLESPOONS BUTTER
2½	CUPS CLAM JUICE		PAPRIKA
⅛	TEASPOON WHITE PEPPER		MINCED PARSLEY

In a large skillet fry the bacon until lightly browned, but not crisp. Remove the bacon from the skillet with a slotted spoon and place on a paper towel-lined plate to drain. Add the yellow onion to the skillet with bacon drippings and sauté over medium heat for approximately 5 minutes or until transparent. Add the green onions during the last minute. Transfer the bacon and onions to a large kettle. Add the potatoes, clams with juice, clam juice, seasonings, half and half, and milk. Simmer over medium heat for approximately 20 minutes, or until warmed through. Do not boil. Stir in the butter. Add additional seasonings to taste. Garnish lightly with paprika and parsley before serving.

YIELDS 6 TO 8 SERVINGS.

TUSCAN BEAN SOUP

★★★★★

"It was a painful situation, and I blushed, gazed uneasily at the newcomers, but hesitated about apologies, as they were my husband's detestation. He relieved us from the awful silence that fell upon all, by a peal of laughter that shook the table and disturbed the poor little steak in its lonesome bed." [Libbie Custer]

1	POUND NAVY BEANS		WATER
⅓	CUP OLIVE OIL	1	BAY LEAF
4	TABLESPOONS BUTTER	8	LARGE TOMATOES, PEELED, SEEDED AND COARSELY CHOPPED
4	CARROTS PEELED AND FINELY DICED		
3	STALKS CELERY, FINELY CHOPPED	⅓	CUP FINELY CHOPPED FRESH BASIL
3	MEDIUM YELLOW ONIONS, MINCED	2	TEASPOONS PESTO, OPTIONAL
3	CLOVES GARLIC, FINELY MINCED		FRESHLY GRATED PARMESAN CHEESE TO GARNISH
12	CUPS BEEF BROTH		

Pick over the beans, removing the stones and other foreign objects. In a non-reactive container soak the beans overnight with sufficient water to cover. The next day, in a large, heavy kettle heat the olive oil and butter. Add the carrots, celery, and onion; cook for approximately 20 minutes or until very tender. Add the garlic during the last minute of cooking time. Drain the soaking water away from the beans. Place the beans in the kettle with the cooked vegetables. Add the broth first and additional water to cover the beans by 2 inches; bring to a boil. Reduce the heat to medium low; add the bay leaf, and simmer until the beans are tender, approximately 1 to 1½ hours.

Stir in the chopped tomatoes; simmer an additional 15 minutes. Add the basil during the last 5 minutes of cooking, and stir in the pesto for extra zing.

YIELDS 12 SERVINGS.

*W*ives often joined their husbands on hunting and fishing expeditions. Intended primarily as a form of entertainment, the fish and game resulting from these expeditions was a welcome addition to their tables. Often, however, a bounty of unexpected fortune was right outside their door.

FRESH MUSHROOM SOUP

★★★★★

"We often found large mushrooms above ground, and these were delicious baked with cream sauce. They would be about the size of an ordinary saucer, but tender and full of rich flavor—and the buttons would vary in size from a twenty-five cent piece to a silver dollar, each one of a beautiful shell pink underneath. They were so very superior to mushrooms we had eaten before—with a deliciousness all of their own."
[Frances Roe]

½	CUP FINELY CHOPPED ONION		PINCH THYME
1	CARROT, PARED AND FINELY CHOPPED	¼	TEASPOON DRY MUSTARD
12	CUPS RICH CHICKEN BROTH	⅛	TEASPOON CAYENNE
½	CUP UNSALTED BUTTER	½	TEASPOON SALT
3	POUNDS FRESH MUSHROOMS, COARSELY CHOPPED	¼	CUP GOOD DRY SHERRY
6	TABLESPOONS ALL-PURPOSE FLOUR	1	CUP HEAVY CREAM
1	TEASPOON FINELY CHOPPED PARSLEY		CHOPPED PARSLEY TO GARNISH

In a large saucepan simmer the onion, carrots, and broth for 1 hour. While the broth is simmering, in a saucepan melt the butter and sauté the mushrooms over low heat for approximately 5 to 6 minutes. Sprinkle with flour and cook, stirring, for 2 to 3 minutes without browning. Gradually add the hot broth mixture, stirring constantly, and blending completely with the flour. Add the parsley, thyme, mustard, cayenne, salt, and sherry, and stir well. Gradually add the cream; reduce the heat to below simmering to warm the soup for an additional 2 to 3 minutes. Garnish with additional chopped parsley, and serve immediately.

YIELDS 12 SERVINGS.

While the transport of food to the new frontier was difficult, the harvest from American farms remained as bountiful as in colonial times, and for that happy circumstance, all Americans gave thanks.

HEARTY CHICKEN VEGETABLE SOUP
★★★★★

"The General was perfectly unmoved . . . setting at ease again, he ask[ed] the guests to do the best they could with the vegetables, bread and butter, coffee and dessert. . . . Eliza thrust her head in at the door, and explained that the cattle had stampeded and could not get them back in time to kill, as they did daily at the post. The next day the beef returned to our table, but alas! The potatoes gave out, and I began to be disturbed about my housekeeping duties . . . an attack of domestic responsibility was upon me." [Libbie Custer]

CHICKEN STOCK

4	QUARTS WATER	2	LARGE ONIONS SLICED
4	POUNDS CHICKEN NECKS, BACKS AND WINGS	1	BAY LEAF
2	STALKS CELERY	2	SPRIGS PARSLEY

Place all stock ingredients in a large stockpot and bring to a boil. Reduce heat, cover pot, and simmer for 3½ to 4 hours. Occasionally skim the surface and add additional water, if necessary, to keep ingredients covered with liquid. Strain stock through a sieve lined with a double thickness of dampened cheesecloth. Allow stock to cool to room temperature before covering and refrigerating it. Discard remaining ingredients. When stock is cold and surface fat has solidified, remove and discard fat. Broth may be refrigerated for up to three days or frozen for up to three months, if tightly covered. Reheat to boiling before using.

YIELDS 4 QUARTS.

SOUP

15	CUPS CHICKEN STOCK	4	STALKS CELERY, CHOPPED
12	OUNCES KALE, WASHED AND CUT INTO SLICES 1 INCH WIDE	2	TABLESPOONS VEGETABLE OIL
¼	CUP VEGETABLE OIL	1	POUND KIELBASA, CUT INTO ½-INCH SLICES
4	CUPS COARSELY CHOPPED ONION	5	CUPS COOKED CHICKEN CUBED
5	MEDIUM LEEKS, CLEANED, TRIMMED AND SLICED THIN (WHITE PART ONLY)	2½	CUPS FROZEN CORN KERNELS
		1½	CUPS CHOPPED TOMATO, PEELED AND SEEDED
5	LARGE CLOVES GARLIC, MINCED	2	TABLESPOONS CHOPPED FRESH PARSLEY
8	TABLESPOONS BUTTER	1¼	TEASPOON SALT, OR TO TASTE
12	LARGE CARROTS, PARED AND CUT INTO ¼-INCH SLICES	1	TEASPOON PEPPER
		3	CUPS COOKED ELBOW MACARONI, AL DENTE

Place the prepared kale in a large saucepan and cover with 3 cups water; bring to a boil. Reduce the heat to medium-low; cover, and simmer for 15 minutes. Next, while the kale is simmering, heat the vegetable oil and butter in a large soup pot over medium heat. When the foam subsides from the melted butter, add the onion, leek, and garlic, and sauté until softened, 2 to 3 minutes. Add the carrots and celery and cook, stirring frequently, for an additional 2 to 3 minutes. Add the stock (see above) and increase the heat to medium-high. Heat to boiling; cover and simmer for 8 to 10 minutes until the carrots are semi-cooked. Rinse kale under cold water, drain, and add to the soup pot. Simmer an additional 15 minutes.

While the soup simmers, prepare the kielbasa. In a large, heavy skillet heat the oil over medium heat. When the oil begins to ripple, add the kielbasa and sauté until brown all over, approximately 3 to 5 minutes. Stir frequently. Use a slotted spoon to remove the kielbasa to a plate covered with a double thickness of paper towels; allow to drain before adding to the soup. Add the chicken and corn. Cover the pot; reduce the heat to low and simmer for 10 minutes. During the last 5 minutes of cooking time add the remaining ingredients and warm through prior to serving.

YIELDS 6 TO 8 SERVINGS.

BACON AND CORNMEAL MUFFINS

★★★★★

"We have no fresh vegetables here, except potatoes, and have to depend upon canned stores in the commissary for a variety, and our meat consists entirely of beef, except now and then when we may have a treat."
[Frances Roe]

1	CUP CORNMEAL	¾	TEASPOON SALT
½	CUP ALL-PURPOSE FLOUR	7	SLICES BACON, FRIED CRISP AND CRUMBLED
1	TABLESPOON FIRMLY PACKED BROWN SUGAR	1	CUP HALF AND HALF
2	TABLESPOONS SUGAR	2	EGGS, WELL BEATEN
3¼	TEASPOONS BAKING POWDER	3	TABLESPOONS BUTTER, MELTED

Preheat the oven to 375°F. In a medium bowl mix together the dry ingredients. (At this point you can place the dry ingredients in a plastic storage bag and set aside in a cool, dry, dark place for use within a week. Fresh is best and I would not suggest making these ahead beyond what was already discussed, but you can line your muffin pans in preparation.) Add the bacon, half and half, eggs, and butter. Mix well and spoon into paper-lined muffin cups. Bake for 20 minutes or until golden.

YIELDS 12 MUFFINS.

JALAPEÑO CHEESE BREAD

✮ ✮ ✮ ✮ ✮

"Faced with the uncertainties of the food supply from the east, obtaining fresh wholesome food on the frontier was a challenge requiring skill, a creative approach, and a certain amount of good-luck." [Libbie Custer]

2	TABLESPOONS ACTIVE DRY YEAST	2¼	CUPS SHREDDED CHEDDAR CHEESE
½	CUP WARM WATER	2½	HEAPING TEASPOONS FRESH JALAPEÑO CHILIES, SEEDED AND MINCED
1½	CUPS BEER		PAPRIKA
1	TABLESPOON SALT		UNSALTED BUTTER
2	TABLESPOONS VEGETABLE OIL	EGG WASH:	
2	TABLESPOONS SUGAR	3	EGG WHITES
5	CUPS UNBLEACHED ALL-PURPOSE FLOUR	1	EGG YOLK

Grease 2 8 x 5-inch bread pans and set aside. In a large bowl dissolve the yeast in water; add the beer, salt, vegetable oil, and sugar. Gradually add 3 to 4 cups of flour and mix until just blended. Turn out on a lightly floured board and knead for approximately 10 minutes. Add flour as necessary to prevent sticking. Place the dough in an oiled bowl; turn over so that both sides of the dough are oiled. Cover with a clean cloth; set aside and allow to rise in a warm place until double in bulk, approximately 1½ to 2 hours.

When the dough has doubled, punch down and divide into 2 equal parts. Allow the divided dough to rest for 5 minutes. Take a rolling pin and roll each part into a 9 x 5-inch rectangle ¼-inch thick. Sprinkle lightly with paprika. Sprinkle evenly with half of the cheese and jalapeño. Roll up tightly, pinch the center seam and place seam side down in the oiled pans. Repeat. For the egg wash, in a small bowl combine the egg whites and yolk, beating until well blended. Brush the dough with egg wash and allow dough to rise until double in bulk. Bake at 400°F for 25 minutes or until done. Turn out onto a wire rack to cool.

YIELDS 2 LOAVES.

HERB BREAD
★★★★★

Libbie was not blessed with the good fortune of Frances Roe, a garrison wife who found an abundance of fresh ingredients just outside the post, where "there was . . . a stable for cavalry horses which was removed two or three years ago, and all around wherever the decayed logs had been, mushrooms sprang up."

1	CUP BUTTER, SOFTENED	½	TEASPOON ONION POWDER
⅓	CUP MINCED PARSLEY	2	LOAVES FRENCH BREAD
¼	CUP CHOPPED CHIVES		

Preheat the oven to 400°F. In a large bowl cream together the butter, parsley, chives, and onion powder until well blended. Cut the bread loaves into 1-inch slices, but do not separate slices; stop cutting within ½ inch of the bottom of the loaf. Place both loaves on a single baking sheet and spread each slice with butter mixture. (Bread may be prepared to this point, tightly wrapped in aluminum foil, and refrigerated overnight. Remove the foil before heating.) Just before cooking, brush the top of the loaf with softened butter and place in the preheated oven for 12 to 15 minutes or until heated through and brown on top. Serve very hot.

YIELDS 6 TO 8 SERVINGS.

GARLIC BREAD
★★★★★

"When it rains is the time to get the freshest [mushrooms], and many a time Mrs. Fiske and I have put on long storm coats and gone out in the rain for them, each bringing in a large basket heaping full with the most delicious buttons." [Frances Roe]

1	CUP BUTTER, SOFTENED	½	TEASPOON ONION POWDER
2	CLOVES GARLIC, MASHED	2	LOAVES FRENCH BREAD

Preheat the oven to 400°F. In a large bowl cream together the butter, garlic, onion powder. Follow the rest of the directions for Herb Bread, above.

YIELDS 6 TO 8 SERVINGS.

At the end of the evening, provide your guests with recipes and disposable containers filled with their favorite soup. Or freeze the leftovers for a month of simmering soup suppers.

Americana: A Harvest Home Supper for Twenty

✦ ✦ ✦ ✦ ✦

Our country has been richly blessed "from sea to shining sea" and autumn is a time of bountiful harvests. The pilgrims adopted the practice of a "thanks-giving" celebration from their Native American neighbors. Every autumn, the Native Americans feasted and gave thanks to their spirits and gods for a bountiful harvest of corn, beans, pumpkins, and other crops.

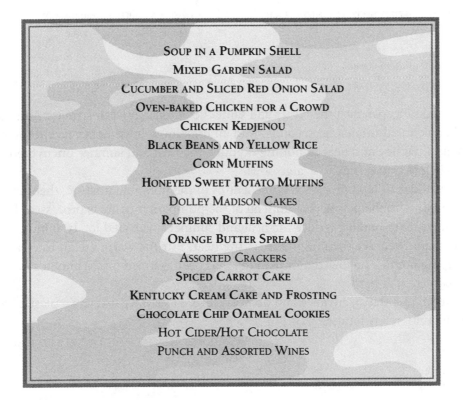

SOUP IN A PUMPKIN SHELL

MIXED GARDEN SALAD

CUCUMBER AND SLICED RED ONION SALAD

OVEN-BAKED CHICKEN FOR A CROWD

CHICKEN KEDJENOU

BLACK BEANS AND YELLOW RICE

CORN MUFFINS

HONEYED SWEET POTATO MUFFINS

DOLLEY MADISON CAKES

RASPBERRY BUTTER SPREAD

ORANGE BUTTER SPREAD

ASSORTED CRACKERS

SPICED CARROT CAKE

KENTUCKY CREAM CAKE AND FROSTING

CHOCOLATE CHIP OATMEAL COOKIES

HOT CIDER/HOT CHOCOLATE

PUNCH AND ASSORTED WINES

PUMPKIN SOUP IN A PUMPKIN SHELL

★ ★ ★ ★ ★

Pumpkin was indeed a staple in the early American diet as reflected in this New England ditty from 1638:

"We had pumpkin in the morning
And pumpkins at noon
If it were not for pumpkins
We'd be undone soon."

Unfortunately, herds of roaming deer were extremely fond of the pumpkin as well, often leaving only the hollow shell. Perhaps early recipes in which the shell was hollowed, filled with milk, and placed in a fireplace for 6 to 7 hours reflected the colonists' creative response to this problem.

4	TABLESPOONS BUTTER		⅛	TEASPOON GROUND ALLSPICE
2	ONIONS, THINLY SLICED		1	TEASPOON WHOLE PEPPERCORNS
3	CLOVES GARLIC, MINCED FINE		⅓	CUP SHERRY
12	CUPS UNSALTED CHICKEN BROTH		1	CUP WHIPPING CREAM, WARMED
4	TO 6 CUPS PARED PUMPKIN, CUT INTO ½-INCH CUBES		2	TEASPOONS SNIPPED FRESH PARSLEY
1	TEASPOON SALT OR TO TASTE		1	MEDIUM PUMPKIN, HOLLOWED
¾	TEASPOON GROUND NUTMEG			
½	TEASPOON GROUND GINGER			

In a covered saucepan melt the butter and sauté the onions until transparent. Add the garlic and cook an additional 30 seconds. Add all remaining ingredients except the sherry, cream, and parsley and heat to boiling. Reduce the heat and simmer uncovered for 20 minutes before transferring to a large bowl.

In a blender or food processor purée 2 cups of the pumpkin mixture, then return the puréed mixture to the pot. Repeat until all of the pumpkin mixture is processed. Heat the puréed mixture to boiling; reduce the heat and simmer uncovered for 10 minutes. Stir in the sherry and remove the mixture from the heat. Stir the warm cream into the soup. Serve piping hot in a hollowed pumpkin that has been warmed for 20 minutes in a 350°F oven. Garnish with parsley.

Make up to 1 day in advance and do not freeze. Place the parsley in a plastic bag and refrigerate until ready for use.

YIELDS 6 TO 8 SERVINGS.

MIXED GARDEN SALAD
★ ★ ★ ★ ★

Cover your table with plaids or prints in bright seasonal colors, or spread across it a charming homemade quilt.

2	HEADS BIBB LETTUCE	1	YELLOW PEPPER, SEEDED AND SLICED
1	SMALL HEAD ICEBERG	2	TABLESPOONS CHOPPED CHIVES
2	CUPS TENDER SPINACH LEAVES	2	HARD BOILED EGGS, CHOPPED
2	CUPS CHERRY TOMATOES, HALVED		

Wash the salad greens in ice water, drain, and pat or spin dry. Tear the greens into bite size pieces and assemble the salad. Refrigerate to crisp while you make the fresh salad dressing.

FRESH SALAD DRESSING

⅓	CUP WATER	⅔	CUP VIRGIN OLIVE OIL
⅓	CUP RASPBERRY VINAIGRETTE	2	TEASPOONS MINCED FRESH CHIVES
¼	TEASPOON SALT	1	TEASPOON MINCED FRESH CHERVIL
¼	TEASPOON BLACK PEPPER	1	TEASPOON MINCED FRESH PARSLEY
⅛	TEASPOON CAYENNE PEPPER		

In a suitable cruet combine all of the ingredients, cover tightly, and shake. Refrigerate before using.

YIELDS 4 TO 6 SERVINGS.

*D*olley Madison, wife of James Madison, who was Thomas Jefferson's Secretary of State, was one of Washington's premier hostesses. At one dinner, Mrs. Merry, the wife of the British prime minister, noted that Dolley's table was "more like a harvest home supper than the entertainment of a secretary of state." Unperturbed, an ever gracious Dolley replied, "The profusion of my table so repugnant to foreign customs arises from the happy circumstances of abundance and prosperity in our country."

SLICED CUCUMBERS AND RED ONIONS
★ ★ ★ ★ ★

Take a moment to hear the echoing footsteps of all those who have gone before you. Bow a head in humility and give thanks.

5	CUCUMBERS, PEELED AND SLICED	1	TEASPOON SUGAR
2	MEDIUM BERMUDA ONIONS, PEELED AND THINLY SLICED	1	TEASPOON COARSELY GROUND PEPPER
1	TEASPOON SALT	1½	TABLESPOONS FRESH LEMON JUICE
1	CUP SOUR CREAM	¼	CUP CHOPPED CHIVES
½	CUP WHOLE MILK	2	TABLESPOONS CHOPPED PARSLEY

In a serving bowl arrange the cucumbers and onion. In a separate bowl mix the remaining ingredients and pour over the salad. Lightly toss and refrigerate until ready to serve.

YIELDS 4 TO 6 SERVINGS.

OVEN BAKED CHICKEN FOR A CROWD
★ ★ ★ ★ ★

Give thanks for what has been given to you. Give thanks with a grateful heart for both the harvest and the hands of the harvesters.

5	3-POUND CHICKENS, CUT UP AS IF FOR FRYING (FREEZE BACKS FOR ANOTHER USE)	2½	TABLESPOONS GROUND PAPRIKA
¾	CUP BUTTER, MELTED	2	TEASPOONS ONION POWDER
1½	TABLESPOONS FRESH-SQUEEZED LEMON JUICE	1	TEASPOON GARLIC POWDER
2½	TABLESPOONS SEASONED SALT	1½	TEASPOONS GROUND BLACK PEPPER

Preheat the oven to 400°F. Wash the chicken and pat dry. Place the chicken in a large bowl. In a small bowl combine the butter and lemon juice and pour over the chicken. Rub the chicken pieces to ensure all are thoroughly coated. In a small bowl combine all of the seasoning ingredients and sprinkle over the chicken. Once again, rub the seasoning into the chicken and ensure that all pieces are thoroughly coated. Place the chicken in a single layer in one or more baking pans. Cover the pans securely with aluminum foil and bake for 20 minutes.

Remove the foil, increase the oven temperature to 450°F, return the uncovered chicken to the oven, and bake an additional 30 minutes.

Turn the chicken and bake an additional 30 minutes.

YIELDS ABOUT 30 SERVINGS.

CHICKEN KEDJENOU
(A DISH FROM THE IVORY COAST)
★★★★★

In West Africa, this dish is cooked in a clay pot or canari. Normally used to keep drinking water cool, the canari, when sealed with a banana leaf and buried in a bed of live embers or cooked on a charcoal fire, produces a uniquely succulent and flavorful dish.

2	CHICKENS, CUT INTO 10 PORTIONS EACH	4	ANAHEIM PEPPERS, SEEDED AND CHOPPED
4	LARGE ONIONS, SLICED	2	BAY LEAVES
3	TABLESPOONS GRATED FRESH GINGER	1	TEASPOON CUMIN
5	CLOVES GARLIC, MINCED	½	TEASPOON SALT
7	TOMATOES, PEELED AND DICED	1	TEASPOON CAYENNE PEPPER

Remove all visible fat from the chicken portions and place the chicken, onions, ginger, garlic, tomatoes, peppers, and bay leaves in a heavy flameproof, enameled or cast–iron casserole. In a separate dish, mix together the spices and use to season the chicken. (May be refrigerated overnight up to this point; this dish is best if refrigerated 1 day before serving, so allow an extra day preparation).

Cover the pan and place it over two burners of your stove. Cook over medium heat for approximately 40 minutes, shaking the casserole every 5 minutes to prevent sticking and to ensure even cooking. Do not open the casserole until the end of the cooking time. For a thicker gravy for this dish, degrease the pan drippings and make a paste of ½ cup of flour and ½ cup water stirred into the pan drippings.

Kedjenou is traditionally served with attieke, a fermented starch. It may also be served with rice.

YIELDS ABOUT 10 SERVINGS.

Remember those patriots from a distant shore who, some even in captivity, gave their last full measure to make this nation one that is free and indivisible under God.

Remember the contributions of the 54th Massachusetts and young Colonel Robert Gould Shaw.

BLACK BEANS AND YELLOW RICE

★ ★ ★ ★ ★

Remember those early farmers, both men and women, who answered the call to arms.

1	POUND DRIED BLACK BEANS	1	HAM BONE OR 2 HAM HOCKS
	WATER	1½	TEASPOONS SEASONED SALT
¼	CUP OLIVE OIL	3	BAY LEAVES
1	CUP DICED ONIONS	1	TEASPOON ONION POWDER
½	CUP DICED GREEN BELL PEPPER	1	TEASPOON GARLIC POWDER
1	SMALL FRESH JALAPEÑO PEPPER, CHOPPED	¼	TEASPOON CUMIN
5	OR 6 CLOVES GARLIC, MINCED		

Wash the beans, removing any foreign objects, and then cover with water and soak overnight or according to the package directions.

In a medium to large pot heat the olive oil and sauté the onion, green pepper, and jalapeño peppers until the onions are transparent. Add the garlic, sauté, and stir an additional minute or two. Add the ham bone, or ham hocks, salt, bay leaves, and sufficient water to cover by 3 inches and bring to a boil. Reduce the heat to low, add the remaining seasonings, and simmer for 1 hour. Add additional water as required to allow the seasoning meat to simmer without sticking. Drain the beans, rinse again, and add to the pot containing the seasoning meat. Add additional hot water, as necessary, to cover the beans by 2 inches or as needed to prevent scorching. Cover the pot and continue to cook over low heat until tender, approximately 2 to 3 hours.

Remove the top during the last half hour of cooking and allow the liquid to "cook down" to the desired thickness.

YIELDS 6 SERVINGS.

YELLOW RICE
★ ★ ★ ★ ★

Remember the personal sacrifice of those who continue to wear the uniform and stand watch at freedom's door.

2½	CUPS CHICKEN BROTH	1	PINCH SAFFRON CRUSHED
2	TABLESPOONS OLIVE OIL	1	CUP CONVERTED RICE

In a saucepan bring the broth, olive oil, and saffron to a boil. Add the rice, cover the pot, and reduce the heat to low. Simmer until all of the water is absorbed, approximately 15 to 20 minutes.

YIELDS 6 SERVINGS.

CORN MUFFINS
★ ★ ★ ★ ★

Give thanks for the sacrifice of those left behind, waiting anxiously, and offering support to the cause.

1	CUP CORNMEAL	3	TABLESPOONS HONEY
½	CUP ALL-PURPOSE FLOUR	1	CUP HEAVY CREAM
3	TEASPOONS BAKING POWDER	3	TABLESPOONS WATER
⅛	TEASPOON GRATED NUTMEG	2	EGGS, WELL BEATEN
¾	TEASPOON SALT	3	TABLESPOONS BUTTER, MELTED

Preheat the oven to 375°F. Mix together the dry ingredients. (At this point you can stop, place the ingredients in a plastic storage bag, and set aside in a cool, dry, dark place for use within a week.) Fresh is best and I would not suggest making these ahead beyond what was already discussed, but you can line your muffin pans in preparation. Add the honey, cream, water, eggs, and butter. Mix well and spoon into paper-lined muffin cups. Bake for 20 minutes or until golden.

YIELDS 12 MUFFINS.

HONEYED SWEET POTATO MUFFINS
★★★★★

Consider that choice is never free; it carries with it a high price paid for by those who laid down their lives in defense of the right to choose.

1	LARGE SWEET POTATO, COOKED	½	CUP WHOLE WHEAT FLOUR
2	EGGS, WELL BEATEN	2	TEASPOONS BAKING POWDER
1	CUP HALF AND HALF	1	TEASPOON GROUND CINNAMON
½	CUP HONEY	¼	TEASPOON GRATED NUTMEG
3	TABLESPOONS BUTTER, MELTED	⅛	TEASPOON GROUND ALLSPICE
2	TABLESPOONS FIRMLY PACKED LIGHT BROWN SUGAR	¾	TEASPOON SALT
1¼	CUPS ALL-PURPOSE FLOUR		

Preheat the oven to 400°F. Line a large muffin tin with foil muffin liners. In a food processor purée the potatoes and transfer 1 cup of the purée to a mixing bowl. Mix in the eggs, half and half, honey, and butter in that order. Add the remaining ingredients and gently stir until just mixed. Spoon the batter into the prepared muffin cups. Bake 20 to 25 minutes or until golden, springy to the touch, and a tester inserted into the center of a muffin comes out clean. Serve hot with butter and additional honey, if desired.

For a great breakfast treat, pour a little milk or cream and additional honey over the muffin. Sprinkle with raisins and sunflower seeds. Heat and serve.

YIELDS 12 MUFFINS.

HONEYED BUTTER SPREAD
★ ★ ★ ★ ★

Choose to live your lives in a manner that honors those who answered freedom's call by making one final choice. . . .

½	CUP BUTTER	½	CUP HONEY
¼	CUP CREAM CHEESE		

In a small bowl cream together the butter and cream cheese. Add the honey and mix thoroughly. Chill slightly before serving.

RASPBERRY SPREAD
★ ★ ★ ★ ★

. . . without hesitation, misgiving, or reservation men and women of every color, creed, and religion—together and undivided—chose freedom.

¼	CUP BUTTER	¼	CUP HONEY
½	CUP CREAM CHEESE	¼	CUP FROZEN RASPBERRIES, THAWED

In a small bowl cream together the butter and cream cheese. Add the honey and raspberries; mix thoroughly. Chill slightly before serving.

ORANGE BUTTER
★ ★ ★ ★ ★

They pledged their lives, their fortunes, and their sacred honor for one great cause.

½	CUP BUTTER	¼	TEASPOON GRATED ORANGE RIND
¼	CUP CREAM CHEESE		
¼	TEASPOON CONFECTIONERS' SUGAR		

In a small bowl cream together the butter and cream cheese. Add the confectioners' sugar and orange rind. Mix thoroughly. Chill slightly before serving.

KENTUCKY CREAM CAKE AND FROSTING
★ ★ ★ ★ ★

Those early patriots honored their pledge by sacrificing what they had for that of which they could only dream.

½	CUP VEGETABLE SHORTENING		1	CUP BUTTERMILK
½	CUP BUTTER		1	TEASPOON VANILLA EXTRACT
2	CUPS SUGAR		1	CUP COCONUT
5	EGG YOLKS, RESERVE WHITES		⅔	CUP CHOPPED WALNUTS
2¼	CUPS ALL-PURPOSE FLOUR		5	EGG WHITES, BEATEN
1	TEASPOON BAKING SODA			

Preheat the oven to 350°F. Grease and flour two 9-inch cake pans and set aside. In a large mixing bowl, cream together the shortening, butter, and sugar. Add egg yolks one at a time. Beat well. Add flour and baking soda, alternating with buttermilk and vanilla. Next, fold in the coconut, walnuts, and beaten egg whites. Place in preheated oven and bake for 35 to 40 minutes or until golden. Cake is done when it is springy to the touch and a tester inserted in the center comes out clean.

YIELDS 8 SERVINGS.

FROSTING

In fulfilling that pledge, they laid down their own lives for that which we hold most dear: Freedom!

1	8-OUNCE PACKAGE CREAM CHEESE		1	POUND CONFECTIONERS' SUGAR
½	CUP BUTTER		1	CUP CHOPPED WALNUTS
1	TEASPOON VANILLA EXTRACT			

In a small bowl cream together the cream cheese, butter, vanilla, and confectioners' sugar, and use to frost cake. Garnish the top with chopped nuts.

SPICED CARROT CAKE WITH RUM SAUCE
★★★★★

"The race is not to the swift, nor the battle to the strong, but the God of Israel is he who gives strength and power to his people." [Abigail Adams]

2	CUPS SUGAR	1⅓	CUPS SALAD OIL
3	CUPS ALL-PURPOSE FLOUR	2	EGGS BEATEN
3	TEASPOONS BAKING SODA	1	CUP CHOPPED PECANS
½	TEASPOON SALT	1	CUP CRUSHED PINEAPPLE, DRAINED
1	TEASPOON GROUND CINNAMON	1	TEASPOON VANILLA EXTRACT
¼	TEASPOON GRATED NUTMEG	1	TEASPOON LEMON EXTRACT
⅛	TEASPOON GROUND ALLSPICE		
2	CUPS COARSELY GRATED CARROTS		

Preheat the oven to 350°F. Grease and flour 1 Bundt pan or 2 large loaf pans and set aside. In a large mixing bowl combine the sugar, flour, baking soda, salt, cinnamon, nutmeg, and allspice. Add the carrots, oil, and eggs. Beat until well mixed. Add the remaining ingredients and stir. Pour the batter into the pan(s). Bake for approximately 1 hour or until a tester inserted in the center comes out clean. Remove the cake from the pan(s) and allow to cool prior to frosting.

YIELDS 8 TO 12 SERVINGS.

CREAM CHEESE FROSTING

1	3-OUNCE PACKAGE CREAM CHEESE, SOFTENED	½	CUP PINEAPPLE JUICE
¼	CUP BUTTER	2	CUPS CONFECTIONERS' SUGAR

In a small bowl cream the butter and cheese together. Add the confectioners' sugar and blend until smooth. Slowly add the pineapple juice until the mixture is just thin enough to drizzle over the cake without being runny.

RUM SAUCE

⅔	CUP BUTTER	1	CUP LIGHT CORN SYRUP
2	CUPS FIRMLY PACKED DARK BROWN SUGAR	⅔	CUP LIGHT RUM
1	CUP HALF AND HALF	1	TABLESPOON VANILLA EXTRACT

In a saucepan melt the butter over low heat. Stir in the brown sugar and mix well. Add the half and half and corn syrup; bring to a quick boil and stir until the sugar dissolves. Remove from the heat and cool to warm while stirring constantly. Stir in the rum and vanilla extract. Serve warm with spiced carrot cake.

CHOCOLATE CHIP OATMEAL COOKIES

★★★★★

"How great the debt we owe to those who went through . . . the suffering of the Revolution so that we might taste the first fruits of freedom." [Sullivan Ballou, killed in the first battle of Bull Run, July 14, 1861]

¾	CUP BUTTER	3	TEASPOONS GROUND CINNAMON
1	CUP FIRMLY PACKED BROWN SUGAR	½	TEASPOON GRATED NUTMEG
½	CUP SUGAR	½	TEASPOON SALT
1	EGG, BEATEN	½	TEASPOON BAKING SODA
¼	CUP WATER	3	CUPS OATMEAL
1	TABLESPOON PLUS 1 TEASPOON VANILLA EXTRACT	1	CUP CHOPPED WALNUTS
1	CUP ALL-PURPOSE FLOUR	½	CUP MINIATURE CHOCOLATE CHIPS

Preheat the oven to 350°F. In a large mixing bowl cream together the butter and sugars. Add the beaten egg, water, and vanilla extract and mix well. In a separate bowl sift together the flour, cinnamon, nutmeg, salt, and baking soda. Combine the butter and flour mixture; blend in the oatmeal. Add the walnuts and chocolate chips; mix well. Drop by heaping teaspoons to an ungreased cookie sheet. Bake in the preheated oven for 12 to 15 minutes or until golden.

*S*ometimes on the sparse frontier the "bounty" of the harvest was equally found in the generous hospitality of the host and hostess who shared in the true tradition of this place we call America.

Thanksgiving was not an officially recognized holiday until Abraham Lincoln proclaimed the last day in November to be a National Day of Thanksgiving. Since that time Americans have continuously given thanks for the bounty of the harvest and gladly shared it with others. The need was great when a flood of bank failures ushered in the Great Depression. And in 1931 the sweeping tide of those failures all but ruined the Arnolds. Both of their fathers were in the banking industry and both banks failed. As a result, the checking account with Hap's father's bank was now defunct. And the children's education fund, held at the bank of Bee's father, was also gone. In addition, her father suffered a stroke. When they arrived on March Field in a drenching rainstorm on Thanksgiving evening, they may have thought there was very little for which to give thanks. "But there on the porch to the house . . . stood . . . Major Carl Spaatz (who commanded a combat wing at March) and his wife, Ruth. A lavish Thanksgiving dinner was waiting for everyone at the Spaatzes' quarters." [Thomas Coffey, *HAP*]

Seafood Casserole Luncheon

★ ★ ★ ★ ★

"We were detained by orders for a little time in New Orleans and the general was enthusiastic over the city. All day we strolled through the streets, visiting the French quarter . . . . [and] dining in the charming French restaurants, where we saw eating made fine art." [Libbie Custer]

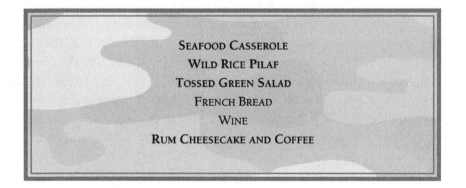

SEAFOOD CASSEROLE
WILD RICE PILAF
TOSSED GREEN SALAD
FRENCH BREAD
WINE
RUM CHEESECAKE AND COFFEE

SEAFOOD CASSEROLE
★★★★★

Libbie Custer wrote, "The seafood was then new to me, and I hovered over the crabs, lobsters, and shrimps." While in New Orleans, the Custers also enjoyed a French dinner with General Sheridan in a beautiful mansion. All of the charms and fine food of New Orleans, however, probably could not compare to the simple hospitality the Custers found among other military families.

1½	CUPS FRESH MUSHROOMS, SLICED	½	CUP SHERRY
¾	CUP THINLY SLICED GREEN ONIONS	1	CUP COOKED CRAB MEAT, PICKED OVER
¼	CUP BUTTER	1	CUP COOKED LOBSTER MEAT
2	CLOVES GARLIC, MINCED	1	CUP SMALL SCALLOPS
¼	CUP ALL-PURPOSE FLOUR	½	CUP SHRIMP, CLEANED AND COOKED
2	CUPS HALF AND HALF	½	POUND PORT WINE CHEESE, CRUMBLED
1¼	TEASPOONS SALT	½	CUP DRY BREADCRUMBS
¼	TEASPOON GRATED NUTMEG	½	CUP CHOPPED PECANS
¼	TEASPOON WHITE PEPPER		

Lightly butter a 2-quart casserole dish and set aside. In a medium saucepan over medium heat sauté the mushrooms and onions in butter; add the garlic and continue to sauté for 2 to 3 minutes. Stir in the flour and cook an additional minute. Add the half and half, salt, nutmeg, and pepper, and continue to stir while cooking until the sauce begins to thicken, an additional minute or two. Add the sherry and stir. Add the seafood, toss lightly and pour into the buttered 2-quart casserole. In a separate bowl combine the cheese, breadcrumbs, and pecans. Sprinkle over the casserole, spread evenly, and refrigerate until prepared to bake. The casserole may be refrigerated overnight or frozen at this point.

Bake in a preheated 350°F oven for 30 to 40 minutes, until the casserole begins to bubble and the top browns. Serve with wild rice, a tossed green salad and crusty bread.

YIELDS 6 TO 8 SERVINGS.

WILD RICE PILAF

☆☆☆☆☆

"We were not surprised, after seeing the other posts below on the river, the guide had praised Fort Sully. . . . The wife of the commanding officer was known throughout the department for her loving Christian character, and the contented life she lived under all circumstances." [Libbie Custer, Boots and Saddles]

3	TABLESPOONS BUTTER		2	CUPS CHICKEN STOCK (FOR HOMEMADE, SEE PAGE 84)
4	TABLESPOONS MINCED PARSLEY		1	CUP WILD RICE

In a large saucepan over medium heat sauté the parsley in butter for approximately 1 minute. Add the chicken stock and bring to a boil. Add the rice to the stock and stir well. Cover and reduce the heat to low. Cook the rice at a slow simmer for an additional 40 minutes or until the liquid is absorbed and the rice is done.

YIELDS 6 TO 8 SERVINGS.

MILITARY BAND IN UNIFORM

TOSSED SALAD
★★★★★

"The post band played outside on the parade ground while we lunched. We had nine kinds of game on the table. Some of it new to us. The goose was . . . served with jelly made from the tart, wild 'bulberries' [sic] that grew near the river." [Libbie Custer]

2	CLOVES GARLIC, CRUSHED		½	CUP COARSELY CHOPPED GREEN PEPPER
1	HEAD ROMAINE LETTUCE (ABOUT 6 CUPS)		½	CUP COARSELY CHOPPED YELLOW PEPPER
1	HEAD BELGIAN ENDIVE (ABOUT 4 CUPS)		½	CUP COARSELY CHOPPED RED PEPPER
½	CUP CHOPPED BERMUDA ONION		¼	CUP CHOPPED PARSLEY

Rub the serving bowl with garlic and discard the cloves (or reserve for the dressing). Wash the greens in ice water, drain, and pat dry. Tear the greens into bite size pieces and place in a serving bowl. Add the remaining ingredients and lightly toss. Place in the refrigerator to crisp while making the salad dressing.

YIELDS 8 TO 10 SERVINGS.

DRESSING

2	LARGE CLOVES GARLIC, CRUSHED		1	TEASPOON ONION POWDER
⅔	CUP VEGETABLE OIL		½	TEASPOON SEASONED SALT
⅓	CUP TARRAGON VINEGAR		¼	TEASPOON PAPRIKA
1	TABLESPOON LIME JUICE		⅓	CUP WATER
1	TEASPOON SUGAR			

In a cruet or jar with fitted cover, combine all of the above ingredients, cover and shake well. Dress the salad immediately before serving.

The hospitality of military wives, learned on an often inhospitable frontier, could be depended upon day or night. "After months of anticipation and days of weary travel we have at last got to our army home. . . . It was dark when we reached the post . . . General and Mrs. Phillips gave us a most cordial reception—just as though they had known us always. Dinner was served soon after we arrived, and the cheerful dining room, and the table with its dainty china and bright silver, was such a surprise—so much better than anything we expected to find here." [Frances Roe, Fort Lyon, Colorado Territory, October 1871]

RUM CHEESECAKE
⭐⭐⭐⭐⭐

"The home-made bread, delightful cake, tender ham, of the garrison's own curing, and the sweets made with cream, fresh butter, and eggs—three unheard of luxuries with us—proved that it is possible for Army people to live in comfort if they do not belong to a mounted regiment." [Libbie Custer, Boots and Saddles*]*

FOR THE CRUST:

¼	CUP PLUS 3 TABLESPOONS FINE GRAHAM CRACKER CRUMBS
¼	CUP SUGAR
½	TEASPOON GROUND CINNAMON
6	TABLESPOONS BUTTER, MELTED

FOR THE FILLING:

1	ENVELOPE UNFLAVORED GELATIN

1	CUP SUGAR, DIVIDED
½	CUP DARK RUM
1	TABLESPOON GRATED LIME PEEL
½	CUP LIME JUICE
¼	TEASPOON LEMON EXTRACT
4	EGGS, SEPARATED (RESERVE WHITES)
16	OUNCES CREAM CHEESE, SOFTENED
1	CUP WHIPPING CREAM

To make the crust, in a medium bowl combine the graham cracker crumbs (reserve 3 tablespoons for future use), sugar, cinnamon, and butter; press into the bottom and sides of a 9-inch springform pan and chill while preparing the filling.

In a medium saucepan over medium heat combine the gelatin, ½ cup of sugar, rum, lime peel, and lime juice. Beat 4 egg yolks and add to the mixture. Continue to cook over medium heat, stirring constantly until slightly thickened, approximately 7 to 8 minutes. Add the cream cheese and beat until smooth. Remove the saucepan from the heat. In a separate bowl beat the egg whites with an electric mixer until foamy; gradually add the remaining sugar; continue to beat until peaks form and set aside. Whip the cream until soft peaks form, fold the egg whites and whipped cream into the creamed cheese mixture. Turn the filling into the crumb-lined pan. Sprinkle with the reserved crumbs, cover, and refrigerate for several hours until chilled.

YIELDS 12 SERVINGS.

Twelfth Night:
A Williamsburg Buffet for Eight

✴ ✴ ✴ ✴ ✴

On the East Coast, it is likely that special occasion menus remained richly steeped in the English heritage of the patriots. Had the Custers accepted an invitation to Virginia for the holidays, it is likely that they would have enjoyed an elegant candlelit dinner such as the Williamsburg Christmas Buffet. Colonial Williamsburg was more than a place, it was an era governed by hospitality and elegance. Eighteenth-century colonials celebrated the Nativity during the season of Advent. December 25 launched an extensive festive season.

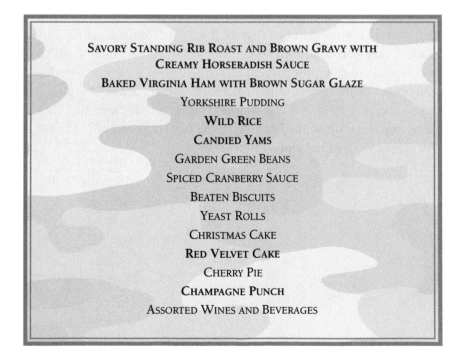

SAVORY STANDING RIB ROAST AND BROWN GRAVY WITH
CREAMY HORSERADISH SAUCE

BAKED VIRGINIA HAM WITH BROWN SUGAR GLAZE

YORKSHIRE PUDDING

WILD RICE

CANDIED YAMS

GARDEN GREEN BEANS

SPICED CRANBERRY SAUCE

BEATEN BISCUITS

YEAST ROLLS

CHRISTMAS CAKE

RED VELVET CAKE

CHERRY PIE

CHAMPAGNE PUNCH

ASSORTED WINES AND BEVERAGES

SAVORY STANDING RIB ROAST
⋆⋆⋆⋆⋆

During the 18th century, the Christmas holiday encompassed twelve days. The Twelfth Day, or Epiphany, occurred on January 6. Colonial Virginians scheduled celebratory occasions such as balls, parties, and weddings for Twelfth Night. From late fall to early winter a variety of fresh meat was available for the table.

1	4 ½- TO 5-POUND RIB ROAST	½	TEASPOON LEAF OREGANO
FOR THE MARINADE:		1	TEASPOON LEAF BASIL
½	CUP LIGHT SOY SAUCE	½	TEASPOON CRUSHED ROSEMARY
¼	CUP OLIVE OIL	1	TEASPOON ONION POWDER
½	CUP DRY SHERRY	**FLOUR MIXTURE:**	
1	LARGE ONION, THINLY SLICED	½	CUP ALL-PURPOSE FLOUR
1	LARGE GREEN BELL PEPPER, SEEDED AND THINLY SLICED	1	TEASPOON SEASON SALT
		½	TEASPOON FRESHLY GROUND PEPPER
5	CLOVES GARLIC, MINCED	¼	TEASPOON GARLIC POWDER
3	BAY LEAVES	½	TEASPOON ONION POWDER

In a large, nonreactive bowl combine all of the marinade ingredients. Rinse the roast under cold running water and pat dry. Place the roast on its side and marinate overnight; turn often. Remove the roast from the refrigerator 2½ hours prior to cooking.

Preheat the oven to 500°F for 20 minutes. Place roast in an open, shallow roasting pan, standing upright on its ribs so that the layer of top fat automatically bastes the meat beneath. Season to taste with salt and pepper. In a small bowl combine the flour and seasonings. Rub the flour mixture into the top fat and lightly dust the sides of the roast with this mixture. Bake for 25 minutes. At the end of 25 minutes, reduce the temperature to 325°, but DO NOT open the oven door. Allow the roast to remain in the oven an additional 2 hours and 10 minutes, approximately 13 minutes per pound. At the end of the cooking time, remove the roast from the oven and insert a meat thermometer into the middle of the roast. Do not allow the thermometer to touch the bone. For a rare roast the temperature should be 135°, for medium rare 140°, and for medium 150°. Allow the roast to set for 10 minutes before carving to serve. Save the pan drippings for the gravy. Serve with gravy and Creamy Horseradish Sauce.

Note: this recipe requires a well-insulated oven.

YIELDS 8 SERVINGS.

BROWN GRAVY
★★★★★

Then as now, beef, goose, ham, and turkey were holiday favorites. Rich sauces and gravies were prepared and served with them as well.

	PAN DRIPPINGS FROM RIB ROAST	2½	CUPS BEEF BOUILLON
2	TABLESPOONS ALL-PURPOSE FLOUR		SALT AND PEPPER TO TASTE

Deglaze the roasting pan. Degrease the pan drippings by skimming the fat with metal spoon or use a fat skimmer. Retain the juice and sediment. Sprinkle flour across the pan contents so that it can absorb any remaining grease and brown slowly over medium heat until the flour is dark brown but not scorched. Stir and scrape the pan to remove sediment and prevent scorching. Add the bouillon. Increase heat to high and bring the mixture to a boil. Reduce the heat to medium high, and allow the gravy to cook down to the desired consistency. Strain into a gravy boat.

CREAMY HORSERADISH SAUCE
★★★★★

1	CUP SOUR CREAM	⅛	TEASPOON PAPRIKA
3	TABLESPOONS HORSERADISH	2	TABLESPOONS MINCED PARSLEY
	SALT AND FRESHLY GROUND PEPPER TO TASTE		

In a small bowl combine all of the above ingredients. Mix well and chill until ready to serve.

BAKED VIRGINIA HAM WITH BROWN SUGAR GLAZE
★★★★★

Meats that could be preserved for the winter were smoked. Consequently, the bounties of these colonial tables also included smoked Virginia ham—always a popular winter holiday fare.

1	12- TO 16-POUND VIRGINIA HAM	1	TEASPOON GROUND ALLSPICE
1	CUP FINE DRY BREADCRUMBS		WHOLE CLOVES
1	CUP DARK BROWN SUGAR	24	MARASCHINO CHERRIES
1	TABLESPOON GROUND CINNAMON		

Cover the ham with cold water and soak for 24 to 36 hours before cooking. Change the water 2 to 3 times during this period. Drain away the soaking water and use a stiff brush to scrub the mold from the surface of the ham. Place the ham in a large kettle with sufficient water to cover it by 1 inch. Slowly simmer 20 to 25 minutes per pound, or until the ham reaches an internal temperature of 150°F. At this point you should be able to easily remove the small bone near the ham's shank. Transfer the ham to a platter, and if you wish, set the cooking water aside for use in cooking vegetables such as green beans or collard greens. Remove the skin while ham is still warm, leaving a ⅛-inch layer of fat intact. (Stop here if cooking ham in advance—up to 2 days. While ham is still warm tightly wrap it in plastic and then again in aluminum foil before placing the ham in the refrigerator.)

Score the remaining fat on the ham surface into diamond shapes. Place a whole clove into each visible diamond. Preheat the oven to 400°F. With your fingers, press enough of the breadcrumbs into the fatty side of the ham to thoroughly coat. In a small bowl combine the brown sugar, cinnamon, and allspice. Sift the brown sugar mixture evenly over the crumbs. Insert cloves where the scoring lines intersect. Alternate with maraschino cherries secured with tooth pick. Place on a rack in the middle of the oven for approximately 20 minutes, or until richly browned. Allow the ham to cool at room temperature and remove the toothpicks before carving the ham into paper-thin serving slices.

YIELDS 12 SERVINGS.

WILD RICE
★ ★ ★ ★ ★

1	CUP THINLY SLICED GREEN ONIONS	2	CUPS WILD RICE
2	TABLESPOONS MINCED CURLY-LEAF PARSLEY	3½	CUPS BEEF BROTH (BOILING HOT)
¼	CUP BUTTER	1	CUP SLIVERED ALMONDS

In a saucepan place the green onions, parsley, and butter and sauté for 10 minutes. Add the wild rice and boiling broth. Cover the saucepan and allow the rice to cook for approximately 30 minutes. Stir occasionally to avoid sticking. When the rice is done, drain away any excess water and test for seasoning. Fluff the rice with a fork and add the almonds before serving. While the rice may be made a day in advance, the almonds should not be added to the reheated rice until just before serving.

YIELDS 6 TO 8 SERVINGS.

CANDIED YAMS
★ ★ ★ ★ ★

The earliest colonials cooked "jacketed" sweet potatoes in the embers and ashes of their hearths. The candied version of these potatoes emerged prior to the Revolutionary War as sugar became more abundant.

8	SMALL SWEET POTATOES, PEELED AND QUARTERED	½	TEASPOON SALT
1½	TABLESPOONS FRESH LEMON JUICE	⅛	TEASPOON GROUND GINGER
½	CUP BUTTER	½	TEASPOON GRATED NUTMEG
¾	CUP SUGAR	1	TEASPOON GRATED LEMON PEEL

In a stock pot place the potatoes in water to cover; add the lemon juice. Bring to a boil and cook until the potatoes are fork-tender. When done, remove the potatoes from the pot and drain. In the same pot melt the butter and sugar over medium heat. Stir constantly and continue to cook until the sugar melts and begins to bubble. Stir constantly to prevent scorching. When the mixture begins to thicken, remove the pot from the heat. Add the spices and grated lemon peel. Mix well and then return the potatoes to pot. Gently coat with the mixture. Serve immediately or transfer to a buttered glass baking dish and keep in a warm oven until ready to serve.

YIELDS 4 TO 6 SERVINGS.

RED VELVET CAKE

★★★★★

Sweet confections and desserts were prepared many weeks in advance. Colonial Virginians looked to the twelve days as a way to extend and more fully savor the most joyful season of the year.

½	CUP BUTTER		1	TEASPOON SALT
1½	CUPS SUGAR		1	TEASPOON WHITE VINEGAR
2	EGGS		1	CUP BUTTERMILK
2½	CUPS SIFTED CAKE FLOUR		1	TEASPOON VANILLA EXTRACT
2	LEVEL TABLESPOONS COCOA		2	TABLESPOONS RED FOOD COLORING
1	TEASPOON BAKING SODA			

Preheat the oven to 350°F. Grease and flour 2 9-inch layer pans and set aside. In a large bowl cream together the butter and sugar. Add the eggs, beating well after each addition. Sift together the flour, cocoa, baking soda, and salt. Add the sifted mixture and remaining ingredients to the creamed mixture and mix well. Pour the batter into the prepared baking pan. Bake for 30 to 35 minutes or until the cake springs back when touched or a wooden tester inserted in the center comes out clean. Turn onto a baking rack to cool.

YIELDS 8 SERVINGS.

FROSTING

16	OUNCES CREAM CHEESE		2	POUNDS CONFECTIONERS' SUGAR
1	CUP BUTTER		1½	TABLESPOONS VANILLA EXTRACT

In a large bowl cream together cream cheese and butter. Gradually add the confectioners' sugar and vanilla, beating until fluffy. When the cake is cool to the touch, frost the cake.

CHAMPAGNE PUNCH
★★★★★

Rum drinks and other libations were generously poured during the Christmas season.

1	12-OUNCE CAN CRUSHED PINEAPPLE WITH JUICE	2	CUPS LIGHT RUM
1	POUND CONFECTIONERS' SUGAR	4	BOTTLES CHILLED CHAMPAGNE
2	CUPS FRESH-SQUEEZED LEMON JUICE	1	QUART LEMON-LIME SODA
1	CUP CURAÇAO	1	QUART FRESH STRAWBERRIES, SLICED
½	CUP MARASCHINO CHERRIES WITH JUICE		PINEAPPLE SLICES
2	CUPS BRANDY		

In a large pitcher combine the crushed pineapple with the confectioners' sugar. Cover the pitcher and allow to stand for 1 hour.

Add the lemon juice, Curaçao, maraschino cherries, brandy, and rum. Stir and allow to stand for an additional hour. To serve, place the mixture in a punch bowl with a block of ice. Stir and add the champagne, lemon-lime soda, strawberries, and pineapple slices.

YIELDS ABOUT 20 SERVINGS.

"*The bal masque is over, the guests have departed and all that is left for us now are the recollections of a delightful ball that gave us full return for our efforts to have it a success. We did not dream that so many invitations would be accepted at far-away posts, that parties would come from Fort Leavenworth, Fort Riley, Fort Dodge, and Fort Wallace. . . . Every house on officer's row was filled to overflowing and scarcely a corner left vacant.*

The new hospital was simply perfect for an elaborate entertainment. The large ward made a grand ballroom, the halls were charming for promenading, and yes, flirting, the dining room and kitchen perfect for supper, and the office and other small rooms were a nice size for cloak rooms. . . . All this necessitated much planning, an immense amount of work, and the stripping of our own houses. Accoutrements were hung everywhere, every bit of brass shining. . . . Much of the supper came from Kansas City—that is the celery, fowls, and materials for little cakes, ices, and so on—and the orchestra consisted of six musicians from the regimental band at Fort Riley. . . . Everybody was en masque and almost everyone wore fancy dress and some of the costumes were beautiful. . . . We had queens and milkmaids and flower girls galore and black starry nights and silvery days, and all sorts of things, many of them were very elegant. . . .

The dancing commenced at nine o'clock, and at twelve supper was served when we unmasked, and after supper we danced again and kept on dancing until five o'clock!" [Frances Roe]

Country Brunch

★ ★ ★ ★ ★

The nicest aspect of this brunch menu is that, for the most part, everything is prepared in advance. In addition, you can take advantage of leftovers from the night before and impress your guests with your level of organization.

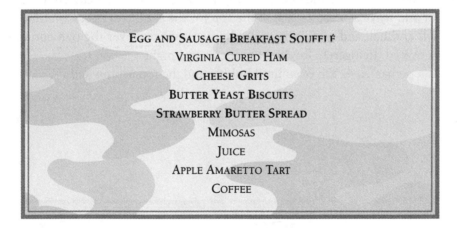

EGG AND SAUSAGE BREAKFAST SOUFFLÉ
VIRGINIA CURED HAM
CHEESE GRITS
BUTTER YEAST BISCUITS
STRAWBERRY BUTTER SPREAD
MIMOSAS
JUICE
APPLE AMARETTO TART
COFFEE

EGG AND SAUSAGE BREAKFAST SOUFFLÉ

★★★★★

Mindful of their precarious situation, these frontier military wives sought to make themselves indispensable. "We know, if the world does not, that the part we are to take on this march is most important. We will see that the tents are made comfortable and cheerful at every camp; that the little dinner after the march and the early breakfast … are each and all as dainty as camp cooking will permit." [Frances Roe, Corinne Utah Territory, 1877]

1½	POUNDS MILD ITALIAN SAUSAGE, CRUMBLED		3½	CUPS HALF AND HALF
16	SLICES DAY-OLD BREAD			SALT AND PEPPER TO TASTE
1	POUND SHARP CHEDDAR CHEESE		3	TEASPOONS DIJON MUSTARD
12	EGGS, BEATEN		¼	TEASPOON TABASCO

Lightly butter a 9 x 13-inch ovenproof baking dish and set aside. In a large skillet over medium heat cook the sausage until done. No pink meat should be visible. Remove the meat to a paper towel-lined plate to drain. While the sausage is draining, trim the crust from the bread and discard the crust. Cube the bread, approximately 6 to 8 cubes per slice. Place half of the bread cubes in a buttered baking dish. Spread the sausage over the bread. Continue by layering the cheese and remaining bread in the casserole; end with a cheese layer and leave at least ½-inch at the top for the soufflé to rise. Combine the eggs with the half and half and remaining ingredients, and pour over the pan contents until just barely covered. Refrigerate for 3 to 4 hours or overnight.

Bake in a preheated 425°F oven until bubbly and the top is browned.

YIELDS 6 TO 8 SERVINGS.

*T*he wives of officers and enlisted men described in army regulations as camp followers had a tenuous status at best. The only status officially recognized was that of laundress—all others could be ordered off the post by the post commander.

CHEESE GRITS
★★★★★

"Yes, we are sometimes called camp followers, but we don't mind. . . . We know all about the comfort and cheer that goes with us, and then—we have not been left behind!" [Frances Roe]

4	CUPS WATER		3	EGGS, SLIGHTLY BEATEN
1	CUP GRITS		⅓	CUP MILK
2	CUPS SHREDDED SHARP CHEDDAR CHEESE			PINCH GARLIC POWDER
¼	CUP BUTTER			SALT AND PEPPER TO TASTE
1	SMALL ONION, MINCED			PAPRIKA TO GARNISH

Preheat the oven to 300°F. Lightly butter a 9 x 13-inch baking dish and set aside. Bring the water to a boil in a medium saucepan over medium-high heat. Slowly stir the grits into the boiling water. Reduce the heat to medium-low and cover. Cook for 16 to 18 minutes or until thickened, stirring occasionally. Add the cheese and remaining ingredients and stir well. Remove from the heat and allow to stand undisturbed for 5 minutes. Garnish with a light sprinkle of paprika before serving.

YIELDS 4 TO 6 SERVINGS.

BUTTER YEAST BISCUITS
★★★★★

"I wish that Eliza was out here to make some nice rolls instead of the solid shot our cook gives us." [Armstrong Custer in an October 18th letter to Libbie Custer. According to Libbie, the cook of which "Autie" spoke was the only woman on the expedition.]

1	PACKAGE ACTIVE DRY YEAST	¼	CUP SUGAR
½	CUP WARM WATER (110°F TO 115°F)	3	CUPS ALL-PURPOSE FLOUR
½	CUP BUTTER	1	TEASPOON SALT
1	EGG	½	CUP BOILING WATER

In a cup dissolve the yeast in warm water. Beat together the butter, egg, and sugar; add the dissolved yeast and stir. Add the flour, salt, and boiling water; mix well. Refrigerate the dough overnight or until well chilled. Roll out the dough to ¼-inch thickness and use a biscuit cutter to cut into biscuits. Re-roll the scraps and cut again until all dough is used. Allow the biscuits to rise for 1½ to 2 hours. Bake in a preheated 350°F oven until golden brown, approximately 12 to 15 minutes.

YIELDS 12 TO 18 BISCUITS.

"And she had been a camp woman many years, and was tanned and toughened by roughing it. When the expedition was attacked at one time, she was cooking by the camp-fire and was heard to mutter when a bullet passed her by, 'Git out, ye divils ye,' and went on with her work as if nothing were happening." [Libbie Custer]

STRAWBERRY BUTTER SPREAD
★ ★ ★ ★ ★

"An officer made me a miniature churn with a bottle, and a little wooden dasher put through a cork. We were at the time marching each day farther and farther into the wilderness, but occasionally came to a ranch where [t]here was a little cream … and as I sat under the tent-fly after we made camp, it was soon transformed into butter in the toy churn." [Libbie Custer, Following the Guidon]

| ¼ | CUP BUTTER | ¼ | CUP HONEY |
| ½ | CUP CREAM CHEESE | ¼ | CUP FROZEN STRAWBERRIES, THAWED |

In a small bowl cream together the butter and cream cheese. Add the honey and strawberries; mix thoroughly. Chill slightly before serving.

MAKES 1 ¼ CUPS.

"The commissary is open Saturday mornings only, at which time we are requested to purchase all supplies we will need . . . for the following week, and as we have no fresh vegetables whatsoever, and no meat except beef we are dependent upon canned goods and other things in the commissary. Last Saturday Mrs. Hunt and I sent over as usual and most supplies were put in a little dug-out cellar we use together. On Sunday morning, cook . . . found . . . the door had been broken open and the shelves as bare as Mother Hubbard.

"Our breakfast that morning was rather light, but as soon as word got abroad . . . true army hospitality and generosity manifested itself. We were invited out to luncheon, and to dinner, and to breakfast the next morning. You can see how like one big family a garrison can be, and how in times of trouble we go to each other's assistance. Of course now and then we will have dissagreeable persons with us—those who will give you only three hours to move out of your house. . . ." [Frances Roe, referencing an unfortunate camp theft and an earlier "ranking" incident mentioned in the introduction]

A Summer Salad Luncheon

★　★　★　★　★

The secret to a successful salad buffet is found in a balance of textures, colors, and flavors. The array of salads should offer a colorful palette of exciting contrasts such as crunchy ingredients served with smooth dressings and spicy bold flavors contrasted against mellow flavors. Each salad should be like a beautiful flower in a garden, individually distinctive, yet part of a beautiful whole. While it is important to have an overall theme, it should be very flexible to allow for interplay between flavors and prevent boredom. The salads of this menu were inspired by the flavors and colors of the Mediterranean simply because they are reminiscent of summer. Set these salads adrift on the sea of a Mediterranean blue tablecloth; accented with sunny yellow napkins.

PANZANELLA (TUSCAN BREAD SALAD)

CRISP CARROT AND TOASTED PECAN SALAD

CREAMY CUCUMBER-MINT SALAD

TORTELLINI SALAD

ZESTY SUMMER SPINACH SALAD

CALIFORNIA CITRUS SALAD

CARROT BREAD

ZUCCHINI BREAD

ASSORTED ROLLS

FRESH FRUIT TRAY WITH HONEYED DRESSING

PANZANELLA

★★★★★

"One afternoon each week the club rooms are at the disposal of the wives of its members, and so popular is this way of entertaining, the rooms are usually engaged weeks in advance. The service is really perfect, and the rooms airy and delightfully cool. Cool rooms are a treasure in this hot place." [Frances Roe, 1888]

1½	LOAVES DAY-OLD ITALIAN BREAD WITH CRUST		¾	CUP SNIPPED FRESH BASIL
12	CUPS TORN LETTUCE LEAVES, A VARIETY		¼	CUP SNIPPED FRESH PARSLEY
2	POUNDS TOMATOES, SEEDED AND COARSELY CHOPPED		4	CLOVES GARLIC, FINELY MINCED
			1½	CUPS FETA CHEESE, CRUMBLED (OPTIONAL)
2	MEDIUM RED ONIONS, HALVED, THINLY SLICED, AND SEPARATED INTO RINGS			**SALAD DRESSING**
2	ENGLISH CUCUMBERS, PEELED AND CUT INTO CHUNKS		⅓	CUP RED WINE VINEGAR
			⅓	CUP OLIVE OIL
1⅓	CUPS SLICED KALAMATA OLIVES		½	TEASPOON SALT
			¼	TEASPOON FRESHLY GROUND PEPPER

Cut the bread into 1-inch cubes and lightly toast. In a large serving bowl combine the salad ingredients except the bread and lightly toss.

In a cruet or a jar with a cover combine the salad dressing ingredients, cover tightly, and shake. Pour over the salad. Allow the dressed salad to sit for 15 minutes to permit the flavors to blend. Immediately before serving, add the bread and toss lightly.

YIELDS 6 SERVINGS.

"Military people are very social."
[Libbie Custer]

In addition to garrison parties, balls and dinner parties, the wives often socialized together at home . . . once again sharing hobbies, interests, and skills. *"During the long summers, when we women were left alone, and had nothing to fill up our time except work that we purposely made to occupy the lonely hours, there came to be a great improvement in our stitchery."* [Libbie Custer]

PORCH PARTY, SHAWNEE LODGE, PLATTE CANYON

CRISP CARROT AND TOASTED PECAN SALAD
★★★★★

"If one of us was plunged into difficulties—for instance, coming from a long march literally in tatters—the rest came in for a 'bee,' and made light work about the sewing machine. We sat on the galleries at work while some read and the delicate fingers of some fashioned the bouillon shoulder straps." [Libbie Custer]

1½	CUPS ORANGE JUICE	½	CUP SALAD OIL
¼	CUP LIME JUICE	3	POUNDS CARROTS, PEELED AND GRATED OR JULI-ENNED
⅛	TEASPOON GROUND CINNAMON		
1	CUP GOLDEN RAISINS	1	CUP CHOPPED PECANS, TOASTED

In a salad bowl combine the orange juice, lime juice, and cinnamon; add the raisins and soak for 30 minutes before adding the salad oil and carrots. Top with toasted pecans.

YIELDS 12 SERVINGS.

THE MILITARY WIVES' COOKBOOK

CREAMY CUCUMBER-MINT SALAD

✯✯✯✯✯

"Each woman coming from leave of absence was prepared to teach a new stitch, lend her fresh designs, or send back to have those she brought reproduced." [Libbie Custer, Following the Guidon]

2½	CUPS SOUR CREAM	1	TABLESPOON SUGAR
½	CUP YOGURT		SALT AND PEPPER TO TASTE
3	ENGLISH CUCUMBERS, PEELED AND QUARTERED		PAPRIKA
⅓	CUP SLICED GREEN ONIONS		MINT LEAF
¼	CUP FINELY CHOPPED FRESH MINT		

In a mixing bowl combine the above ingredients and season with salt and pepper to taste. Transfer to a serving bowl, and garnish with paprika and a mint leaf. Cover tightly and refrigerate until served.

YIELDS 4 TO 6 SERVINGS.

"Everyone has been most hospitable—particularly the Army people at Fort Omaha.. . . . There have been afternoon and evening receptions, and several luncheons, the most charming luncheon of all having been the one given by my friend, Mrs. Schuyler, at the Union Club." [Frances Roe, 1888]

TORTELLINI SALAD
★★★★★

"Those women who cared for fancy-work would beautify their quarters, and there was much leisure for needle work accompaniments." [Libbie Custer]

2	9-OUNCE PACKAGES CHEESE TORTELLINI	½	POUND FRESH ASPARAGUS SPEARS, BIAS-SLICED INTO 1½-INCH PIECES
3	TABLESPOONS OLIVE OIL		
1	POUND MEDIUM-SIZED SHELLED SHRIMP, TAILS INTACT	24	SMALL CHERRY TOMATOES, HALVED
		1	TABLESPOON CHOPPED FRESH BASIL
2	6-OUNCE JARS MARINATED ARTICHOKE HEARTS, UNDRAINED	½	TABLESPOON PARSLEY, MINCED
2	16—OUNCE CANS PITTED BLACK OLIVES, DRAINED AND HALVED		

In a large saucepan bring one quart of water to a boil. Add the shrimp and cook until pink and opaque, approximately 4 to 5 minutes. The shrimp is done when it is opaque throughout and the tail just begins to curl. Drain and refrigerate to cool before adding to the tortellini. Cook the tortellini according to the package directions, rinse, and drain well. Place the tortellini in a mixing bowl and toss with olive oil. Add the artichoke hearts, black olives, asparagus, tomatoes, basil, and parsley. Gently toss in the shrimp and transfer to a serving dish.

YIELDS 12 SERVINGS.

DRESSING

1	CUP BOTTLED ITALIAN DRESSING	½	TEASPOON ONION POWDER
½	TEASPOON DIJON MUSTARD		SALT AND PEPPER TO TASTE
1	TEASPOON GARLIC POWDER	⅓	CUP FRESHLY GRATED PARMESAN CHEESE

In a jar or cruet with a fitted lid combine the Italian dressing, mustard, garlic powder, and onion powder. Shake well and pour over the salad. Cover the salad tightly and refrigerate overnight. Add salt and pepper to taste and sprinkle with grated Parmesan just prior to serving.

ZESTY SUMMER SPINACH SALAD

★★★★★

"Harper's Bazaar was as thoroughly read out there as at any point in its wide wanderings. . . . It was rather difficult to teach ourselves to be dress-makers . . . and things looked pretty homemade for a long time after we had begun to do such work." [Libbie Custer]

	RIND FROM 1 FRESHLY PRESERVED LEMON RIND (SEE RECIPE ON PAGE 232)	1	RED BELL PEPPER, SEEDED AND CHOPPED
8	CUPS SLICED STRAWBERRIES	1	YELLOW BELL PEPPER, SEEDED AND CHOPPED
1½	CUPS MANDARIN ORANGES, DRAINED	2	PURPLE ONIONS, THINLY SLICED
¼	CUP MINCED FRESH MINT	8	CUPS STEMMED, WASHED, BITE SIZE PIECES SPINACH
1½	CUPS THINLY SLICED FRESH MUSHROOMS	½	CUP TOASTED PINE NUTS

Rinse the preserved lemon, remove the pulp, and discard. Cut the rind into 1/4-inch cubes. In a small bowl combine the lemon rind with the remaining ingredients; toss gently and refrigerate while preparing the salad dressing.

YIELDS 4 TO 6 SERVINGS.

DRESSING

½	CUP SUGAR	⅓	CUP FRESH LIME JUICE
1	TEASPOON DIJON MUSTARD	1	CUP VEGETABLE OIL
1	TEASPOON ONION JUICE		

In a cruet or jar with a fitted lid, combine the above ingredients; close tightly and shake well.

Prior to serving, pour the dressing over the salad, toss lightly, and sprinkle with pine nuts.

CALIFORNIA CITRUS SALAD
★★★★★

"Others painted, or drew or learned new guitar accompaniments. In addition, there were afternoon socials, musicals and amateur theatricals." (Libbie Custer, Following the Guidon]

4	SEEDLESS ORANGES	3	SMALL AVOCADOS
4	RUBY-RED GRAPEFRUIT		BIBB LETTUCE
5	KIWI FRUIT, PEELED AND SLICED		

Peel and section the oranges and grapefruit, removing the bitter membranes. Drain in a colander set over a bowl to reserve the juices. Peel and slice the kiwi. Peel, pit, and slice the avocados. Dip the avocados in the reserved juices to prevent discoloration. Place a bed of lettuce on a serving plate. Arrange sliced avocado on the lettuce bed. Drizzle any reserved fruit juices on the avocado to prevent discoloration. Add the fruit.

DRESSING

½	CUP HONEY	1	TEASPOON DIJON MUSTARD
1	CUP VEGETABLE OIL	1	TABLESPOON POPPY SEEDS
⅓	CUP LIME JUICE	¼	TEASPOON SALT
1	TEASPOON PAPRIKA		

In a jar or cruet with fitted lid combine the dressing ingredients. Cover and shake well. Chill thoroughly.

Pour the dressing over the salad just before serving.

ZUCCHINI BREAD
★★★★★

By 1898, America had become an empire. It was during this period that the women's club movement was born in the civilian sector of American life. They were ideally suited to frontier wives who had already forged strong friendships and alliances, learned to organize, and recognized the importance of working together toward common objectives.

3	EGGS	1	TEASPOON BAKING SODA
2	CUPS SUGAR	¾	TEASPOON BAKING POWDER
1	TABLESPOON VANILLA EXTRACT	3	TEASPOONS GROUND CINNAMON
1	CUP VEGETABLE OIL	½	TEASPOON GRATED NUTMEG
2	CUPS ALL-PURPOSE FLOUR, SIFTED	¼	TEASPOON GROUND ALLSPICE
1	CUP WHOLE WHEAT FLOUR	2½	CUPS UNPEELED GRATED AND WELL DRAINED ZUCCHINI
1	TEASPOON SALT		

Preheat the oven to 350°F. Grease and flour two 9 x 5-inch loaf pans and set aside. In a large bowl beat the eggs until light and fluffy. Add the sugar, vanilla, and oil. Blend well. In a separate bowl sift together the flours, salt, baking soda, baking powder, cinnamon, nutmeg, and allspice. Blend the dry ingredients into the beaten eggs. Fold in the zucchini. Pour into the prepared pans. Bake for 45 minutes until golden and a testing pick inserted in the center comes out clean.

YIELDS 2 LOAVES.

CARROT BREAD

★ ★ ★ ★ ★

Members of these once purely social clubs began addressing the important social issues of their day. Moreover, they took the lead on issues such as education, temperance, and suffrage reform!

1	CUP BUTTER, SOFTENED	1	TEASPOON BAKING SODA
¼	CUP SUGAR	1	TEASPOON SALT
¾	CUP FIRMLY PACKED LIGHT BROWN SUGAR	2	TEASPOONS GROUND CINNAMON
3	EGGS	½	TEASPOON GROUND ALLSPICE
2	CUPS ALL PURPOSE FLOUR	3	CUPS GRATED CARROT
1	TEASPOON BAKING POWDER	1	CUP COARSELY CHOPPED PECANS

Preheat the oven to 350°F. Butter and lightly flour a 9x5x3-inch loaf pan and set aside. In a large bowl cream together the butter and sugars. Beat well. Add the eggs one at a time, beating well after each addition. In a separate bowl sift together the dry ingredients, and beat into the egg mixture. Fold in the carrots and pecans. Mix well and fold into the prepared baking pan. Bake for approximately 1 hour or until golden. Turn out on a wire rack to cool.

YIELDS 1 LOAF.

*T*oday, the social aspect of wives clubs continues to include structured activities, games and luncheons. These social opportunites were received with great relish as indicated by excerpts taken from letters of this World War II bride:

Dear People;—
. . . In Army terms, Blythe is a "splinter town," which is a post of hastily constructed barracks.
. . . but there is no actual post complete with recreational facilities. . . . Splinter towns, lacking in the above mentioned features, make it necesssary for the officers to find their own ways and means of entertainment. . . . Guess that I will have to make out a program of parlor games, work up a vaudeville act, . . . run classes on how to play Gin Rummy, or something. . . .
Missing you
Betty
[Betty Utley St. John, excerpted from Excess Baggage or Adventures of an Army Wife*]*

PEANUT BUTTER COOKIES

★ ★ ★ ★ ★

The social and service traditions of military wives have, like heirloom china, passed through many hands. Numerous women have added to a trunk now filled with the customs, traditions, and social activist legacies of the military wives who have gone before us.

1¼	CUPS ALL-PURPOSE FLOUR	½	CUP SUGAR
¾	TEASPOON BAKING SODA	½	CUP FIRMLY PACKED BROWN SUGAR
¼	TEASPOON SALT	1	EGG
½	CUP BUTTER	1	TEASPOON VANILLA EXTRACT
½	CUP SMOOTH PEANUT BUTTER		SUGAR

In a large bowl combine flour, baking soda, and salt; set aside. In a separate bowl beat the butter until creamy, approximately 20 to 30 seconds. Add the peanut butter and sugars, beating well after each addition. Add the egg and vanilla, and beat well. Shape the dough into 1-inch balls, roll in sugar, and place 2 inches apart on an ungreased baking sheet. Press the flat tines of a fork against the surface of the dough balls, first in one direction and then the opposite direction. Exert sufficient pressure to slightly flatten the ball and form a criss-cross pattern on its surface. Bake for 10 minutes until golden. Cool for 1 minute before removing to a wire rack.

YIELDS 3 DOZEN COOKIES.

While in the White House, Mamie Eisenhower enjoyed relaxing over a game of canasta. She played every free afternoon with friends from her days as an "army wife." Their strong friendships remained firm.

I am certain that Betty would have thoroughly enjoyed the summer fete described by Katherine Tupper Marshall, wife of General George C. Marshall, in *Together: Annals of a Military Wife*: "A French cruiser on a goodwill trip of the United States made Charleston its last port of call on the tour . . . and [General Marshall] arranged a dinner for forty at our quarters, followed by a reception and dance at the Officer's Club.

"The young officers' wives did all the decorating, made the punch and sandwiches, then hurriedly dressed in their best dance frocks. . . . The Captain was so pleased over the Southern hospitality . . . that he in turn invited the garrison and many Charlestonians to a reception and dance aboard the cruiser."

Mah Jongg Luncheon at Evie Foster's
(April 7, 2000)
★ ★ ★ ★ ★

The tradition continues. Evie set the table with her finest linen, china, and crystal, collected during many years of service as a military wife. She regaled us with charming stories and then we shuffled the Mah Jongg tiles.

Mah Jongg, an ancient Chinese game of skill and chance, has been a favorite of military wives for many years. It was first introduced to America in 1920 by an American businessman. When Wright Patterson was still known as McCook Field, Mah Jongg players there began compiling their own rules under the guidance of Sylvia Bauer and Helene Morris. Copyrighted in 1963, these standardized rules allowed players to transfer from" Base to Port to Post" and still play the same game.

BROCCOLI CHICKEN STRATA
AMERICAN MAH JONGG CASSEROLE
CRANBERRY SALAD
DEVILED EGGS
CRESCENT ROLLS
BLUEBERRY MUFFINS
FROZEN PEPPERMINT CHEESECAKE
ASSORTED RELISHES AND JAMS

BROCCOLI CHICKEN STRATA

★★★★★

A defensive game requiring strategic thinking, Mah Jongg traces its origins to ancient China and the time of Confucius. During the postwar years it was largely popular, as evidenced by Eddie Cantor's hit song "Since Ma Is Playing Mah Jongg" and a song called "Mah Jongg Blues" contained in a Broadway revue.

15	OUNCES FROZEN BROCCOLI		3	EGGS
6	SLICES WHITE BREAD		2	CUPS MILK
1½	POUNDS SKINLESS CHICKEN TENDERS OR BREASTS, COOKED		1	MEDIUM ONION, CHOPPED
			1	TABLESPOON PREPARED MUSTARD
6	SLICES SWISS CHEESE		½	TEASPOON PAPRIKA

Grease a 9 x 13-inch casserole dish and set aside. Cook the broccoli according to the package directions and drain. Arrange the bread slices on the bottom of the baking dish. Cut the chicken into 1-inch cubes and place on top of the bread. Layer the broccoli over the chicken. Top with cheese.

In a medium bowl combine the eggs, milk, onions, mustard, and paprika; mix well and pour over the strata. Tightly cover the casserole and refrigerate for at least 1 hour.

Bake the casserole in a preheated 350°F oven for 60 to 70 minutes or until a knife inserted in the center comes out clean. Allow to stand a few minutes before serving.

Other vegetables such as grated carrots or zucchini may be substituted for the broccoli. Turkey or roast beef may be substituted for the chicken.

YIELDS 6 SERVINGS.

EVIE FOSTER AND FAMILY

"No matter where the four winds may carry us, we will never forget the 'Pung' nor the great 'Chow' enjoyed here today." [Vandenberg wives' Mah Jongg toast]

AMERICAN MAH JONGG CASSEROLE
★★★★★

Recipes, such as this one, also paid tribute to the game. It calls for ingredients representing the three suits of the game: red tomatoes for the "craks," green pepper for "bams" or "bamboos," and white rice representing the "dots" or "pearls."

1	CUP UNCOOKED LONG GRAIN RICE		½	TEASPOON GROUND BLACK PEPPER
4	CUPS CANNED TOMATOES		2	TEASPOONS SALT
1	CUP CHOPPED GREEN BELL PEPPER		1	TEASPOON GROUND TURMERIC
1½	CUPS (6 OUNCES) GRATED SHARP AMERICAN CHEESE		1	BAY LEAF, CRUMBLED
1	CUP PIMIENTO-STUFFED OLIVES, CHOPPED		1	CUP HOT WATER
¼	CUP INSTANT MINCED ONION			

In a large bowl combine all of the ingredients. Turn into a buttered 2-quart casserole. Cover and bake at 325°F for 2 hours or until the rice is tender. Serve hot as a main dish.

YIELDS 8 SERVINGS.

CRANBERRY SALAD
★★★★★

At Vandenberg Air Force Base, Mah Jongg veterans Jinny Donald and Evie Foster share the game with a new generation of enthusiasts. Each fall Jinny teaches a demanding class and Evie soothes bruised egos.

1⅓	POUNDS CRANBERRIES		2	CUPS SUGAR
4	SMALL APPLES WITH SKINS		2	3-OUNCE PACKAGES FLAVORED GELATIN
4	SMALL ORANGES WITH PEELS			

In a food processor or grinder chop together the cranberries, apples and oranges. Add the sugar and mix well. Prepare the gelatin according to the package directions. Pour the gelatin into a 9x9-inch serving dish and refrigerate. When slightly set add the cranberry mixture and refrigerate until firm.

"When cranberries were plentiful last fall and winter, I ground together the apples, oranges, and cranberries. I then added the sugar and froze in amounts needed for one recipe." [Evie Foster]

DEVILED EGGS
★★★★★

Mah jongg is most akin to the card game gin rummy. However, the game tiles are slightly smaller than domino tiles and identified by distinctive Chinese characters. Winning hands are formed with specific combinations of these tiles and have unique, atmospheric names such as "Sukiyaki" or "Pung Chow." Play begins with four double-tiered walls designated as East, South, West, and North Winds.

1	DOZEN BOILED EGGS	SALT AND PEPPER TO TASTE	
1	TABLESPOON SWEET PICKLE RELISH	PINCH CAYENNE PEPPER	
1½	TEASPOONS DIJON MUSTARD	PAPRIKA	
3	TABLESPOONS MAYONNAISE	PARSLEY	
1	TEASPOON FRESH LEMON JUICE		

Halve the boiled eggs; remove the yolks to a bowl and mash. Add the remaining ingredients except the paprika and parsley; mix well and return the mixture to each egg white half, a teaspoonful per half. Garnish each egg with a sprinkle of paprika and a parsley sprig.

YIELDS 24 HALVES.

FROZEN PEPPERMINT CHEESECAKE
★ ★ ★ ★ ★

Although Mah Jongg is a fast-paced and competitive game, when the tiles are shuffled, hands touch and stories and recipes are exchanged, and friendships are formed. Words cannot describe the sadness I felt when the inevitable orders arrived that would separate me from my Mah Jongg friends.

1	8-OUNCE PACKAGE CREAM CHEESE, SOFTENED	3	DROPS RED FOOD COLORING
1	14-OUNCE CAN SWEETENED CONDENSED MILK	2	CUPS WHIPPING CREAM
1	CUP CRUSHED PEPPERMINT CANDY	2	PREPARED 9-INCH CHOCOLATE PIE SHELLS

In the bowl of an electric mixer beat the cream cheese until light and fluffy. Add the condensed milk, crushed peppermint candy, and red food coloring. Continue to beat at high speed until the mixture turns a "pretty pink" color. If necessary, add more food color. In a separate bowl whip the cream until soft peaks form; fold into the cream cheese mixture and divide between the shells. Tightly cover the pies and freeze until firm. Prior to serving, garnish with whipped cream or crushed peppermint.

YIELDS 12 TO 16 SERVINGS.

Constance Baker:
MILITARY SPOUSE ON THE MOVE BUILDS DREAM CAREER
WITH VOLUNTEER EXPERIENCE

On average, military wives earn three dollars less per hour than civilian spouses, and their unemployment rate is three times as much, due in part to the fact that only about 10 percent of military wives stay in the same home for five years, while most move to a different state with different career licensing and certification requirements. The impact of the mobile military lifestyle on employment opportunities for spouses may be viewed as either a blessing or a curse. Fortunately, there is support in the community and creative solutions that transform a potential curse into a blessing. Some turn to volunteer work.

Volunteerism was the key to Constance Baker's future. As a result of her commitment to improving the lives of others, she gained experience that prepared her for the professional opportunity of her dreams. Today, she is the assistant director for the Combined Federal Campaign–Overseas in Europe (CFC). As a young military spouse and mother, she stayed at home and managed the household, raised her children, and supported her husband's career. Occasionally, she did volunteer work, but she also began thinking about a career of her own.

She faced an additional disadvantage in that her schooling and job training was accomplished in Germany, and her skills and training did not translate easily into something familiar and usable in the States. She tried several home-based businesses and part-time jobs while training herself to be computer literate. Constance found that she had talent and enjoyed graphic design. A friend suggested that the nearby Red Cross could use someone. So she became a Red Cross volunteer, filling many different positions. Although they were sometimes demanding, as a volunteer, she maintained the flexibility needed to take care of her family. Frequently, others asked her why she chose to work for free. Constance valued the experience she was gaining and free training courses in technology and other areas.

When there was a job opening for a marketing assistant–Web master, she applied. Although it did not happen right away, she was eventually hired. Of course, it did not last forever. After another military transfer, she was job hunting again. A manager she had worked with in the past alerted her to a job opening of assistant director for the CFC. She's been with the CFC Overseas for several years now. As the director for the European Command, Central Command, and Africa Command, she directs a staff of four as well as thousands of volunteers. In 2007, they raised $11 million for national and international charities.

Her husband will retire soon, and their years of moving will come to an end. Constance is proof that while military life can be difficult, it is full of opportunity if one focuses on finding fulfillment.

A TASTE OF HOME: DINNER FAMILY STYLE

"Every house where love abides and friendship is a guest, is surely home, and home sweet home; for there the heart can rest." [Henry Van Dyke]

"I must tell you that I had a foretaste of home yesterday. We were on a picket about five miles from camp and . . . went to a house near where our post was and engaged us a supper."

Simmering Soup Pot Dinner
★ ★ ★ ★ ★

Service was foremost in the mind of Sarah Borginis when the shelling resumed at Fort Texas. She never left her post as the cook and even found time to assist in the battle. During the evening, she served the men savory soup, hot and as tasty as she could manage with her dwindling supplies.

BEAN POT SOUP
HEARTY WHOLE WHEAT CORN BREAD
TOSSED SALAD
TEXAS SHEET CAKE

BEAN POT SOUP
★★★★★

At a June banquet, Lieutenant Braxton Bragg, a long-time friend, offered a toast to Sarah. With loud cheers of approval for the valor and courage of Sarah Borginis, the men sprung to their feet and cried, "Huzzah!"

2	CUPS PINTO BEANS		2	TABLESPOONS SEASONING MIX (SEE RECIPE BELOW)
4	SLICES BACON		2½	QUARTS UNSALTED CHICKEN BROTH
1	JALAPEÑO PEPPER, DICED		2	CUPS CHOPPED CANNED TOMATOES
1	LARGE BELL PEPPER, DICED		1¼	POUNDS HOT SMOKED SAUSAGE, SLICED
1	LARGE ONION, DICED		1¼	POUNDS COOKED HAM, CUT INTO ½-INCH CUBES
1	CUP DICED CELERY		2	POTATOES, DICED
3	CLOVES GARLIC, MINCED			

Soak the beans overnight in sufficient cold water to cover. In an 8-quart or larger stock pot fry the bacon until crisp and remove from the pan. Add the peppers, onion, celery, and garlic to the bacon fat, and sauté until tender. Add the unsalted broth and seasoning.

Drain and rinse the beans and add them to the pot, ensuring the beans are covered by 2 to 3 inches of liquid. Bring to a boil. Reduce the heat; cover, and simmer for 2 hours or until the beans are tender. Add additional water as needed to ensure the free boiling of the beans.

Add the sausage, ham, and potatoes; simmer an additional 30 minutes. Add additional water if necessary. Season with salt and pepper to taste. Serve with Hearty Whole Wheat Corn Bread.

YIELDS 6 TO 8 SERVINGS.

SEASONING MIX

¼	CUP FIRMLY PACKED BROWN SUGAR		1	TEASPOON CELERY SEED
1	TABLESPOON CHILI POWDER		1	TEASPOON DRIED OREGANO
1	TEASPOON SEASON SALT		½	TEASPOON GROUND THYME
1	TEASPOON CRUSHED BAY LEAF		1	TEASPOON DRIED BASIL

In a small bowl combine the seasoning ingredients. If not used immediately, cover tightly and store in a cool, dry place.

In addition to serving as laundresses and cooks, women, some with very little training, also provided nursing services. And of course, when necessary, they took up arms.

LT CHARLES C. DERUDIO STANDING BETWEEN TWO DAUGHTERS

Service was also foremost on the mind of Susie King Taylor. Taylor was married to a sergeant in the First South Carolina Volunteers, a U.S. black regiment, where she served as a nurse and laundress. According to Susie, "We had fresh beef once in a while, and we would have soup, and the vegetables they put in the soup were dried and pressed; they looked like hops." [Susie King Taylor, Laundress, 33rd United States Colored Troops, 1864]

THE MILITARY WIVES' COOKBOOK

HEARTY WHOLE WHEAT CORN BREAD
★★★★★

"Salt beef was our standby. Sometimes the men would have what we called slap-jacks. This was flour made into bread and spread thin on the bottom of the mess-pan to cook; each man had one of them with a pint of tea for his supper." [Susie King Taylor, Laundress, 33rd United States Colored Troops, 1864]

¼	CUP SHORTENING		1	TABLESPOON BAKING POWDER
1	CUP YELLOW CORNMEAL		½	TEASPOON SALT
1	CUP WHOLE WHEAT FLOUR		1 ½	CUPS MILK
2	TABLESPOONS SUGAR		1	EGG, BEATEN

Preheat the oven to 425°F. Place the shortening in a 10½-inch cast-iron skillet and heat in a preheated oven for approximately 10 to 15 minutes. While the skillet heats, in a large mixing bowl combine dry ingredients. Add the milk and egg; mix until well blended. Remove the skillet from the oven, turn, and tilt to evenly coat the sides and bottom of the skillet with the shortening. Pour the shortening into the batter and mix well. Pour the batter into the skillet. Bake for 20 to 25 minutes or until a wooden pick inserted into the center comes out clean.

YIELDS 6 SERVINGS.

> *"My work now began, I gave my assistance to alleviate their sufferings. . . . My services were given at all times for the comfort of these men. I was on hand to assist wherever needed."* [Susie King Taylor, Laundress 33rd United States Colored Troops 1864]

TEXAS SHEET CAKE
★★★★★

"The regiment was ordered to Morris Island between June and July 1864. About four o'clock, July 2, the charge was made. The 103rd New York suffered the most. They wanted soup, but that I could not get; but I had a few cans of condensed milk and some turtle eggs. I thought I would try to make some custard. I had some doubts as to my success, for cooking with turtle eggs was something new to me. . . . The result was a very delicious custard. This I carried to the men who enjoyed it very much." [Susie King Taylor, Laundress, 33rd United States Colored Troops, 1864]

2	CUPS SUGAR		1	CUP WATER
2	CUPS ALL-PURPOSE FLOUR		½	CUP SOUR CREAM
½	TEASPOON SALT (OPTIONAL)		2	EGGS, WELL BEATEN
1	CUP BUTTER		1½	TEASPOONS VANILLA EXTRACT
4	TABLESPOONS COCOA		1	TEASPOON BAKING SODA

Preheat the oven to 350°F. Grease and flour a 9 x 13-inch baking pan and set aside. In a large mixing bowl sift together the sugar, flour, and salt, and set aside. in a small saucepan combine the butter, cocoa, and water and bring to a boil over medium-high heat, stirring constantly. Immediately pour into the flour mixture; using an electric mixer, beat for 3 to 5 minutes until well blended. Pour the batter into prepared baking pan. Bake for 20 to 25 minutes or until a toothpick inserted in its center comes out clean. Allow to cool for 15 minutes, but frost while warm.

YIELDS 8 TO 12 SERVINGS.

FROSTING

6	TABLESPOONS MILK		1½	TEASPOONS VANILLA EXTRACT
1	CUP BUTTER		1	POUND CONFECTIONERS' SUGAR
4	TABLESPOONS COCOA		1	CUP CHOPPED WALNUTS

In a medium saucepan over medium-high heat combine the milk, butter, and cocoa. Bring to a boil, taking care not to burn, and remove from the heat. Add the vanilla. Add the confectioners' sugar, a little at a time, beating well after each addition. Finally, add the nuts and beat until smooth. Pour over the warm cake.

"I often got my own meals and would fix some dishes for the noncommissioned officers also." [Susie King Taylor, Laundress, 33rd United States Colored Troops 1864, from Reminiscences of My Life in Camp with the 33rd United States Colored Troops, *Boston, 1902]*

A Foretaste of Home

★ ★ ★ ★ ★

Home-cooked meals were morale boosters for soldiers of every war and every generation. Thoughts of home were reflected in their writings. All that "home" represented was never far from their hearts and minds.

FRESH SPINACH AND FRUIT SALAD

TOSSED SALAD

CHICKEN POT PIE

APPLE BETTY

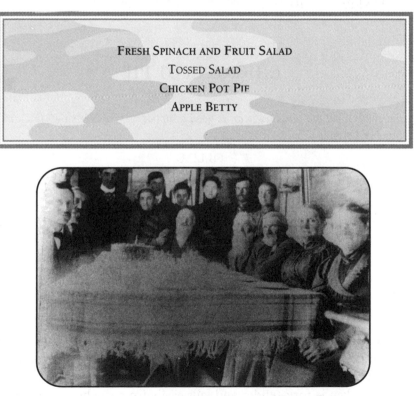

CHRISTMAS

FRESH SPINACH AND FRUIT SALAD
⭐⭐⭐⭐⭐

"Dear wife, I hasten to write you again a few lines. I am glad to inform you that all is well with me and I enjoy excellent health. Someone has remarked that we cannot properly estimate our individual blessings until we are deprived of them. So it is with me now. My absence has taught me that deprived of you the world would be a wilderness and life a blank. I have to meditate here in solitude the many joys you have brought me, strewing my pathway with happiness and exalting my soul to a just prescription of the good and beautiful in life. A few months and I hope to be with you.

Your husband, Edgar

1	CUP SLICED STRAWBERRIES	8	THIN SLICES BERMUDA ONION, SEPARATED
½	CUP MANDARIN ORANGES, DRAINED	2	BOILED EGGS, CHOPPED
½	CUP THINLY SLICED FRESH MUSHROOMS	4	CUPS SPINACH, STEMMED, WASHED, AND TORN INTO
½	SLICES COOKED BACON, CRUMBLED		BITE-SIZE PIECES

In a serving bowl combine all of the ingredients. Cover and refrigerate. Just prior to serving dress with poppy seed dressing. (See the recipe on page 124.)

CHICKEN POT PIE
⭐⭐⭐⭐⭐

"We engaged a chicken pot pie and had near as good a supper as you ever saw." [Edgar Clark, Camp Upson Hill, October 1, 1862]

FILLING

1	5-POUND STEWING CHICKEN	½	CUP SIFTED ALL-PURPOSE FLOUR
1½	QUARTS WATER	½	TEASPOON ONION POWDER
	CHICKEN BOUILLON CUBES AS DESIRED	½	TEASPOON GARLIC POWDER
¼	TEASPOON SALT	¼	TEASPOON CELERY SEED
¾	CUP CHOPPED ONION	¼	TEASPOON WHITE PEPPER
3	CARROTS, DIAGONALLY SLICED INTO 1-INCH PIECES	3	DROPS YELLOW FOOD COLORING
1	STALK CELERY, CHOPPED	½	CUP FROZEN GREEN PEAS
1	SMALL BAY LEAF		CREAM BISCUIT DOUGH (RECIPE FOLLOWS)

in a large kettle and add the water, bouillon, salt, onion, carrot, celery, and bay leaf. Cover and simmer until tender, 3 to 3½ hours. (Toward the end of the cooking time, begin preparing cream biscuit dough.)

When the chicken is fork-tender and falls easily from the bones remove it from the pot. Strip the meat from the bones, and refrigerate it. Discard the bones. Remove any excess oil from the surface of the broth. In a medium bowl combine the flour, onion powder, garlic powder, celery seed, and white pepper. Add to this mixture 1 cup of water and stir smooth. Add 3 cups of hot broth removed from the stewing pot, whisking well to prevent lumps. Remove any remaining broth from the pot and freeze for future use. Return the flour mixture to the pot and cook over medium heat, stirring constantly until the mixture is smooth. Continue to cook in this manner until the mixture thickens. Add the food coloring, stirring until well blended. Add the peas and return the chicken and carrots to the pot.

CREAM BISCUIT DOUGH

2	CUPS SIFTED ALL-PURPOSE FLOUR	6	TABLESPOONS BUTTER
½	TEASPOON SALT	2	CUPS HEAVY CREAM
2	TEASPOONS BAKING POWDER		

In a bowl sift together the dry ingredients and using a fork or pastry cutter, cut in the butter. Add the cream, working the dough well for several minutes. Turn out the dough onto a flat, floured surface; dust lightly with flour and roll into 2 circles ⅛-inch thick. Line a 9-inch deep-dish pie shell with one of the circles of dough.

Preheat the oven to 400°F. Fill the prepared deep-dish pie pan with the chicken mixture. Place the top crust over the pie. Cut steam vents and flute the edges. Bake for 45 minutes to 1 hour or until golden brown.

Note: This dish may be frozen, however, allow the filling to completely cool before placing it in the shell. Follow the preparation directions up to the point of baking and then freeze. To serve, place the frozen pie in the oven and bake according to the directions.

YIELDS 6 TO 8 SERVINGS.

*H*usbands far from home and their loved ones missed the nourishing meals their wives provided. However, they also missed the nurturing hearts from which an abundance of love flowed.

APPLE BETTY
★ ★ ★ ★ ★

"You cannot tell how much good your last letter done me. . . . I have nearly learned it by heart. I wish I could have seen Carrie when she was pot black as you told. I would give $5 to see both the children. You said Lydia wished I was at home to help eat some of their ripe peaches and apples. I wish I was there . . . Abraham Lincoln has issued a proclamation freeing all the slaves in rebellion . . . I think it will . . . produce peace." [Edgar Clark, October 1, 1862]

5 CUPS PEELED, CORED, AND SLICED MACINTOSH APPLES	⅛ TEASPOON GROUND ALLSPICE
½ CUP WATER	⅛ TEASPOON GRATED NUTMEG
1 CUP FIRMLY PACKED BROWN SUGAR	¾ CUP ALL-PURPOSE FLOUR
1¼ TEASPOONS GROUND CINNAMON	½ CUP BUTTER, CUT INTO SMALL PIECES

Preheat the oven to 350°. Layer the apples in the bottom of a 9 x 9 x 2-inch lightly buttered baking dish. In a separate bowl combine the remaining ingredients. Mix with a fork or cut with a pastry cutter until the mixture resembles small peas. Spread the topping mixture over the apples and press lightly. Bake for 20 to 25 minutes or until golden brown and crisp. Serve warm with whipped cream or vanilla ice cream.

YIELDS 6 TO 8 SERVINGS.

Chicken and Dumpling Delight

★ ★ ★ ★ ★

Far from home and their relatives, military families were formed. Libbie Custer also experienced the sense of family associated with military life. From the very beginning of the general's career, the Custers shared quarters in military encampments wherever possible. According to Libbie, she was the only army wife who always followed the regiment.

SOUTHERN CHICKEN AND DUMPLINGS

HOMEMADE WALNUT BROWNIES WITH

VANILLA ICE CREAM AND CHOCOLATE SYRUP

SOUTHERN CHICKEN AND DUMPLINGS
★★★★★

And in later years, while noting that her "husband's camp was always meager," she recalled that "the wives of some of the Michigan Brigade had given some touches to the barren place, draping the high-poster with calico curtains . . . it looked homey." [Libbie Custer, Boots and Saddles*]*

2½	QUARTS CHICKEN STOCK		2	STALKS CELERY, SLICED (¼-INCH)
2	BOUILLON CUBES		4	CARROTS, PEELED AND SLICED (¼-INCH)
3	DROPS YELLOW FOOD COLORING (OPTIONAL)		1	TEASPOON SALT
5	CHICKEN BREAST HALVES, WASHED		1	CUP GARDEN PEAS, FRESH OR FROZEN
1	SMALL ONION, CHOPPED		1	TABLESPOON PARSLEY, CHOPPED FINE FOR GARNISH (OPTIONAL)

In a stock pot bring the chicken broth to a boil. Add the bouillon cubes, food coloring, chicken breasts, onion, and celery. Boil for 10 minutes. Reduce the heat to low, add the carrots, and simmer over low heat for an additional 30 to 35 minutes.

Remove the chicken breasts from the water and set aside to cool. Once cooled, skin, bone, and cut the chicken into ½-inch cubes. Discard the skin and bones and refrigerate the chicken.

DUMPLINGS

1½	CUPS ALL-PURPOSE FLOUR		½	TEASPOON SALT
¾	ROUNDED TEASPOON BAKING POWDER		⅓	CUP PLUS 2 TABLESPOONS ICE COLD WATER
¼	CUP BUTTER			

In a medium bowl blend the above ingredients to form a dough. Place the dough on a lightly floured surface. Dust the dough's surface with flour. Roll out thin and cut into 3 x 2-inch strips. If necessary, add additional broth to the chicken pot to make 2 quarts. Bring to a rapid boil and drop the dough strips in quickly. Cook until done, approximately 10 to 12 minutes. Add the diced chicken breast. Season with salt and pepper to taste. Cover and simmer a few additional minutes. After the dumplings have been cooked, if you desire a thicker gravy, mix 2 tablespoons of flour with ¼ cup of cold water and slowly add to the mixture; stirring until smooth.

YIELDS 4 SERVINGS.

HOMEMADE WALNUT BROWNIES
★★★★★

¾	CUP SIFTED ALL-PURPOSE FLOUR	2	EGGS
1	CUP SUGAR	1¼	TEASPOONS VANILLA EXTRACT
¼	TEASPOON SALT	1	TABLESPOON WATER
½	CUP BUTTER, SOFTENED	½	CUP WALNUTS, CHOPPED

Preheat the oven to 350°F. Grease the bottom of an 8 x 8 x 2-inch baking pan and set aside. In the bowl of an electric mixer combine all of the ingredients except the nuts and beat on medium-high speed for 3 minutes. Add the nuts to the mixture and stir in by hand. If the mixture is too difficult to stir, add an additional tablespoon of water. Pour the mixture into the prepared pan. Bake for 30 minutes or until the brownies spring quickly back when pressed with an index finger.

YIELDS 9 TO 12 SERVINGS.

SOLDIERS OF THE SEVENTH CAVALRY AND WIVES

Nanna's Chicken-Fried Steak and Biscuits

★ ★ ★ ★ ★

"I had hardly breathed a long breath . . . before all the troops had swept out of camp. The camp that I could not see knew that I was alone, but I could see no signs of any troops. I neither heard a sound nor could see a tent." [Libbie Custer, Boots and Saddles]

CHICKEN-FRIED STEAK AND BISCUITS
BUTTERED GARDEN PEAS
GLAZED CARROTS
AUTIE'S APPLE PIE

NANNA'S CHICKEN-FRIED STEAK
★★★★★

"A clash of sabers and looking out the window the yard seemed full of troops, for each officer had his order-lies mounted on those horses children see in military pictures, chomping on the bit, standing on their hind legs in their very best uniforms." [Libbie Custer]

4	THICK CUBE STEAKS	1	TEASPOON SEASONED SALT
	ALL-PURPOSE FLOUR FOR DREDGING	1	TABLESPOON BAKING POWDER
¾	CUP ALL-PURPOSE FLOUR	1	EGG
3	TABLESPOONS SUGAR	2	CUPS EVAPORATED MILK, DIVIDED

Season the steaks to taste. Thoroughly flour each steak, shake off the excess, and set aside. In a medium bowl combine the flour, sugar, salt, egg, and 1 cup of milk. Stir until smooth; add as much of the remaining cup of milk as necessary to reach a good dipping consistency (1¼ cups is usually sufficient). Place approximately ½ inch of oil in the bottom of a large skillet and heat over medium-high heat. Dip each of the floured steaks in the batter. Hold the steak above the bowl and allow the excess batter to drip back into the bowl. Just before the oil begins to smoke, add the steaks, but do not crowd the pan. Reduce the heat to medium. Fry for 3 to 5 minutes on each side or until golden brown. Remove the steaks to a paper towel-covered platter and keep warm.

YIELDS UP TO 8 SERVINGS.

GRAVY

"Their spurs and accoutrements jingled up the rickety stairs and Eliza threw the door open to several of General Sheridan's staff." [Libbie Custer]

4	TABLESPOONS BUTTER	1	CUP ALL-PURPOSE FLOUR
8	CUPS MILK		SALT AND PEPPER TO TASTE
½	CUP VEGETABLE OIL		

In a large saucepan completely melt the butter. Add the milk and stir. Bring this mixture to a boil. Blend the flour and oil and add to the heated milk mixture. Stir until smooth and thickened. Remove from the heat. Season with salt and pepper to taste. Serve with steak and biscuits.

BISCUITS
★★★★★

"General Sheridan's staff filled the upstairs room and I was made to sit on the one chair while they offered congratulations, praised my husband, wished us all joy, and were, of course, absolutely silent about the expedition." [Libbie Custer]

2	CUPS ALL-PURPOSE FLOUR	5	TABLESPOONS BUTTER
1	TEASPOON SALT	¾	CUP MILK
3	TEASPOONS BAKING POWDER		

Preheat the oven to 425°F. Into a medium bowl sift together the dry ingredients. Cut in the butter until the mixture resembles coarse cornmeal. Add the milk and mix until smooth. Knead the dough on a floured board. Roll and cut out biscuits with a floured biscuit cutter or glass rim. Arrange the biscuits on a baking sheet. Bake for 12 or 15 minutes or until the tops brown.

YIELDS APPROXIMATELY 18 BISCUITS.

CARROTS
★★★★★

8	TO 10 SMALL FRESH CARROTS OR 3 CUPS QUICK-FROZEN CARROTS	¼	CUP SUGAR
		¼	TEASPOON GRATED NUTMEG
1	CUP ORANGE JUICE PLUS ADDITIONAL WATER TO COVER CARROTS BY 2 INCHES	3	TABLESPOONS BUTTER

Scrape carrots and cut into 1/4-inch pieces. Place in a medium-sized saucepan; add water, orange juice, and sugar; bring to a boil and cook until fork-tender. Drain carrots; add butter and nutmeg; serve hot.

YIELDS 4 TO 5 SERVINGS.

Eliza, who figured prominently in the Custers' lives, was a former slave who began working for the Custers during the Civil War. According to Eliza, she joined the general at Amosville, Rappahannock County, in August 1863. And despite loneliness, hardship, and danger that included being captured by the enemy and taken behind enemy lines, she "set out to see the war, beginning and end. I helped free myself. I was all ready to step to the front whenever I was called upon, even if I didn't shoulder the musket."

Eliza often cooked under fire. One of the general's staff would later describe her efforts to prepare the general's dinner in the field. "A shell would burst near her; she would turn her head in anger at being disturbed, unconscious that she was being observed, begin to growl to herself about being obliged to move, but take up her kettle and frying pan, march further away, make a new fire, and begin cooking as unperturbed as if it were an ordinary disturbance instead of a sky filled with bits of falling shell."

Eliza did continue with Custer. According to Eliza, "I went to the end, and there's many folks says that a woman can't follow the army without throwing themselves away, but I know better. I went in and I come out with the respect of the officers."

According to Libbie, Eliza's "whole heart was wrapped up in our interests, and many a device she resorted to in concocting some new dish with which to surprise us. I remember when we were very far out in the wilderness, having tomato catsup to add to the flavor of the ever-recurring beef. Eliza's face shone with pleasure when we called her in and found that she had used canned tomatoes, which the commissary always has, to get up this treat for us.

"Once I had what seemed to me old-fashioned peach preserves, carrying me back in memory . . . to my mother's table when I was a child. Again, it was one of Eliza's surprises with canned peaches—which like tomatoes are always good at the commissary. Sometimes we saw no eggs all summer long, after the supply that we had brought from the last town we passed through on our way to camp was exhausted. The cook-books were maddening to us, for a casual glance at any of them proves how necessary eggs, butter and cream are to every recipe. In those days when the army lived beyond the railroad, it would have been a boon if some clever army woman could have prepared a little manual for use of the house-keepers stranded on the frontier.

"However, Eliza really needed few suggestions, for her mind was intent on inventions, and ready to improve every opportunity that presented itself. While we were encamped near Fort Hays, General Miles offered us many civilities, and among other kindnesses we received ice occasionally from the post ice-house. Eliza, in order to celebrate the arrival of some Eastern guest whom she wished to impress with our resources, served as a surprise one day peach ice cream. Investigation revealed that it was made of condensed milk, with canned peaches, and frozen in a bucket which her milling 'Man Friday' manipulated, no one knows for how long a time during the freezing process."

ELIZA WITH THE CUSTERS

Eliza knew of the general's extreme fondness for apples and according to Libbie "when the supply sent out began to decay, she took the utmost pains to put them up in glass jars; and when spring came around and there was a dearth of everything in our snowbound home, and we were aggravated by reading of strawberries in the States, Eliza brought the jars out from their concealment, setting the apples before the head of the house."

Heart of the Home: Beef Stew Dinner

★ ★ ★ ★ ★

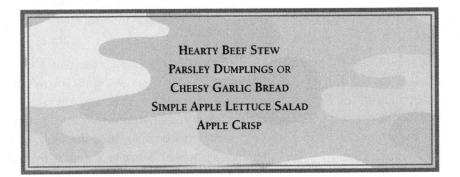

HEARTY BEEF STEW
PARSLEY DUMPLINGS OR
CHEESY GARLIC BREAD
SIMPLE APPLE LETTUCE SALAD
APPLE CRISP

HEARTY BEEF STEW
★★★★★

"[We] hadn't seen service before the war and hadn't our claim to loving even. I must confess that I was awed, but after having been thoroughly disciplined by these women, I received some excellent hints as to my future military life." [Libbie Custer]

2	TEASPOONS SEASONED SALT	2	CUPS APPLE JUICE OR CIDER
1	TEASPOON ONION POWDER	1	CUP WATER
½	TEASPOON GARLIC POWDER	1	TABLESPOON CIDER VINEGAR
1	TEASPOON BLACK PEPPER	½	TEASPOON DRIED THYME
2½	POUNDS BEEF STEW MEAT, CUT INTO 1-INCH PIECES	3	LARGE CARROTS, CUT INTO 1-INCH PIECES
¼	CUP ALL-PURPOSE FLOUR	2	RIBS OF CELERY, CUT INTO 1-INCH PIECES
1	LARGE ONION, PEELED AND CHOPPED	3	LARGE RED POTATOES, QUARTERED
2	TABLESPOONS COOKING OIL		

In a large bowl combine the seasoning ingredients; mix well. Rub the beef with the seasoning mix. Dredge the beef with flour. Set aside. In a large saucepan brown the onion and beef over medium-high heat. Add the cider, water, vinegar, and thyme; bring to a boil. Reduce the heat, cover, and simmer for 1 hour and 20 minutes or until fork-tender.

Add the carrots, celery, and potatoes; return to a boil. Reduce the heat, cover, and simmer for 20 minutes or until the vegetables are tender. Remove the stew from the heat while preparing the parsley dumpling mix, or omit the dumplings, preheat the oven to 400°F and prepare Cheesy Potato Garlic Bread.

PARSLEY DUMPLINGS
★★★★★

"From the first day of our marriage, General Custer celebrated every order to move with wild demonstrations of joy." [Libbie Custer]

1½	CUPS ALL-PURPOSE FLOUR	2½	TABLESPOONS MINCED FRESH PARSLEY
2¼	TEASPOONS BAKING POWDER	1	LARGE EGG
½	TEASPOON ONION SALT	½	CUP MILK

In a large bowl sift together dry ingredients. Add the minced parsley to dry ingredients. In a separate bowl beat the egg and mix in the milk to blend. Pour the egg mixture into flour mixture and mix just until evenly moistened. Drop by ¼-cup portions evenly across the gently boiling stew. Cook uncovered for approximately 15 to 20 minutes. Turn frequently to baste with gravy.

YIELDS 12 DUMPLINGS.

CHEESY POTATO GARLIC BREAD
★★★★★

The general came home one day whooping, shouting and breaking furniture. From experience, Libbie knew that they would be moving soon.

2	PACKAGES ACTIVE DRY YEAST		1	TEASPOON GARLIC POWDER
2	TABLESPOONS SUGAR		⅛	TEASPOON CAYENNE PEPPER
½	CUP WARM WATER (110°F TO 115°F)		2	TEASPOONS DRIED CHIVES
1	CUP HALF AND HALF		5½	TO 6 CUPS ALL-PURPOSE FLOUR, DIVIDED
6	TABLESPOONS BUTTER, DIVIDED		2	CUPS FINELY SHREDDED, PEELED POTATOES
1	TABLESPOON SALT		1	CUP SHREDDED CHEDDAR CHEESE

In a large mixing bowl dissolve the sugar and yeast in warm water; let stand until foam forms on the surface, approximately 5 minutes. Add the half and half, half of the butter, salt, garlic powder, cayenne, chives, and 2½ cups of flour; beat for 2 minutes. Stir in the potatoes and enough of the remaining flour to form a soft dough. Turn onto a floured board; knead until smooth and elastic, approximately 8 to 10 minutes. Place in a greased bowl and allow to rise in a warm place until almost doubled, approximately 1 hour.

Punch the dough down and pat into a ½-inch-thick rectangle. Sprinkle the cheese evenly over the dough. Fold the dough over the cheese and knead into the dough. Shape into 2 round loaves; place in 2 greased 9-inch round baking pans. Cover and allow to rise until doubled in bulk, about 45 minutes.

Cut an X on top of each loaf; brush with the remaining butter. Bake in a preheated 400°F oven for 35 to 40 minutes or until golden. Remove from pans to cool on wire racks.

YIELDS 2 LOAVES.

SIMPLE APPLE LETTUCE SALAD

★★★★★

"[We] went to Dakota in the spring of 1873. General Custer was delighted! I know that it would surprise a well-regulated mover to see what short work it was for us to prepare for our journeys. We began by having a supply of hay and gunnysacks brought in from the stable. . . ." [Libbie Custer, Boots and Saddles]

4	CUPS BIBB LETTUCE, TORN INTO BITE-SIZE PIECES	⅓	CUP RAISINS
2	UNPEELED RED APPLES, DICED	⅓	CUP CHOPPED WALNUTS

In a salad bowl combine the lettuce, apples, raisins, and walnuts. Toss gently. Refrigerate until needed.

YIELDS 4 SERVINGS.

DRESSING

"On moving day the kitchen utensils were plunged into the barrels generally left uncovered in the hurry; rolls of bedding, encased in waterproof cloth or canvas, were strapped and roped, and the few pictures and books were crowded into chests and boxes." [Libbie Custer, Boots and Saddles]

½	CUP MAYONNAISE	1	TABLESPOON HONEY
¼	CUP BUTTERMILK	1	PINCH CAYENNE PEPPER
2	TABLESPOONS PINEAPPLE JUICE		

In a small bowl or jar with a tight-fitting lid, combine the mayonnaise, buttermilk, pineapple juice, honey, and cayenne pepper, and blend well. Remove the salad from the refrigerator and dress just prior to serving.

APPLE CRISP
★★★★★

"When these possessions were loaded upon the wagon, at the last moment there always appeared the cook's bedding to surmount the motley pile. Her property was invariably tied up in a flaming quilt representing the souvenirs of her friends' dresses." [Libbie Custer, Boots and Saddles]

5	CUPS APPLES, CORED, PARED AND SLICED	¾	CUP BUTTER
2	TABLESPOONS FRESH LEMON JUICE	½	CUP FIRMLY PACKED LIGHT BROWN SUGAR
¾	CUP SUGAR	1	CUP ALL-PURPOSE FLOUR
1	TEASPOON GROUND CINNAMON		

In a large bowl combine the apples and lemon juice and lightly toss to coat. Add the sugar and cinnamon, and mix well. Arrange in a buttered 1½-quart baking dish. Melt the butter, and combine with the brown sugar and flour. Spread over the apples. Bake for 35 to 40 minutes or until the apples are fork-tender and the topping is slightly browned and crisp. Serve warm with ice cream or whipped cream.

YIELDS 6 SERVINGS.

Southern Fried Chicken Dinner

★ ★ ★ ★

"In all this confusion no one was cross. We rushed and gasped through the one day given us for preparation, and I had only time to be glad with my husband that he was going back to the life of activity that he so loved." [Libbie Custer]

BUTTERMILK FRIED CHICKEN AND GRAVY
JOHN'S HOME FRIED POTATOES
FRESH GARDEN PEAS
BUTTERMILK BISCUITS WITH HONEY
OLD-FASHIONED BANANA PUDDING

THE CUSTERS

BUTTERMILK FRIED CHICKEN AND GRAVY
★ ★ ★ ★ ★

"Steamers were ready for us at Memphis, and we went thither by rail to embark. People cannot go up and down the face of the earth together for nine years of hardships, trials and deprivation without being nearly as like one family as is possible." [Libbie Custer]

1	FRYER, CUT UP	2	TEASPOONS SEASONED SALT
	BUTTERMILK, SUFFICIENT TO COVER THE CHICKEN (APPROXIMATELY 1 QUART)	¼	TEASPOON POULTRY SEASONING
		1¼	TEASPOONS GROUND BLACK PEPPER
2	TEASPOONS GARLIC POWDER	1	CUP ALL-PURPOSE FLOUR
1	TEASPOON ONION POWDER		SHORTENING

Wash the chicken pieces and place in a glass or plastic bowl. Cover with buttermilk and refrigerate for 1 hour. In a double strength paper bag combine the seasonings and flour. Drain the chicken pieces. Using additional seasoned salt and pepper, lightly season the chicken to taste. Place the chicken in the bag one piece at a time. Shake well until thoroughly coated. Remove and shake the excess flour from the chicken. Place on a sheet of waxed paper. Repeat until all of the chicken pieces are coated in this manner. Allow the chicken to rest for 15 minutes to dry.

Place shortening in a cast-iron frying pan to a depth of about ½ inch. Heat to about 370°F. Place the chicken in the hot shortening. Fry 4 to 5 pieces of chicken at a time for approximately 15 minutes or until golden. Test doneness by piercing the thickest part of the chicken. When done, the juice should run clear.

YIELDS 6 SERVINGS.

GRAVY

¼	CUP FRIED CHICKEN DRIPPINGS	3	TABLESPOONS ALL-PURPOSE FLOUR
2	TABLESPOONS CHOPPED ONION	1	QUART CHICKEN BROTH

In a medium saucepan heat the drippings and sauté the onions until almost transparent. Add the flour and stir constantly until it turns golden brown. Add the chicken broth and continue stirring and cooking over medium-high heat until the gravy reaches the desired consistency.

JOHN'S HOME FRIED POTATOES
★★★★★

"Thankful once more to be reunited, we entered again, heart and soul into the minutest detail of one another's lives." [Libbie Custer, Boots and Saddles]

3	MEDIUM BAKING POTATOES	¼	TEASPOON SEASONED SALT
1	LARGE ONION, SLICED THIN	¼	TEASPOON GARLIC POWDER
3½	TABLESPOONS BACON DRIPPINGS	¼	TEASPOON PEPPER

Peel the potatoes and place in a medium saucepan with sufficient water to cover. Bring to a boil over medium heat and cook until fork-tender. Use additional water if necessary to continue the boiling process. When the potatoes have completed cooking; drain and refrigerate.

When the potatoes are thoroughly chilled, slice thinly. In a large cast-iron skillet heat the bacon drippings and sauté the onions until tender. In a small bowl combine the seasoned salt, garlic powder, and pepper; mix well. Add the potatoes and seasoning mix to the skillet. Periodically shake the pan over medium heat until the potatoes are golden all over. Adjust seasonings to taste.

YIELDS 4 TO 6 SERVINGS.

BUTTERMILK BISCUITS
✮✮✮✮✮

"Three steamers were at last loaded and we went on to Cairo, where we found the trains ready to take us into Dakota." [Libbie Custer]

2	CUPS ALL-PURPOSE FLOUR	3	TABLESPOONS BUTTER, SOFTENED
½	TEASPOON SALT	3	TABLESPOONS SHORTENING
½	TEASPOON BAKING SODA	⅔	CUP BUTTERMILK

Preheat the oven to 450°F. Into a large bowl sift together the dry ingredients. Add the shortening and butter, and cut in lightly until the mixture resembles coarse cornmeal. Add the milk gradually; mix until a soft dough is formed. Mound the dough onto a floured board and knead for 30 seconds, turning it over 2 or 3 times during the process. Be careful not to overwork the dough, as it will make the biscuits tough. Roll the dough out to a thickness of 1 inch; use a floured biscuit cutter or glass rim to cut out biscuits; place on an ungreased baking sheet. (If biscuits are placed close together, the sides will be softer). Bake for 12 to 15 minutes or until golden.

YIELDS ABOUT 12 BISCUITS.

"Fort Ellis, Montana Territory
June 1880
Night before last an unusual pleasant dancing party was given by Captain Andrews, where Faye and I were guests of honor. It was such a surprise and very kind in Captain Andrews to give it, for he is a bachelor. Supper was served in his own quarters. . . . Mrs. Adams, wife of the commanding officer, superintended all of the arrangements and also assisted in receiving. The supper was delicious—as all army suppers are—and I fancy that she and other ladies of the garrison were responsible for the perfect salads and cake." [Frances Roe]

OLD-FASHIONED BANANA PUDDING

★★★★★

"We were a week or more on the route. Our days were varied by the long stops necessary to water the horses, and occasionally take them out of the cars for exercise. My husband and I always went on these occasions to loose the dogs and have a frolic and a little visit with our own horses." [Libbie Custer]

⅔	CUP SUGAR	2	TABLESPOONS BUTTER
½	CUP ALL-PURPOSE FLOUR	2	TABLESPOONS VANILLA EXTRACT
½	TEASPOON SALT	1	12-OUNCE BOX VANILLA WAFERS
2	CUPS HALF AND HALF	2	CUPS SLICED RIPE BANANAS
3	EGG YOLKS, LIGHTLY BEATEN		MERINGUE TOPPING (RECIPE BELOW)

Preheat the oven to 350°F. In the top of the double boiler combine the sugar, flour, and salt over boiling water. Add the half and half and stir for 10 minutes or until the mixture thickens; remove from the heat. Stirring constantly, pour half of the hot cream into the egg yolks. Return the egg yolks to the rest of the cream mixture and cook over the simmering water until thickened. Remove from the heat; stir in the butter and vanilla. Cool slightly. While the mixture is cooling, place a layer of vanilla wafers on the bottom of a casserole dish. Alternate wafers with layers of banana slices and cooled pudding mixture, ending with the pudding on top. Make the meringue topping. Spread over the pudding top and bake for 10 to 15 minutes or until golden.

YIELDS 6 SERVINGS.

MERINGUE TOPPING

2	EGG WHITES	½	TEASPOON VANILLA EXTRACT
¼	TEASPOON CREAM OF TARTAR	¼	CUP CONFECTIONERS' SUGAR

In the bowl of an electric mixer whip the egg whites with the cream of tartar until they hold a peak without being dry. By hand, beat in the vanilla extract and sugar.

Emerald Isle Dinner

★ ★ ★ ★ ★

September 19
Fort Stevens

"Yesterday Andrew received a note from General Sherman saying he would be at Fort Garland today, so Andrew went to see him on business relating to the fort." [Eveline M. Alexander]

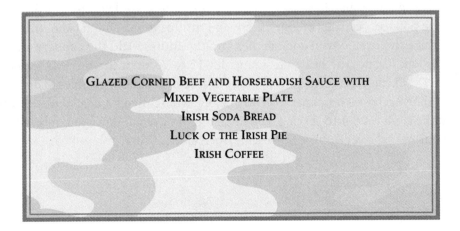

GLAZED CORNED BEEF AND HORSERADISH SAUCE WITH
MIXED VEGETABLE PLATE
IRISH SODA BREAD
LUCK OF THE IRISH PIE
IRISH COFFEE

GLAZED CORNED BEEF AND HORSERADISH SAUCE
WITH MIXED VEGETABLES

☆☆☆☆☆

"Have been busy all day fixing up my abode so that it looks pleasant. . . . Carroll received a dispatch this afternoon telling him to prepare for General Sherman's reception. So, although I have some things to attend to myself, I had to go to work making bags for blank cartridges to give the General a salute." [Eveline M. Alexander]

1	5- TO 6-POUND CORNED BEEF BRISKET		2	TABLESPOONS CHOPPED CELERY LEAVES
3	TEASPOONS PICKLING SPICE		3	TURNIPS, PEELED AND CUT INTO WEDGES
	WHOLE CLOVES		1	LARGE CABBAGE, CUT INTO QUARTERS
6	TO 8 SMALL RED POTATOES		½	POUND FRESH GREEN BEANS
6	MEDIUM CARROTS		½	CUP BUTTER
1	POUND SMALL WHITE ONIONS		¼	CUP CHOPPED PARSLEY
3	CELERY RIBS, CUT INTO 2-INCH PIECES			

Wash the brisket and place it in an 8-quart Dutch oven with pickling spice. Cover with water and bring to a boil. Reduce the heat and simmer for 4 hours or until tender.

Place the Dutch oven containing the brisket in the refrigerator to cool. When cooled, remove the brisket from the pan juices, pat dry and place on a rack in a shallow baking pan, fat side up. Score the fat in 1-inch diamonds and stud each diamond with a whole clove. Spoon half of the Glaze (see the recipe below) over the brisket and bake at 350°F for 25 minutes. Remove the brisket from the oven and spoon the remaining Glaze over the top. Bake an additional 20 minutes until the brisket is glazed and browned.

Add the potatoes, carrots, onions, celery, and turnips to the Dutch oven, and return to a boil. Reduce the heat, cover, and simmer for 20 minutes. Add the cabbage and beans; return to a boil. Reduce the heat and simmer for 15 to 20 minutes or until the vegetables are tender. Drain the vegetables; return to low heat and toss the vegetables to dry.

Drain the vegetables on paper toweling before arranging on a heated platter with the brisket in the center. Prior to serving, melt the butter in a small saucepan; mix in the parsley and pour over the vegetables. Serve with Horseradish Sauce.

YIELDS 6 TO 8 SERVINGS.

GLAZE

"This has been a wild and stormy evening, but I have been quite comfortable. I have a large hospital tent pitched in front of my small tent with a wide chimney and a fire place with a roaring fire, and I have been sitting in front of it writing home." [Eveline M. Alexander, 1866]

2	TEASPOONS CIDER VINEGAR	¼	CUP DARK KARO SYRUP
2	TEASPOONS DIJON-TYPE MUSTARD	¼	TEASPOON GROUND ALLSPICE
½	CUP FIRMLY PACKED BROWN SUGAR		

In a small bowl combine all of the ingredients, mix well, and spread over the brisket according to the directions above.

HORSERADISH SAUCE

"'The general is coming sir!' . . . About eleven o'clock small Jacob came galloping up to the tent with the information. Whereupon Andrew fastened on his sash and sabre and started out at the head of the company to meet the lieutenant general. General Sherman entered the tent and greeted me warmly." [Eveline M. Alexander]

1	CUP SOUR CREAM	2	TABLESPOONS PREPARED HORSERADISH

In a small serving container combine all of the ingredients and mix well. Cover with plastic wrap and refrigerate until ready to serve.

"September 22
Have been looking around to see what preparation I could make for the entertainment of the general, who is expected tonight or tomorrow morning. Housekeeping with a fly tent for a kitchen is a rather sorry affair, however. Last evening, just at dinner, the soup overturned, and today I was deep in some blanc mange when a sudden gust of wind blew all over me and destroyed my morning's work. Also, one of my dinner plates broke, leaving me with only five to entertain my guests. Nothing will be left for the great general directly but a tin plate." [Eveline M. Alexander]

IRISH SODA BREAD
★★★★★

"I had a large table made just the day before that would just seat eight comfortably. Soon after their arrival we had lunch in the mess tent. General Sherman occupied the seat of honor on my left, on the end of a trunk. I spent nearly all evening tete-a-tete with him." [Eveline M. Alexander, 1866]]

1	CUP WHOLE WHEAT FLOUR	1½	TEASPOONS SALT
1	CUP ALL-PURPOSE FLOUR	2	CUPS MILK
1	TEASPOON BAKING SODA	1	EGG, LIGHTLY BEATEN
2	TEASPOONS BAKING POWDER		

Preheat the oven to 375°F. In a large bowl sift together the flours, soda, baking powder, and salt. In a separate bowl combine the milk and egg; stir into the flour mixture. Knead the dough until smooth. Shape into a flat cake on a cookie sheet; cut a deep cross in the top, cover, and allow to rise until double in bulk.

Bake for 35 to 45 minutes until golden.

YIELDS 1 LOAF.

LUCK OF THE IRISH PIE
★★★★★

"We had dinner about six o'clock. . . . It is the fashion after entertaining great men to publish your bill of fare, so I will note mine here. First course, beef vegetable soup; second, saddle of mutton with jelly, green peas, kirshaw squash, cabbage and beets; third, soft custard, blanc mange with cream and sugar and coffee." [Eveline M. Alexander, 1866]

1	8-OUNCE PACKAGE CREAM CHEESE	1	16-OUNCE CARTON COOL WHIP
1	14-OUNCE CAN SWEETENED CONDENSED MILK	1	9-INCH GRAHAM CRUST PIE SHELL
5	DROPS GREEN FOOD COLORING	1	LIME, THINLY SLICED AND TWISTED
⅓	CUP LIME JUICE		CHOCOLATE CURLS
⅓	CUP FROZEN LIMEADE CONCENTRATE, THAWED		

In a large mixing bowl beat the cream cheese until light and fluffy. Slowly add the condensed milk, beating until smooth. In a small bowl or cup combine the food coloring and lime juices. By hand, stir in the juice mixture and fold in the whipped cream. Lightly fill the crust, garnish with lime and chocolate curls. Refrigerate for a minimum of 2 hours prior to serving.

YIELDS 6 TO 8 SERVINGS.

IRISH COFFEE
★★★★★

"Everything was cooked to perfection and the general declared he had not tasted so fine a saddle of mutton since he left Saint Louis and said it was the King of dishes. I must say they all ate with a good appetite, and our chief honored the mutton so far as to return to it a third time." [Eveline M. Alexander]

1	TABLESPOON KAHLUA LIQUEUR	STRONG BLACK COFFEE	
1	JIGGER IRISH WHISKEY	HEAVY CREAM LIGHTLY WHIPPED	
1	TEASPOON RAW SUGAR, ADDITIONAL TO TASTE		

Heat a heavy coffee mug with hot water and then discard water. Add Kahlua, whiskey, and sugar. Add the very hot coffee to within an inch of the rim of the mug. Top with a head of cream.

YIELDS 1 SERVING.

My Grandmother's Favorite Meatloaf Dinner

★　★　★　★　★

For military families, home is where military orders send you. Libbie accompanied her husband on almost every assignment. The Seventh camped at Yankton, Dakota Territory. While other wives took rooms in St. Charles Hotel, Libbie remained in camp with her husband, who soon after became extremely ill. Having rented a cabin, she sent Mary Adams to town to purchase a stove and supplies. The merchant would not deliver the stove that night and shortly after Mary returned to the cabin, empty-handed, an April blizzard arrived.

MY GRANDMOTHER'S MEATLOAF (AS FINANCES PERMIT) OR
SECOND LIEUTENANT'S MEATLOAF
MASHED POTATOES AND GRAVY
GREEN BEANS
BUTTERED CORN ON THE COB
POTATO ROLLS
FRESHLY SQUEEZED LEMONADE
GRANDMOTHER'S LEMON POUND CAKE

MY GRANDMOTHER'S MEATLOAF
★★★★★

"Outside the door, [Mary] . . . tried to light a fire. The wind and the muffling snow put out every little blaze that started, however, and so, giving it up, she went into the house and found the luncheon-basket we had brought from the car, in which remained some sandwiches, and these composed our supper."

2	POUNDS GROUND CHUCK, OR 88% TO 92% LEAN GROUND BEEF	½	TEASPOON PEPPER
½	POUND GROUND VEAL	3½	TEASPOONS WORCESTERSHIRE SAUCE
½	POUND GROUND PORK (DO NOT USE SAUSAGE)	1	MEDIUM ONION, CHOPPED
1½	TEASPOONS GARLIC POWDER	2	SLICES WHITE BREAD, CRUSTS REMOVED
¾	TEASPOON ONION POWDER	¾	CUP HALF AND HALF
1	TEASPOON SALT	1	EGG, SLIGHTLY BEATEN

In a large bowl combine the beef, veal, pork, seasonings, and Worcestershire. Add the onion. Place the bread on top of the meat mixture. Slowly pour the half and half over the bread to soften it. Add the egg and then gently mix into the meat. Shape and place into an ungreased 9x5x3-inch loaf pan. Bake at 375°F for approximately 45 minutes to 1 hour, or until done.

YIELDS 6 TO 8 SERVINGS.

GRAVY

3	TABLESPOONS BACON DRIPPINGS OR VEGETABLE OIL	2	CUPS WATER
¼	CUP MINCED ONION	1	TEASPOON GRANULATED BEEF BOUILLON
3	TABLESPOONS ALL-PURPOSE FLOUR	1	CAN SLICED MUSHROOMS
⅓	CUP RIPPINGS FROM MEAT LOAF, OR VEGETABLE OIL	2	TABLESPOONS HALF AND HALF

In a medium-sized saucepan heat the drippings or oil over medium-high heat. Add the onion and sauté until onion is translucent. Add the flour and brown to a nice rich tawny-brown color. (Most people fail to allow the flour to sufficiently brown, resulting in white gravy.) Combine the drippings, water, and bouillon. Add to the pan, stirring constantly. Add the mushrooms and allow the gravy to cook down to desired consistency before adding the half and half.

"Every minute seemed a day; every hour a year. When daylight came I dropped into an exhausted slumber, and was awakened by Mary standing over our bed with a tray of hot breakfast. I asked if help had come, and finding that it had not, of course I could not understand the smoking food."

SECOND LIEUTENANT'S MEATLOAF

★★★★★

This old army recipe, designed to stretch meat, was certainly economical. The name is likely a reference to the limited financial resources of these young officers. It's included for historical purposes, but certainly provides for a tasty family meal.

2	SLICES WHOLE WHEAT BREAD, CRUSTS REMOVED		FRESHLY GROUND BLACK PEPPER
½	CUP TOMATO PURÉE	½	TEASPOON GRATED NUTMEG
1	CUP GRATED CARROT	¼	TEASPOON GROUND CLOVES
¾	CUP GRATED GREEN PEPPER	1	MEDIUM ONION, SLICED
½	CUP CHOPPED GREEN BEANS	1	BAY LEAF
¼	CUP ZUCCHINI	2	TABLESPOONS ALL-PURPOSE FLOUR
2	POUNDS GROUND BEEF CHUCK		WORCESTERSHIRE SAUCE
1	EGG		CHILI SAUCE
1	TEASPOON SALT		

Preheat the oven to 375°F. In a medium bowl soak the bread in the tomato purée. In a large bowl combine the bread mixture, vegetables, meat, egg, and remaining ingredients. Gently mix; place in a casserole and shape into a loaf. Add sufficient water to cover the bottom of the casserole dish. Add the onion slices and crumbled bay leaf. Lightly sprinkle additional flour over the loaf. Bake for 1 hour and 15 minutes, basting every 15 minutes. After the first 15 minutes, the loaf should be slightly set.

In a small bowl combine the Worcestershire and chili sauce to continue basting. Do not allow the casserole to bake dry. If necessary, add additional water or beef-stock to the casserole dish.

YIELDS 6 TO 8 SERVINGS.

CREAMY MASHED POTATOES
★★★★★

"[Mary] told me that . . . it had come to her . . . [to] cut up the large candles . . . and try if she could to cook over the many short pieces placed close together, so as to make a large flame." [Libbie Custer]

5	MEDIUM RUSSET BAKING POTATOES	2	TABLESPOONS BUTTER
1	CUP HEAVY CREAM	1	TEASPOON SALT, OR TO TASTE

Bring a large pot of water to boil. Wash the potatoes and place in boiling water. Bring to a second boil and cook for 30 to 45 minutes or until soft. When done, drain and return the potatoes to the pot, cover, and allow to steam an additional 30 seconds until dry. Allow the potatoes to cool. Remove the skins; add butter and cream. Using an electric mixer, whip the potatoes until smooth. Add additional butter, cream, or seasoning as necessary.

YIELDS 6 SERVINGS.

GREEN BEANS
★★★★★

The result was hot coffee and some bits of the steak she had brought from town, fried with slices of potatoes. [It] revived the general so much that he began to make light of the danger in order to quiet me." [Libbie Custer]

2	TABLESPOONS BACON DRIPPINGS	½	TEASPOON ONION POWDER
1	SMALL ONION, CHOPPED	1	TEASPOON BROWN SUGAR
1	QUART WATER	1	HAM HOCK
1	TEASPOON SEASON SALT	2	POUNDS GREEN BEANS, ENDS AND STRING REMOVED

In a medium saucepan sauté the onion in bacon drippings over medium heat. Add the water, spices, brown sugar, and ham hock; bring to a rapid boil over high heat. Reduce the heat to low and simmer the ham hock for 1 hour.

Add the beans, cover, and cook an additional 45 minutes. If necessary, add additional water. Old-fashioned beans were cooked so long because they were tougher. Today's beans require less cooking and you may adjust the cooking time according to your taste.

YIELDS 6 TO 8 SERVINGS.

POTATO ROLLS
★ ★ ★ ★ ★

Libbie was huddled under blankets when several officers and citizens of Yankton arrived with a stove and food. Fearing for the Custers' welfare, the officers and other soldiers returned to camp after being ordered to seek emergency shelter for themselves and their horses with the Yankton citizens. Determinedly, they ploughed through the snow bringing with them camp stoves, parcels, and baskets of food.

1	LARGE BAKING POTATO, COOKED, PEELED, AND MASHED (1 CUP)	¾	CUP SHORTENING
1	PACKAGE YEAST	1	CUP HALF AND HALF, SCALDED
1	CUP WARM WATER	2	EGGS, WELL-BEATEN
1	CUP SUGAR	5	CUPS ALL-PURPOSE FLOUR
1	TEASPOON SALT	1	CUP BUTTER, MELTED

Place the mashed potato in a large bowl and set aside. In a separate bowl combine the yeast with warm water and set aside to proof. Add the sugar, salt, and shortening to the potato. Pour scalded half and half over the mixture. Add the yeast, half and half, eggs, and flour, and mix well. Cover with a cloth tea towel and allow to rise overnight, or at least 8 hours.

Roll the dough out to ½-inch thickness and cut with a biscuit cutter. Dip each roll into melted butter; fold in half; and place in a lightly greased baking pan approximately ½ inch apart. Allow to rise 1 hour. Bake at 350°F for 20 minutes.

YIELDS 2 DOZEN DELICIOUS ROLLS.

LEMONADE
★★★★★

By May the regiment was again on the move. Although most of the women traveled by steamer, Libbie Custer and a few of the other women accompanied their husbands on a long overland march filled with dangerous encounters with the Sioux.

8	LEMONS (ONE THINLY SLICED)	3	CUPS HOT WATER
1½	CUPS SUGAR	1	QUART COLD WATER

Cover half of the lemon slices with sugar. Reserve the remainder for later use as a garnish. Squeeze the 7 remaining lemons, straining the seeds from the juice. Add the juice to the sliced lemons in the bowl. Cover with 3 cups of hot water. Do not stir. Allow to cool at room temperature. Remove the sliced lemons and transfer the mixture to a serving container. Add the water and stir. Adjust the flavor to personal taste. Chill and serve over ice in frosted glasses. Garnish with fresh lemon slices.

To frost glasses, place them on a tray in the freezer compartment until well chilled and covered with frost. Next, dip the rims in sugar and fill with lemonade or return the unfilled glasses to the freezer for the sugar to firmly set.

YIELDS 6 SERVINGS.

GRANDMOTHER'S LEMON POUND CAKE
★★★★★

"The day at last came for our march of 500 miles to terminate. After 6 weeks of marching, the Seventh Cavalry reached Rice where the gracious hospitality of the post commander's wife brought welcome respite from weeks of marching and camping. She met us as cheerfully as if she were in the luxurious home from which we knew she had gone as a girl to follow a soldier's life." [Libbie Custer]

2	CUPS SUGAR	3	CUPS ALL-PURPOSE FLOUR
1	POUND BUTTER	1	CUP EVAPORATED MILK
6	EGGS	1	TABLESPOON LEMON EXTRACT
3	TEASPOONS BAKING POWDER	1	LEMON, SLICED THIN

Preheat the oven to 325°F. Grease and flour a tube or Bundt pan and set aside. In a large bowl cream together the sugar, butter, and eggs. In a separate bowl sift together the baking powder and flour. Add the flour mixture to the butter mixture 1 cup at a time. Add the milk and extract; beat well. Pour the mixture into the prepared pan and bake for approximately 1 hour. When the cake is cool, glaze with lemon glaze (see recipe below) and garnish with lemon slices.

YIELDS 8 TO 12 SERVINGS.

GLAZE

And perhaps while Libbie enjoyed the earnest hospitality of this post commander's wife she dreamed of a home "that might be hers, with so many dozen spoons, 'solid,' so many sheets and pillow slips, closets filled with jars of preserved fruit, . . . where peaches ripened on [a] garden wall."

1	CUP SUGAR	2	TABLESPOONS BUTTER
¼	CUP CORNSTARCH	2	TABLESPOONS GRATED LEMON PEEL
1	CUP FRESH LEMON JUICE		

In a saucepan combine the ingredients and cook, stirring constantly, over medium heat until the sugar completely dissolves and the mixture is smooth. Add the butter and grated lemon. Continue to cook over low heat until the mixture is thick and glossy. Drizzle over the cake while warm.

Yankee Doodle Pot Roast Dinner

★ ★ ★ ★ ★

Finally, after nine years, Libbie Custer had a home of her own! "In the dim light I could see the great post of Fort Lincoln, where only a few months before we had left a barren plain." As she drove though the gates of Fort Lincoln, her expectations were exceeded as she saw before her a brightly lit furnished home.

YANKEE DOODLE POT ROAST

GREEN BEANS WITH CORN ON THE COB

CORN MUFFINS (SEE PAGE 95)

CHOCOLATE AMARETTO CAKE

CUSTERS' FIRST RESIDENCE, FORT LINCOLN

YANKEE DOODLE POT ROAST
★★★★★

"Our quarters were lighted . . . our friends had lighted it all, and built fires in the fireplaces. The garrison had gathered to welcome us. . . . We found our new quarters admirable for the garrison gayety." [Libbie Custer]

1	3- TO 4-POUND POT ROAST (RUMP, HEEL OF ROUND, OR SIRLOIN TIP)	½	CUP CHOPPED GREEN PEPPER
1½	TEASPOONS SALT	¾	CUP CHOPPED ONION
½	TEASPOON COARSELY GROUND PEPPER	3	CLOVES GARLIC, MINCED
¼	TEASPOON GARLIC POWDER	3	TEASPOONS GRATED ORANGE RIND
½	TEASPOON ONION POWDER	2	BAY LEAVES
⅛	TEASPOON GROUND CINNAMON	¾	CUP BEEF BOUILLON
¼	TEASPOON GROUND CLOVES	12	MEDIUM NEW POTATOES, HALVED
⅛	TEASPOON CAYENNE	8	CARROTS, PARED AND CUT INTO 1 INCH SLICES
¼	TEASPOON GRATED NUTMEG	½	POUND MUSHROOMS, STEMS REMOVED
4	TABLESPOONS BACON DRIPPINGS OR SHORTENING	3	TABLESPOONS ALL-PURPOSE FLOUR
		1	CUP COLD WATER

Wash the roast under cold running water and pat dry. In a cup combine the salt, pepper, garlic powder, onion powder, cinnamon, cloves, cayenne, and nutmeg. Mix well, and rub into the roast. In a large Dutch oven or heavy saucepan heat the drippings and braise the meat on both sides. Remove the meat from the pot and add the green pepper, onion, and

garlic. Sauté until the onion and bell pepper become soft. Add the orange rind, bay leaves, and beef bouillon; return the meat to the pot. Cover and simmer for 3½ to 4 hours.

Add the potatoes and carrots during the last hour of cooking. Add the mushroom caps during the last 10 minutes.

To make gravy, remove the roast and vegetables from the pan. In a small bowl combine the cold water and flour and mix well, ensuring that there are no lumps in the mixture. Add to the pan juices while constantly stirring over medium heat until the gravy reaches the desired thickness.

YIELDS 6 TO 8 SERVINGS.

ELIZABETH CUSTER

THE MILITARY WIVES' COOKBOOK

GREEN BEANS WITH CORN ON THE COB
★ ★ ★ ★ ★

Libbie's new home, "had large double parlors on the right with folding doors . . . and it was insulated throughout with warm paper. A warm fire blazed in the fireplace, while outside the band played Gerry Owen and . . . Home Sweet Home . . . and on the dining room table, Mary Adams had spread a feast."

3	POUNDS GREEN BEANS	4	CUPS WATER
3	STRIPS BACON	2½	TABLESPOONS SALT
½	CUP CHOPPED ONION	½	TEASPOON DRIED BASIL
1	CLOVE GARLIC, MINCED	6	3- TO 4-INCH PIECES CORN ON COB, FRESH OR FROZEN

Clean the green beans by removing the stems and strings, if necessary. Wash the beans and set aside in a colander to drain. While the beans are draining, in a large pot over medium-high heat, render the drippings from the bacon. Remove the bacon; add the onion and garlic, and sauté until the onion is soft. Add the water, salt, and basil. Bring the water to a boil. Reduce the heat to low. Add the green beans, cover the pot, and cook for 20 minutes. Add the corn pieces and cook an additional 20 to 30 minutes, or until the beans reach desired tenderness.

YIELDS 6 TO 8 SERVINGS.

The Custers' home became the center of the garrison's decidedly brisk and gay social life. The couple hosted frequent dinners and Libbie befriended the officers' wives and sweethearts. "How we chattered and gloried over the regiment having a home at last. It seemed too good to believe that the 7th Calvary had a post of its own." [Libbie Custer]

CHOCOLATE AMARETTO CAKE
★ ★ ★ ★ ★

According to Katherine Garret, who was a visitor at the fort, Libbie was "slim—girlish looking in a light-colored, out-of-date frock" with "quiet intelligent eyes that met one with interest rather than criticism and warmed one with her friendliness."

2	CUPS SUGAR		⅓	CUP WATER
2	CUPS ALL-PURPOSE FLOUR, SIFTED		⅔	CUP AMARETTO LIQUEUR
	PINCH SALT		½	CUP SOUR CREAM
½	CUP BUTTER		2	EGGS, SLIGHTLY BEATEN
¼	CUP COCOA		1	TEASPOON BAKING SODA
¼	TEASPOON GROUND CINNAMON		1	TEASPOON VANILLA EXTRACT

Preheat the oven to 350°F. Grease and flour a Bundt pan. In a large mixing bowl combine the sugar, flour, and salt, and set aside. In a small saucepan bring the butter, cocoa, cinnamon, and water to a boil. Remove the pan from the heat. Add the Amaretto and pour into the dry ingredients; mix well. Add the sour cream, eggs, baking soda and vanilla, stirring after each addition. Pour into the prepared pan and bake for 50 to 55 minutes or until a pick inserted into the center comes out clean.

YIELDS 10 TO 12 SERVINGS.

GLAZE

½	CUP SUGAR		¼	CUP AMARETTO
⅛	CUP WATER		¼	CUP BUTTER

In a small saucepan combine the sugar, water, Amaretto, and butter. Cook over medium-high heat until the butter has melted and the sugar is dissolved. Drizzle over the cake.

*U*pon learning of Katie's engagement to Lieutenant Francis Gibson she, as had been done for her years earlier, prepared Katie for life as a soldier's wife. She shared with her the reality of living in drab stockade posts, poor pay, frequent separations, and the pain and uncertainty of being left behind during dangerous campaigns.

ELIZABETH CUSTER

In the end, Libbie noted, "nothing mattered if you loved your man." They were, according to Libbie, "pioneer army women who were keeping the home fires burning while the soldiers guard[ed] the railroad engineers and surveyors . . . as mile by mile, in the face of almost insurmountable obstacles, they are building the railroads straight across our continent . . . which will open our country to civilization. . . . Yes, we are military women and we are proud of it. Proud to have created homes amidst primitive conditions of the American frontier."

Company's Coming Lasagna Dinner

✦ ✦ ✦ ✦ ✦

To this day, commanders' wives open their homes to their husbands' officers and spouses, and in their own way help to prepare them for "the seriousness of the husband's command" and their future as military wives.

OLIVE CHEESE TOASTS

ANTIPASTO PLATTER

GARLIC BREAD (SEE THE RECIPE ON PAGE 88)

SALAD GREENS

LASAGNA

CAPPUCCINO CHEESECAKE

OLIVE CHEESE TOASTS
★★★★★

Betty Karle was the Air War College vice-commandant's wife. She and the commandant's wife, Suzanne Smith, were wonderful role models and I have tried to emulate their example.

1	CUP MAYONNAISE	½	TEASPOON SALT
1	CUP SHREDDED MOZZARELLA CHEESE	¼	TEASPOON CURRY POWDER
¼	CUP GRATED FRESH PARMESAN	¼	TEASPOON ONION POWDER
1½	CUPS PITTED BLACK OLIVES, CHOPPED		MELBA TOAST ROUNDS
¼	CUP DRAINED AND CHOPPED PIMIENTO		OLIVE OIL
1	TEASPOON PEPPER		

In a medium bowl mix the mayonnaise, mozzarella, Parmesan, olives, pimiento, pepper, salt, curry powder, and onion powder. Lightly brush the toast rounds with olive oil. Spread the cheese mixture over the toast rounds. Broil until bubbly.

YIELDS 8 TO 10 SERVINGS.

SALAD GREENS
★★★★★

I have served this menu on various social occasions and it is always well received. In fact, when we invite a squadron or the group over for an evening social, this is the menu I most often prepare.

1	CLOVE GARLIC, CRUSHED	3	BOILED EGGS, CRUMBLED
	MIXTURE OF ARUGULA, RADICCHIO, AND BOSTON LETTUCE	1	14-OUNCE JAR MARINATED ARTICHOKES, DRAINED (CANNED MAY BE USED)
3	CUPS FRESH SPINACH LEAVES	½	CUP PITTED OLIVES, SLICED IN HALF
	BIBB LETTUCE		ITALIAN DRESSING
3	TABLESPOONS CAPERS	½	CUP PARMESAN CHEESE
½	CUP SLICED GREEN ONIONS, INCLUDE TOPS		PARMESAN FOR GARNISH AND PASSING TO GUESTS

Rub a salad serving bowl with garlic, discard the used clove and then toss the above ingredients with your favorite Italian dressing. (Use any combination of the above salad greens; however, use sufficient amount to equal a 1-cup serving per guest). Use additional Parmesan to garnish.

YIELDS 4 TO 6 SERVINGS.

LASAGNA
★★★★★

An ice-breaking game at one of our socials required maintaining possession of a clothespin worn on our clothing by simply refraining from saying "yes" or "no" during the course of our social. Well, by the end of the social, Betty had teased, cajoled, and charmed everyone's clothespins from them. The "Worrisome Lasagna" recipe shared by Betty certainly reflects her own humor and wit. However, in the true tradition of military wives, I have made changes that resulted in the "Because I Am Worried Lasagna" recipe.

2	POUNDS ITALIAN SAUSAGE	2	EGGS
5	CLOVES GARLIC, MINCED	2	15-OUNCE CONTAINERS RICOTTA CHEESE
1	TABLESPOON BASIL	½	CUP FRESHLY GRATED PARMESAN CHEESE
2	TABLESPOONS DRIED ROSEMARY	2	TABLESPOONS PARSLEY FLAKES
2	14-OUNCE CANS TOMATOES	½	TEASPOON BLACK PEPPER
3	6-OUNCE CANS TOMATO PASTE	1	TEASPOON TABASCO SAUCE
½	CUP DRY RED WINE (OPTIONAL)	5	CUPS SHREDDED MOZZARELLA CHEESE
1	10-OUNCE PACKAGE LASAGNA NOODLES		

Preheat the oven to 375°F. Dear Betty, thanks for the "Worrisome" Lasagna recipe. I am writing to you while the meat is slowly browning in a large frying pan. I share your regret that sausage is not good for you, but the flavor is sooooo good, I doubled the amount. As you noted, it really does give the lasagna a better flavor than lean ground beef. However, although I did feel some trepidation, I took your advice and "moved on," spooned off the excess fat, and added garlic (as you know, I love garlic so I increased the amount from 3 to 5 cloves). Betty, I thought rosemary added a little extra zest, so I added it. I then continued with your recipe by adding the basil (crushing the herbs between my palms to release the flavor as you suggested). Next, I added the tomatoes and tomato paste. Now Betty, I know you were concerned that if I bought unpeeled whole tomatoes, I would worry that they'd lie in the sauce in big clumps; or if I bought peeled and diced tomatoes, I'd fret that they would not add enough heft. Well, I neither fretted nor worried and frankly, Betty, that worries me. Maybe I am not sufficiently committed to the process and my lack of commitment will be reflected in the lasagna's flavor. While pondering this potential problem, I allowed the sauce to simmer for 30 minutes.

I disagree that you should only add the wine if you are "in the mood and have on hand." That wine is the big red bow that makes this lasagna a present to your palate. So I say, add the wine and allow it to simmer 10 minutes more before removing it from the heat. Cook the noodles in boiling salted water until tender. You were absolutely on point about the challenge of overcooking the noodles. Packaged noodles do always taste a little overcooked. And fresh lasagna noodles do seem to cook even before they are immersed in the boiling water. It's a dilemma, you warned. A dilemma? It's more like an enigma, wrapped in a cryptogram, answered by a puzzle. Nevertheless, what is a cook to do? Acknowledge her shortcomings and move on, I suppose. Like you, I just drained and rinsed the noodles, while hoping for the best.

In a large mixing bowl I beat in the eggs, stirred in the ricotta, Parmesan, parsley flakes, and pepper. I added the Tabasco for even more zest. Ricotta is so bland—don't you agree?

Betty, you recommended that I layer half the noodles in a 13 x 9 x 2-inch baking dish, overlapping each one by about half. (I had a little extra meat sauce, so I put a thin layer of sauce on the bottom of the pan before I began layering the lasagna.) At your suggestion I did tear two or three noodles to fit that empty space at the end of the dish. (ingenious!) and then, using a spatula, evenly spread about half of the ricotta mixture over the noodles. However, we once again parted company on the issue of the mozzarella slices which you instructed be spread over the ricotta mixture. I prefer shredded for the very reason you gave: "The cheese slices never really fit, so you must tear them into strips to fit where needed." I then spread on half of the meat sauce. And I did worry that I would miscalculate what constitutes half, because, as you indicated, the sauce sometimes rearranges itself in the pan.

By the time I repeated the previous paragraph, I was running out of everything and, as you anticipated, "worried that I divided wrong." However, it was too late, so I moved on. I had exactly three noodles left over. And I just couldn't help myself Betty; despite your admonition to "not to try to think of uses for them," I couldn't throw them out as you suggested. I twisted, twirled, and rolled them, but could think of no use for them. Finally I refrigerated them and worried that they would just sit and mold, creating a bigger mess. However, it's easier to throw them away in that condition without feeling as if you are being wasteful. I then placed the lasagna in the preheated oven and baked it for 30 to 40 minutes.

Finally, I hope you are happy, because I did worry that the lasagna would bubble over, creating a mess for me to clean up. I wish now that I had placed foil on the bottom of the oven, or placed another pan under the lasagna pan, but that creates a whole subset of additional problems. While pondering this latest quandary, I removed the lasagna and allowed it to stand 10 minutes before serving.

Although you promised it would serve between 8 to 10 people, I began to worry that maybe I should have made two pans because as you indicated, people always want seconds. Oh my! Company's here. Maybe I should have made two pans!

CAPPUCCINO CHEESECAKE

★ ★ ★ ★ ★

Everything is consumed so voraciously, especially the lasagna, that I have learned to double everything, regardless of the size of the group. I receive special satisfaction when a young, single airman compares the meal favorably with that prepared by his or her mother. No higher accolade could be given.

32	OUNCES CREAM CHEESE, SOFTENED	¼	CUP BOILING WATER
1¼	CUPS SUGAR	½	TEASPOON VANILLA EXTRACT
3	TABLESPOONS UNBLEACHED ALL-PURPOSE FLOUR	¼	TEASPOON ALMOND EXTRACT
4	LARGE EGGS	1	9-INCH GRAHAM CRACKER PIE CRUST
1	CUP SOUR CREAM		WHIPPED CREAM
1	TABLESPOON INSTANT COFFEE		TOASTED ALMONDS
¼	TEASPOON GROUND CINNAMON		

Preheat the oven to 450°F. In the bowl of an electric mixer combine the cream cheese, sugar, and flour, mixing at medium speed until well blended. Add the eggs one at a time, mixing well after each addition. Blend in the sour cream. Dissolve the coffee granules and cinnamon in water; add the extracts. Cool. Gradually add to the cream cheese mixture, mixing until well blended. Pour into the pie crust. Bake for 10 minutes, then reduce the oven temperature to 250°F. Continue baking for 1 hour. Chill. Garnish with whipped cream and toasted almonds.

YIELDS 8 SERVINGS.

Military families often share a deep and abiding faith, a legacy from generations past, which recognizes a country founded on a desire for religious freedom and self-determination. We also understand that freedom is never free but often comes at great sacrifice.

THE MILITARY WIVES' COOKBOOK

Sunday Family Dinner

★ ★ ★ ★ ★

There was no chapel at Fort Lincoln. Therefore, on Sundays, officers and their wives gathered in the Custers' parlor. In opening her home for Sunday service, Libbie was following the advice of ministers such as Samuel Phillips and writers such as Harriet Beecher Stowe, who encouraged American women to think of their homes as alternative places of worship.

ROASTED ROSEMARY CHICKEN AND GRAVY
CORN BREAD DRESSING
BROCCOLI IN BUTTER LEMON SAUCE
HONEY GLAZED CARROTS
GREEN BEANS AND TOMATOES
POTATO ROLLS
CRANBERRY SAUCE
RUBY HOWINGTON'S ITALIAN CREAM CAKE

ROASTED ROSEMARY CHICKEN
☆☆☆☆☆

"Our women's hearts fell when the fiat went forth that there was to be a summer campaign with actual fighting. . . . The morning for the start came only too soon." [Libbie Custer]

1	3-POUND ROASTING CHICKEN	4	TABLESPOONS COLD BUTTER, DIVIDED
2	LEMONS, QUARTERED	2	STALKS CELERY, WASHED AND HALVED
2	TABLESPOONS SEASONED SALT	3	SMALL CLOVES GARLIC, PEELED AND CRUSHED
1	TABLESPOON PLUS 1 TEASPOON ONION POWDER	1	LARGE ONION, GRATED
2	TEASPOONS GARLIC POWDER	1	LARGE BELL PEPPER, SEEDED AND QUARTERED
1	TABLESPOON DRIED ROSEMARY, CRUSHED	1	16-OZ CAN CHICKEN BROTH
1	TEASPOON RUBBED SAGE		

Preheat the oven to 375°F. Thoroughly wash and rinse the chicken. Pat dry. Rub the chicken inside and out with lemon juice (reserve used lemon quarters). In a small bowl combine the seasoned salt, onion powder, garlic powder, rosemary, and sage, and season the chicken to taste (I generally use all of the seasoning mix). Stuff the cavity with the celery, onion, bell pepper, and reserved lemon quarters. Bake for 1½ hours, basting periodically with broth. Serve with gravy and Creamy Horseradish Sauce (see page 108).

YIELDS 6 SERVINGS.

GRAVY

"On Sunday the 14th of May, the Seventh Cavalry prepared to depart on a long campaign. Three days of rain delayed their departure. However, in the early morning fog of June 17th, Custer prepared to lead his men to the Little Bighorn River. The Seventh marched onto the Dakota plains, while the regimental band played 'The Girl I Left Behind Me.'" [Libbie Custer]

2½	CUPS HOT CHICKEN BOUILLON	SALT AND PEPPER TO TASTE
2	TABLESPOONS ALL-PURPOSE FLOUR	

Degrease the pan drippings, retaining all juice and sediment. Sprinkle the flour across the surface of the pan juices, and whisk until well-blended; brown over medium heat until flour turns a rich dark brown color; take care not to scorch it. Stir constantly and scrape the bottom of the pan to prevent sticking. Add hot bouillon; increase heat to high, while constantly stirring. Allow the mixture to cook to the desired consistency and strain into a warm gravy boat.

In hurried words her name I bless'd;
I breathed the vows that bind me,
And to my heart in anguish press'd
The girl I left behind me.

THE MILITARY WIVES' COOKBOOK

CORN BREAD DRESSING

★★★★★

"When our band struck up 'The Girl I Left Behind Me,' the most despairing hour seemed to have come."
[Libbie Custer]

1	PAN J.R.'S SKILLET CORNBREAD (RECIPE FOLLOWS)	1	TEASPOON DRIED THYME LEAVES
¼	CUP BACON DRIPPINGS OR VEGETABLE OIL	2	TEASPOONS GARLIC POWDER
1½	CUPS CHOPPED ONION	1½	TEASPOONS COARSELY GROUND PEPPER
1	CUP CHOPPED CELERY	2	TEASPOONS SEASONED SALT
1½	CUPS CHOPPED BELL PEPPER	1	LARGE EGG, LIGHTLY BEATEN
2	TEASPOONS RUBBED SAGE	3½	CUPS CHICKEN BROTH

Preheat the oven to 350°F. Oil an 11½ x 7½ x 1½-inch baking pan and set aside.

Place cooled cornbread in a large mixing bowl and break into pieces. Then crumble it by rubbing between palms. Continue this process until all bread is crumbled. Place hands firmly on either side of the bowl and sift the contents by moving the bowl in rapid circular motions against the counter top. Large pieces of bread should spin to the top. Repeat the crumbling and spinning process, until crumbs are of uniform size. (My brother-in-law, Bill, uses this process and it always results in a very smooth dressing.)

In a large skillet over medium-high heat, melt the bacon drippings or vegetable oil and sauté the onion, celery, and bell pepper until the onion is transparent. Place the pan contents in the bowl with the breadcrumbs. Add the remaining ingredients and mix well. Pour into the prepared pan. Bake for 1 hour or until golden.

YIELDS 6 TO 8 SERVINGS.

THE CUSTERS' PARLOR

J. R.'S SKILLET CORN BREAD
★★★★★

"All the sad-faced wives of the officers who had forced themselves to their doors to try and wave a coura-geous farewell and smile bravely to hide the anguish of their breaking hearts, gave up the struggle at the sound of the music." [Libbie Custer]

1	CUP ALL-PURPOSE FLOUR		PINCH GRATED NUTMEG
½	CUP YELLOW CORNMEAL	1	CUP WHOLE MILK
¼	CUP SUGAR, OPTIONAL	1	EGG, BEATEN
¾	TEASPOON SALT, OPTIONAL	¼	CUP VEGETABLE OIL
3	TEASPOONS BAKING POWDER		

Preheat the oven to 425°F. In a large bowl mix the dry ingredients. Slowly add the milk, beaten egg, and vegetable oil; mix well. Set aside. Coat a 10-inch cast-iron skillet with approximately 2 tablespoons of oil and place in the oven for approximately 10 to 15 minutes (the oil should smoke slightly). Remove the skillet and fill with batter. Reduce the oven temperature to 400°F and bake for 20 to 25 minutes. Remove the bread from the oven, check, and brown under the broiler, if necessary. Turn out onto a plate and cool before using.

YIELDS 6 TO 8 SERVINGS, OR ENOUGH CORN BREAD FOR CORN BREAD DRESSING.

BROCCOLI IN BUTTER LEMON SAUCE
★★★★★

"The first notes made them disappear to fight out alone their trouble, and seek to place their hands in that of their heavenly father, who at such hours was their never-failing solace." [Libbie Custer]

2	POUNDS FRESH BROCCOLI SPEARS	¼	TEASPOON DIJON MUSTARD
¼	CUP BUTTER	1¾	CUPS MILK
¼	CUP ALL-PURPOSE FLOUR	½	CUP GRATED PARMESAN CHEESE
	SALT TO TASTE	2	TABLESPOONS LEMON JUICE

Place the broccoli in boiling salted water; cook until bright green and crisp-tender (10 to 15 minutes).

Remove from the pot; drain well, and place on a warmed serving platter. In a small saucepan over medium heat melt the butter; blend in the flour, salt, and mustard to form a smooth paste. Gradually blend in the milk. Stir constantly and continue to cook until the mixture thickens and begins to boil. Stir in the Parmesan and lemon juice. Spoon over the broccoli prior to serving.

YIELDS 6 TO 8 SERVINGS.

HONEY GLAZED CARROTS
★★★★★

Libbie and her sister-in-law, Maggie Calhoun, accompanied their husbands on the first day of the expedition. "At every bend of the road, as the column wound its way round and round the low hills, my husband glanced back to admire his men, and could not refrain from constantly calling my attention to their grand appearance." [Libbie Custer]

3	CUPS FROZEN BABY CARROTS, COOKED	¼	TEASPOON GRATED NUTMEG
3	TABLESPOONS HONEY	3	TABLESPOONS BUTTER
3	TABLESPOONS BROWN SUGAR		

Cook the carrots according to package directions, drain and set aside. In a medium saucepan combine the honey, sugar, nutmeg, and butter. Cook over low heat until the sugar is melted and the mixture begins to bubble. Add the carrots, mix well to thoroughly coat, and serve.

YIELDS 6 SERVINGS.

GREEN BEANS WITH TOMATOES

★★★★★

Unaware of impending tragedy, Annie Yates played with her children running "up the hill bareheaded and laughing with her abundant black hair escaping from its fastenings and her husband was to die that day, although she knew it not." [Mary Manley, twelve-year-old daughter of an Infantry Officer]

The women met on that Sunday afternoon to sing their usual hymns. It was not until the day after the country celebrated its centennial that they heard the first rumors of the massacre. With a 2 a.m. knock at Libbie's door, rumors and speculation were confirmed by Captain William McCaskey as he read a dispatch to Libbie and other waiting wives who had been left behind.

¼	CUP BUTTER	1	TABLESPOON LEMON JUICE
¼	CUP FINELY CHOPPED ONION	2	MEDIUM TOMATOES, SEEDED AND COARSELY CHOPPED
1	SMALL CLOVE GARLIC, MINCED		
3	POUNDS GREEN BEANS, COOKED	1	TABLESPOON FIRMLY PACKED BROWN SUGAR
½	TEASPOON DRIED OREGANO	1	TEASPOON SALT

In a large skillet melt the butter. Add the onions and sauté for 3 minutes. Add the remaining ingredients and heat thoroughly. Toss lightly and serve.

YIELDS 6 TO 8 SERVINGS.

More than a place of sanctuary, Libbie's home became a place of solace and refuge following the Massacre at Little Bighorn, on Sunday, June 25. As the post commander's wife, Libbie knew she must accompany the soldiers notifying other waiting wives. Despite the July heat, a wrap was placed around her shivering shoulders as she stepped into the darkness of the Dakota night.

… "But should I ne'er return again,
still worth thy love thou'lt find me;
dishonor's breath shall never stain
the name I'll leave behind me"

"*Native Americans have a proud heritage of military service. During World War II the . . . U.S. Marine Corps utilized Americans from the Navajo tribe to pass secret U.S. messages throughout Europe and the Pacific. Known as 'Code Talkers,' these Navajo Americans spoke in their native language while transmitting military secret information. The U.S. Marines recruited over 300 Navajos who were praised for their skill, speed, and accuracy in secret communications throughout the war. One of the key battles attributed to their skill was the battle of Iwo Jima. Major Howard Connor, 5th Marine Division signal officer, declared, 'Were it not for the Navajos, the Marines would never have taken Iwo Jima.' The Japanese, who were skilled code breakers, remained baffled by the Navajo language.*

"*Although that is just one example, native Americans have served in many vital roles in all U.S. conflicts; helping secure the freedom we all cherish today. In fact in the 20th Century, five Native Americans have been among those receiving the United States' highest military award: The Medal of Honor.*" [*Colonel Duane L. Lamb, Remarks at Native American Luncheon, Vandenberg AFB, November 8, 2000*]

Custer clan; a hunting party in 1875, seated under a tent

ALFRESCO DINING

After "Autie" erected a hospital tent for Libbie Custer's parlor, he attached an over-hanging tarpaulin for dining and relaxing with friends. There, Libbie, Autie, and Tom spent their evenings, enjoying their "beer garden."

Grilled Artichokes and Shrimp with Pesto Pasta
✶ ✶ ✶ ✶ ✶

In later years it is almost certain that Libbie remembered the time during which she and "Autie" tented the plains and slept beneath the stars.

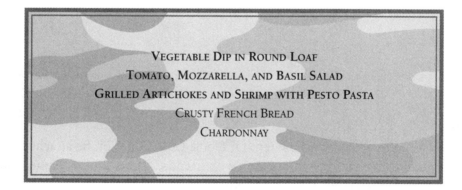

VEGETABLE DIP IN ROUND LOAF
TOMATO, MOZZARELLA, AND BASIL SALAD
GRILLED ARTICHOKES AND SHRIMP WITH PESTO PASTA
CRUSTY FRENCH BREAD
CHARDONNAY

VEGETABLE DIP IN ROUND LOAF
★★★★★

"Our summer camp was between two and three miles from Fort Hays, on Big Creek. The place selected for our tents was under a fringe of good sized cotton-wood trees." [Libbie Custer, Boots and Saddles]

1	10-OUNCE BOX FROZEN CHOPPED SPINACH, THAWED	1¼	CUPS SOUR CREAM
1	ROUND LOAF BREAD	½	CUP SOFTENED CREAM CHEESE
1	PACKAGE DRIED VEGETABLE SOUP MIX	3	GREEN ONIONS, THINLY SLICED
½	CUP MAYONNAISE		

Place the spinach in a colander to drain. While the spinach is draining, hollow the bread. Freeze for at least 1 hour, and keep frozen until ready to use.

Press the spinach to remove the excess water. In a large mixing bowl combine the drained spinach with the remaining ingredients. Fill the cavity of the frozen bread and refrigerate for at least 8 hours prior to serving. Serve with vegetable crudités and slices of French bread.

YIELDS 6 TO 8 SERVINGS.

TOMATO, MOZZARELLA, AND BASIL SALAD
★★★★★

"It was most gratifying to have this protection, and after a hot ride on the arid plain, we came under the boughs and saw, with a real home feeling, the white tents gleaming in the shade." [Libbie Custer]

4	SLICES SOURDOUGH BREAD	5	ITALIAN TOMATOES, SLICED
	BUTTER	2	TABLESPOONS FINELY CHOPPED FRESH BASIL
4	⅛-INCH SLICES MOZZARELLA CHEESE	2	TABLESPOONS MINCED CHIVES

Use a biscuit cutter to cut 4 rounds from the bread; butter both sides and broil until golden. Remove from the broiler and set aside to cool. Cut 4 rounds from the cheese; top the bread with cheese. Place 3 to 4 slices of tomato on each toast round. Sprinkle lightly with Italian-vinaigrette salad dressing. Garnish with basil and chives before serving.

YIELDS 4 SERVINGS.

GRILLED ARTICHOKES

★★★★★

"The sitting-room was a hospital tent which is perhaps fourteen by sixteen. Opening out at the rear of our sitting room was our own room, a wall tent, ten by twelve." [Libbie Custer]

4	ARTICHOKES, 3½ TO 4 INCHES WIDE	¼	TEASPOON DRIED BASIL
½	CUP OLIVE OIL	¼	TEASPOON GARLIC POWDER

Remove the small outer leaves and discard. With a sharp knife remove the upper tip of each artichoke and, using scissors, remove the thorn from each remaining leaf. Trim the stem and remove the coarse fibers from the stem. Cut the artichokes in half, rinse, and drain well. In a medium bowl combine the remaining ingredients and artichokes. Roll the artichokes in oil to coat and set aside until prepared to grill.

YIELDS 4 SERVINGS.

TENT EXTERIOR

GRILLED SHRIMP
★★★★★

"In pitching these tents General Custer had an eye for a tree with wide-spreading branches to shade us, and in order to use it he put the tents on the side bank running down to the stream." [Libbie Custer]

2	POUNDS LARGE, PEELED SHRIMP	¼	CUP OLIVE OIL
¾	TEASPOON SUGAR	12	OUNCES PENNE RIGATE PASTA
3	TABLESPOONS LIME JUICE	1	CUP LARGE, PITTED BLACK OLIVES, DRAINED AND HALVED
½	TEASPOON GARLIC POWDER		
¼	TEASPOON ONION POWDER	¼	CUP PESTO (SEE THE RECIPE ON PAGE 198)

Two hours before grilling, soak the mesquite chips in sufficient water to cover or according to the package directions. Wooden bamboo skewers should also be soaked to prevent burning.

Peel and devein the shrimp. In a large, nonreactive bowl combine the shrimp with the next four seasoning ingredients and olive oil; mix well and refrigerate for at least one hour prior to grilling. At the end of one hour, remove shrimp from refrigerator and allow to stand at room temperature for 20 minutes.

Bring 4 quarts of water to a boil. While waiting for the water to boil, place 4 to 6 shrimp on a wooden skewer. Repeat the process until all shrimp are used. When the water comes to a boil, add the pasta. When the embers are glowing, spread about 2 cups of chips evenly over the coals. While the pasta is cooking place the shrimp on the hot grill and cook for 3 to 5 minutes or until pink and opaque; take care not to overcook the shrimp. When the pasta has completed cooking, drain away the water and return the pasta to the cooking pot; toss with the olives and pesto. Place the pasta on serving plates. Add the grilled artichokes and shrimp. Serve with tomato salad, French bread, and Chardonnay.

YIELDS 4 TO 6 SERVINGS.

PESTO
★★★★★

"Our regimental quartermaster made requisition for the tents, which would be returned to the post in the fall. We felt very rich . . . we had as many rooms as some houses have—that is by calling each tent a room." [Libbie Custer]

¾ CUP FRESHLY GRATED PARMESAN CHEESE

¾ CUP CHOPPED PINE NUTS

2¼ CUPS PACKED FRESH BASIL LEAVES, STEMS REMOVED

7 CLOVES GARLIC

¼ CUP OLIVE OIL

1 TEASPOON SALT

¾ TEASPOON FRESHLY GROUND PEPPER

Place all ingredients in a food processor and pulverize until a thick sauce is formed. This recipe may be made ahead and frozen. Fill a lightly oiled ice cube tray with the pesto mixture and freeze completely. Remove the pesto cubes and store in a freezer bag. This method allows you to retrieve just the amount needed.

YIELDS APPROXIMATELY 2¼ CUPS.

THE BEER GARDEN

Lobster Dinner for Four

★ ★ ★ ★ ★

"Of course it was necessary to build up a rough embankment of stones and earth, and that left the tent floor at the rear almost up to the limbs of the tree. We then thought how foolish of us not to continue the floor around the tree." [Libbie Custer]

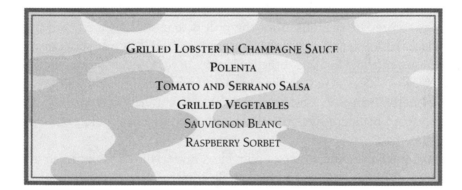

GRILLED LOBSTER IN CHAMPAGNE SAUCE
POLENTA
TOMATO AND SERRANO SALSA
GRILLED VEGETABLES
SAUVIGNON BLANC
RASPBERRY SORBET

GRILLED LOBSTER IN CHAMPAGNE BUTTER SAUCE
★★★★★

"The company carpenter built such a comfortable platform, with a railing that we felt as if we had a real gallery to our canvas house." [Libbie Custer]

6	CUPS CHAMPAGNE ("BRUT" OR "EXTRA-DRY")		SALT AND FRESHLY GROUND BLACK PEPPER TO TASTE
4	TABLESPOONS FINELY CHOPPED SHALLOTS	4	1½- TO 2-POUND LOBSTERS
1	CUP UNSALTED BUTTER, DIVIDED		OLIVE OIL
½	CUP SOUR CREAM		MELTED BUTTER
¼	CUP ALL-PURPOSE FLOUR		

In a large saucepan combine the champagne and shallots, and bring to a boil over high heat. Reduce the heat to medium and simmer until the liquid is reduced by half, approximately 20 minutes. Slowly whisk in the butter, 1 tablespoon at a time. Next, thoroughly mix the flour with the sour cream and add to the champagne butter in the pan, stirring to combine thoroughly. Bring the liquid to a boil and continue to boil over high heat until it has the consistency of heavy cream. This process may take from 2 to 5 minutes. Keep warm until time to serve.

In selecting a lobster, look for the one that is most lively in the tank. The most humane way to prepare the lobster for the grill is to sever its spinal cord just prior to cooking. Place the lobster on a cutting board with its back towards you. Use a dishtowel to hold the lobster firmly in place at the back of its head. Quickly insert a knife crosswise where the back of the head and the shell meet and push until the knife strikes through to the cutting board. Turn each lobster on its back and butterfly and crack claws. Because they are protected by dense shell, the claws will take longer to cook; cracking the claws hastens the process.

In a small bowl combine olive oil and melted butter. Brush the exposed lobster flesh with the olive oil/butter mixture and place it flesh side down on the grill, approximately 4-inches from the heat source. Cook for 5 minutes and carefully turn the lobsters over. Brush with additional butter, and continue cooking until the lobster is cooked through, approximately 5 additional minutes. Spoon some of the champagne butter sauce over the exposed flesh of the lobster and put the remainder in a dipping bowl.

YIELDS 4 SERVINGS.

GRILLED VEGETABLES
★★★★★

"Sitting out there, Tom smoking, I sewing, and General Custer reading, we imagined Big Creek to be the Hudson, and the cotton-wood whose foliage is anything but thick, to be a graceful maple or a stately, branching elm." [Libbie Custer]

3	MEDIUM ONIONS, QUARTERED AND SKEWERED	3	YELLOW SQUASH, CUT LENGTHWISE TO A THICKNESS OF ½ INCH
3	ZUCCHINI, CUT LENGTHWISE TO A THICKNESS OF ½ INCH		OLIVE OIL

Brush the vegetables with olive oil and place on a grill, approximately 4 inches from the heat source, for 7 to 8 minutes, turning frequently to prevent burning, or until the desired degree of doneness is reached.

YIELDS 6 TO 8 SERVINGS.

TOM, GEORGE, AND LIBBIE

POLENTA
★ ★ ★ ★ ★

"A huge tarpaulin of very thick canvas, used to cover the grain and military stores, was spread over the large tent and extended far in front so that we had a wide porch, under which we sat most of the time."

1	CUP YELLOW CORNMEAL		¼	CUP CHOPPED ONION
2	TABLESPOONS BUTTER		¼	CUP CHOPPED MUSHROOMS
4½	CUPS CHICKEN BROTH		¾	CUP SHREDDED FONTINA CHEESE
2	TABLESPOONS OLIVE OIL			

Prepare 1 day prior to serving. In a 3- to 4-quart pan over medium-high heat stir the cornmeal and butter into the broth and continue to stir as the polenta comes to a boil. Reduce the heat to medium and continue to cook until the polenta is soft to bite (like cream of wheat or grits), approximately 10 minutes. In a saucepan heat the olive oil over medium heat and sauté the onion and mushrooms. Add to the polenta; stir in the cheese. Spoon into buttered individual ramekin dishes and smooth level. Place in a preheated 350°F oven and bake for 25 to 30 minutes.

YIELDS 4 TO 6 SERVINGS.

The efforts of these brave cavalry men and their wives opened the West as far as California, to future generations of men and women of every nationality and belief—pioneers in their own right.

TOMATO AND SERRANO SALSA
★★★★★

"Our brother Tom, while he enjoyed our arbor, refused to call it anything but the 'beer-garden'—but calling names did not destroy our delight."

¼	CUP FINELY CHOPPED WHITE ONION		1	TEASPOON OLIVE OIL
½	CUP FINELY DICED PLUM TOMATOES		½	TEASPOON LIME JUICE
½	TEASPOON MINCED SERANNO CHILI		¼	TEASPOON SUGAR
¼	TEASPOON MINCED FRESH CILANTRO			

One day prior to serving combine the above ingredients. Cover tightly and refrigerate.

YIELDS ABOUT ¾ CUP.

SOLDIERS AND WIVES

Santa Maria Style Barbecue

★ ★ ★ ★ ★

As an Air Force brat, I have had unique opportunities to travel the world and experience many different cuisines. For me, it was the ultimate "melting pot" experience. Every duty station presented matchless learning opportunities. However, some of my most cherished memories were created in my mother's kitchen. There she and various international friends exchanged and prepared various ethnic recipes. Now I no longer consider these recipes "ethnic," because they have become family favorites that evoke fond memories.

I continue to travel the world as the wife of an Air Force officer and experience various regions through their food. In Alabama, I renewed my acquaintance with traditional Southern food and wrote my best-selling cookbook, The African-American Heritage Cookbook. In Texas, I discovered traditional Mexican cooking as well as Tex-Mex (which is what occurs when the regional flavors of Texas and Mexico meet).

Upon my husband's reassignment to Vandenberg Air Force Base in California, I rediscovered the unique flavor of central coast dining, especially Santa Maria-style barbecue. Its early association is with the open-air cooking of the indigenous Chumash tribe, but the first local barbecues are said to have originated during the early 1800s. European immigrants received large land grants from the Mexican government and established huge ranches. Cattle ranching became the backbone of the fledgling economy. Here, under the serene Santa Maria oaks, the rancheros, the vaqueros (America's first cowboys), and their friends gathered for large Spanish-style barbecues. These barbecues, held following every cattle roundup, were celebratory in nature.

Traditionally, Santa Maria-style barbecue consists of top block sirloin, which is seasoned with salt, pepper, and garlic powder and cooked slowly over native red oak wood coals. The main course is served with tossed salad, beans, salsa, French bread toasted on the pit and then dipped in garlic butter, and sometimes macaroni and cheese. Included here are some excellent recipes for a Santa Maria barbecue.

SANTA MARIA STYLE BARBECUE
SANTA MARIA STYLE SALSA
SANTA MARIA STYLE BEANS
SANTA MARIA STYLE MACARONI AND CHEESE

SANTA MARIA STYLE BARBECUE
★★★★★

Begin with a 3-inch cut of boneless top sirloin, weighing 3 to 4 pounds, allowing approximately 1 pound per person. Although some purist may protest its "authenticity," you may also use the smaller tri-tip cut. Also known as a bottom cut, no one knew what to do with this triangular cut until a Santa Maria butcher used the now legendary seasoning and placed it on a rack in his rotisserie. The rest is history.

Combine 1 tablespoon of salt with ½ teaspoon coarse ground pepper and ½ teaspoon garlic salt. Traditionally, oak-wood logs are placed in a pit with a moveable grate. However, backyard chefs can also use charcoal mixed with oak-wood chips. The fire should be hot but not blazing. Place your hands two to three inches over the grill. If you can count to ten before removing your hand then the fire is ready.

Tips for Success: Do not trim off the fat before putting the meat on the grill. If cooking more than one cut and using steel rods, alternate fat and lean sides for an even distribution of the juices.

Otherwise, place meat on grill and adjust grill so the meat is 2 to 3 inches from the coals. Sear the lean part of the meat over the fire for the first 5 to 10 minutes to seal in the juices. Move the meat to 6 to 8 inches from the coals. Then flip over to the fat side for another 30 to 45 minutes. When juice appears at the top of the meat, it is time to flip it again. Cook to the desired degree of doneness (130°F for rare).

Finally, it is important to slice tri-tip against the grain, the long way, not across the triangle. It will not be a uniform cut, but it will be more tender. This cut of meat is best when served immediately after cooking.

YIELDS 3 TO 4 SERVINGS.

SANTA MARIA SALSA
★★★★★

The historic Santa Maria Club was incorporated in 1920. A huge pit was built and at the club's first Stag Barbecue, the beef, beans, green salad, salsa, garlic bread, and coffee were offered for a mere $1.25. This salsa recipe is best if prepared a day in advance.

3	MEDIUM TOMATOES, CHOPPED	1	TABLESPOON VINEGAR
½	CUP FINELY CHOPPED CELERY	1	DASH WORCESTERSHIRE SAUCE
½	CUP FINELY CHOPPED GREEN ONIONS	1	PINCH GARLIC SALT
½	CUP FINELY CHOPPED MILD GREEN CHILIES	1	PINCH DRIED OREGANO, CRUSHED
2	TABLESPOONS CHOPPED FRESH CILANTRO		A FEW DROPS HOT PEPPER SAUCE

In a serving bowl combine all of the ingredients. Cover and let stand at least 1 hour to blend flavors.

YIELDS 3½ CUPS.

SANTA MARIA BEANS
★★★★★

The pinquito bean is a small, pink bean unique to Santa Maria. I have never seen it outside of California. No one is quite sure how the pinquito first came to Santa Maria Valley. Some say it started with a bag of beans given as a gift to one of the early Swiss/Italian families, others say a European woman brought several plants with her when she migrated to the area many years ago.

1	POUND PINQUITO BEANS	¼	CUP RED CHILE SAUCE (LAS PALMAS BRAND, NOT TO BE CONFUSED WITH CHILI SAUCE, WHICH IS LIKE HOT CATSUP)
1	STRIP BACON, DICED		
½	CUP DICED HAM	1	TEASPOON DRY MUSTARD
1	CLOVE GARLIC, MINCED	1	TABLESPOON SUGAR
¾	CUP TOMATO PURÉE	1	TEASPOON SALT
		1	PINCH MSG OR ACCENT (OPTIONAL)

Pick through the beans to remove any small stones. Place in a pot, cover with water, and let soak overnight. Drain the beans, cover with fresh water, and simmer for 2 hours, or until tender.

In a skillet sauté the bacon and ham until lightly browned. Add the garlic and sauté for 1 to 2 minutes longer. Add the tomato purée, Chile sauce, sugar, mustard, salt, and MSG. Drain and save the liquid from the beans. Stir the sauce into beans and simmer for 30 minutes. Add some of the saved liquid if the beans get too dry.

YIELDS 6 TO 8 SERVINGS.

SANTA MARIA MACARONI AND CHEESE
★ ★ ★ ★ ★

These barbecues quickly came to nearby Vandenberg AFB where they remain a traditional part of hail and farewell parties, promotions, and other festive activities. In fact, it was a long time before I realized that it was not Vandenberg-style barbecue. When we moved to Colorado, I quickly called the commissary to complain that I could not find tri-tip anywhere. In a deeply consoling tone, the butcher advised me that it was only available in Santa Maria and the surrounding area, then urged me to hurry "home."

1½	CUPS ELBOW MACARONI	1	PINCH PEPPER
2	TABLESPOONS BUTTER	2	CUPS HOT MILK
2	TABLESPOONS ALL-PURPOSE FLOUR	1½	CUPS SHREDDED SHARP CHEDDAR CHEESE
¾	TEASPOON SALT		

Cook the macaroni according to the directions on the package. In a saucepan make a roux of the butter, flour, and salt. Melt 1 cup of the cheese in the hot milk. Add the pepper and hot milk to the butter and flour mixture. Cook in a double boiler until thickened and bubbly, stirring constantly. Combine the macaroni and cheese sauce, and place in a 1½-quart casserole. Sprinkle the remaining ½ cup of cheese on top. Bake at 350°F for 35 to 40 minutes.

YIELDS 6 TO 8 SERVINGS.

*T*hese recipes have appeared in numerous cookbooks, brochures, and newspaper articles. To quote an article in the *Santa Maria Times,* "A copyright, held by the Santa Maria Valley Chamber of Commerce (http://www.santamaria.com), protects the name, the concept, and the menu. This action came to stop commercial ventures from advertising their barbecue when it wasn't 'the real thing.'"

Picnic on the Potomac

★ ★ ★ ★ ★

"I would have our basket packed in the late afternoon when George arrived at the house, we would drive over the foot of 35th Street, hire a canoe and paddle up the Potomac as far as Chain Bridge. Then we would let the canoe drift back while I served the picnic dinner, with a lantern hanging at the stern after dark."

FRIED CHICKEN

HOT DROP BISCUITS

TOSSED SALAD

ICE CREAM

BRANDIED PEACHES

COFFEE

FRIED CHICKEN
★★★★★

"We took the Secretary of War and Mrs. Stimson on one of our evenings on the river. We hired two canoes and the Secretary, who loved to exercise, paddled my canoe all the way up to Chain Bridge. He was 73 then." [Katherine Tupper Marshall]

3	POUNDS CHICKEN, CUT UP	1	TEASPOON PAPRIKA
2	PACKAGES ZESTY ITALIAN SALAD DRESSING MIX	½	TEASPOON SAGE
1½	CUPS ALL-PURPOSE FLOUR	1	TEASPOON PEPPER
¼	TEASPOON BAKING POWDER	1½	CUPS VEGETABLE OIL
2	TEASPOONS SALT		

Wash the chicken and pat dry with paper towels. In a large plastic bag mix the dry dressing mix, flour, baking powder, salt, paprika, sage, and pepper. Add the chicken a few pieces at a time, and shake to coat. In a 12-inch skillet heat the oil over medium-high heat, to approximately 350°F. Add the chicken pieces, being careful not to crowd the pan. If necessary, cook the chicken in batches. Decrease the heat to medium. Cook uncovered until well browned on the underside, about 15 minutes. Reduce the heat to 275°, cover, and cook for 25 minutes. Uncover and cook an additional 5 minutes. Drain. Transfer the chicken to double-thick paper towels.

YIELDS 6 SERVINGS.

HOT DROP BISCUITS
★★★★★

"Under the bridge we lashed two canoes together and drifted back down stream." [Katherine Tupper Marshall]

2	CUPS SIFTED BREAD FLOUR	2	EGGS, WELL BEATEN
3¾	TEASPOONS BAKING POWDER	¾	CUP HEAVY CREAM
1	TEASPOON SALT		

Preheat the oven to 400°F. In a large mixing bowl sift together the dry ingredients. Add the eggs and cream, and stir just until combined. At this point the mixture should be lumpy and soft. Drop by heaping teaspoonfuls onto an ungreased baking sheet. Bake for 15 minutes or until golden. Serve with honey butter and additional honey, if desired.

YIELDS ABOUT 12 BISCUITS.

TOSSED SALAD
★★★★★

"I had brought my usual picnic supper of fried chicken, hot biscuits and green salad, topped off with ice cream, brandied peaches and coffee."

2	CUCUMBERS, PEELED AND CUT INTO BITE-SIZED QUARTERS		1	CUP SEASONED RICE VINEGAR
1	RED ONION, THINLY SLICED		1	SMALL HEAD ICEBURG LETTUCE, WASHED, CRISPED, AND TORN IN BITE-SIZED PIECES
2	CUPS CHERRY TOMATO HALVES		1	BUNCH WATERCRESS, WASHED, CRISPED, AND STEMS REMOVED
1	YELLOW BELL PEPPER, CUT IN STRIPS		¼	CUP VEGETABLE OIL
⅓	CUP SNIPPED CHIVES		2	TABLESPOONS MINCED PARSLEY

In a large mixing bowl combine the cucumbers, onion, tomatoes, yellow pepper, chives, and rice vinegar. Toss well. Cover and refrigerate for 4 to 8 hours.

To serve, drain the cucumber mixture. Add the lettuce and toss with oil. Adjust the salt and pepper to taste. If substituting plain vinegar for seasoned rice vinegar, add additional sugar and salt to taste.

YIELDS 4 TO 6 SERVINGS.

BRANDIED PEACHES
★★★★★

"Mrs. Stimson said as we arrived at the boathouse, 'This is the nicest evening I ever had in Washington.'"
[Katherine Tupper Marshall]

FOR VANILLA SUGAR:

1⅔ CUPS SUGAR

1 VANILLA BEAN, CHOPPED

1 CINNAMON STICK

COMPOTE:

1 CUP WATER

⅓ CUP BRANDY (KOSHER FOR PASSOVER)

2 TABLESPOONS APRICOT PRESERVES

12 FRESH OR FROZEN UNSWEETENED RASPBERRIES

8 MARASCHINO CHERRIES

2 TABLESPOONS MARASCHINO SYRUP

1¼ POUNDS FROZEN UNSWEETENED SLICED PEACHES (ABOUT 5 CUPS), THAWED

ICE CREAM

First, make the vanilla sugar: In a food processor combine the sugar and vanilla bean. Blend for 2 minutes. Sift to remove any vanilla pieces. (Can be made ahead and stored for up to 2 weeks in an airtight container.)

In a heavy medium saucepan combine ¼ cup of vanilla sugar, water, brandy, apricot preserves, raspberries, maraschino cherries, and syrup. Cook over medium-high heat, stirring, until the sugar dissolves. Add the peaches and cinnamon stick, and bring to a boil. Reduce the heat and cook until the peaches are barely tender, about 5 minutes.

With a slotted spoon, transfer the peaches to a strainer set over a bowl. Boil the syrup until very thick and reduced to a scant ⅓ cup, approximately 15 minutes, returning any juices that drain from the peaches. Strain the syrup into a bowl and mix in the peaches. Cool. Cover and refrigerate.

Spoon over ice cream and serve.

YIELDS 8 SERVINGS.

A Sunday Reunion with Very Dear Friends

★ ★ ★ ★ ★

Our friendship was fully formed from the moment we met as young second lieutenants at Sheppard Air Force Base in Texas. Flora Tate Davidson was there to attend budget school and I to attend transportation school. Warm, friendly, and beautiful, she was easy to talk to from the start.

Imagine our amazement when we learned that we were both expecting our first child and that we were both assigned to Whiteman Air Force Base in Knob Noster, Missouri! In many ways Flora was the sister I never had. We shopped till we dropped, making the one-hour drive to Kansas City on a moment's notice. We talked for hours on the telephone. Our families shared every holiday. Over the years, we talked less often, but whenever the conversation resumed, it was as if no time passed. As always, much of our conversation was seasoned with favorite recipes. I barbecued for her in Colorado and prepared a sit-down dinner in Washington, D.C. Together we reviewed the manuscript for my first book, The African-American Heritage Cookbook. Last year when my husband was assigned to Lackland Air Force Base, Flora was the first to call with a dinner invitation.

MIXED GRILL PLATTER (CHICKEN AND BEEF)

FLORA'S BAKED BEANS

GARDEN SALAD (SEE THE INDEX FOR SALAD CHOICES)

OLD-FASHIONED BANANA PUDDING (SEE THE RECIPE ON PAGE 162)

FLORA'S BAKED BEANS
★★★★★

My family loved these beans so much that I finally had to ask Flora for the recipe. We have always had a very friendly cooking competition, so when my family kept complimenting her meal, I teased that she was never to cook for them again . . . and then she brought out the banana pudding!

2   CANS VAN DE CAMP PORK AND BEANS (PLAIN), REMOVE PORK PIECES

½   POUND JIMMY DEAN GROUND PORK SAUSAGE

¼   CUP CHOPPED SMOKED CHICKEN BREAST

¼   CUP HICKORY-SMOKED BARBECUE SAUCE

Fry crumbled ground sausage until thoroughly cooked over medium heat (do not fry crispy). Drain on paper towels. Chop chicken from an earlier barbecue. Drain 1 can of beans and mix with the remaining undrained can. In a large casserole dish mix all of the ingredients. Bake at 350°F for 1 hour.

YIELDS 8 SERVINGS.

Fajita Festival

★ ★ ★ ★ ★

Sometimes referred to as the "Texification" of Mexican food, Tex-Mex cooking probably began in the mid-1800s with San Antonio street vendors who offered tamales, chili, and tacos for sale.

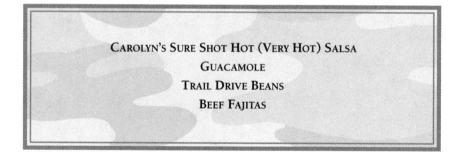

CAROLYN'S SURE SHOT HOT (VERY HOT) SALSA
GUACAMOLE
TRAIL DRIVE BEANS
BEEF FAJITAS

CAROLYN'S SURE SHOT HOT (VERY HOT) SALSA
★★★★★

When the zesty spices and peppers of Mexico were blended with Texas cooking, a whole new dimension was added to regional recipes.

5	TOMATOES, CHOPPED	¾	TEASPOON SALT
1	MEDIUM ONION, CHOPPED	8	TO 9 FRESH JALAPEÑO PEPPERS, SEEDED AND CHOPPED
1½	TEASPOONS MINCED CILANTRO		
8	CLOVES GARLIC, MINCED	3	TABLESPOONS RED HOT PEPPER SAUCE
½	TEASPOON ONION POWDER	¼	TEASPOON CAYENNE PEPPER
¼	TEASPOON GARLIC POWDER	3	TABLESPOONS LIME JUICE
		¼	CUP PLUS 2 TABLESPOONS OLIVE OIL

In a serving bowl combine all of the above ingredients (for milder salsa use fewer peppers and less hot pepper sauce) and refrigerate, preferably overnight.

Serve with tortilla chips, plenty of cold beer, and icy margaritas.

YIELDS ABOUT 5 CUPS.

GUACAMOLE
★★★★★

With only a young servant girl, Long survived the winter by digging oysters from a frozen beach and, on occasion, firing a canon to frighten away Indians. Upon learning of her husband's death, she opened a boarding house to support her family. Convinced her husband would return to retrieve her and his new daughter, Jane Long, known as the "Mother of Texas," remained at a small fort on Galveston Island after soldiers and settlers abandoned it.

4	RIPE AVOCADOS	1	TEASPOON ONION POWDER
1	LARGE TOMATO, SEEDED AND CHOPPED	1½	TABLESPOONS FRESH LEMON JUICE
1	TABLESPOON MINCED ONION	⅛	TEASPOON CHILI POWDER
1	TEASPOON GARLIC POWDER	½	TEASPOON SALT

In a large bowl mash the avocados until smooth. Add the remaining ingredients and mix well. Refrigerate until ready for use.

YIELDS 6 TO 8 SERVINGS.

TRAIL DRIVE BEANS
★★★★★

The chuck wagon evolved from wagons used during the Civil War. Cowmen acquired the government's surplus wagons and adapted them for use on trail drives. As the drives grew larger and longer, trail bosses began to take cooks with them. Charlie Goodnight was one such cook and is credited with turning one of those surplus wagons into what we would come to know as the chuck or grub wagon.

3	CUPS PINTO BEANS		1	16-OUNCE CAN TOMATOES, CHOPPED
7	SLICES BACON, SLICED INTO 1 ½-INCH STRIPS		¼	TEASPOON BLACK PEPPER
¾	CUP CHOPPED ONION		1	TABLESPOON SALT
½	CUP CHOPPED GREEN BELL PEPPER		1	TABLESPOON CHILI POWDER
2	TABLESPOONS CHOPPED JALAPEÑO PEPPER (OPTIONAL)		¼	TEASPOON GARLIC POWDER
5	CLOVES GARLIC, MINCED		⅛	TEASPOON CUMIN

The night before preparing, pick over the beans, removing and discarding any foreign objects. In a large pot cover the beans with sufficient water to cover them by 2 inches and soak them overnight.

The next day, drain and rinse the beans. Return them to the pot and cover them with fresh water; bring to a boil over medium-high heat. Reduce the heat to low, cover, and allow to simmer while preparing the remaining ingredients.

In a large saucepan sauté the bacon over medium-high heat until crisp. Remove the bacon and set aside; add the onion, bell pepper, jalapeño, and garlic to the bacon drippings, and sauté until the onion becomes transparent. Add the remaining ingredients, cover, and simmer for 10 minutes. Add to the bean pot and simmer until the beans are tender, approximately 2 hours. Add additional water as needed to prevent the beans from sticking. Crumble the bacon over the beans just prior to serving.

YIELDS 8 SERVINGS.

BEEF FAJITAS
★★★★★

Sarah Borginis accompanied her husband and enlisted into the 8th cavalry as a cook. Arriving at Ft. Brown, Texas, with a two-pony wagon and pots and pans, she later became the principal cook and was among those accompanying General Zachary Taylor when he moved most of his troops to the Rio Grande. However, the 8th remained behind when the general took a force of about 600 to secure a supply depot.

2	POUNDS BEEF SKIRT STEAK (¼ POUND PER PERSON)		½	TEASPOON CHILI POWDER
			¼	TEASPOON CUMIN
1	8-OUNCE BOTTLE ZESTY ITALIAN SALAD DRESSING		1	TEASPOON GARLIC POWDER
½	CUP LIME JUICE		2	CUPS SEEDED AND SLICED THIN GREEN BELL PEPPERS
1	12-OUNCE CAN BEER			
2	TABLESPOONS LEMON PEPPER		1	LARGE ONION, SLICED INTO THIN WEDGES
1	TABLESPOON MEAT TENDERIZER (SEE NOTE, BELOW)			TORTILLAS
¼	TEASPOON OREGANO			

Trim the flank steak, then wash it under cold running water. Pat dry and place in a nonreactive bowl. In a small bowl combine the salad dressing, lime juice, and beer. Pour the mixture over the steak, tightly cover; and refrigerate, allowing to marinate overnight; turn often.

The next day, combine the lemon pepper, tenderizer, and garlic pepper; rub the meat with the mixture; and allow it to sit at room temperature for 1 hour prior to grilling. Grill over hot charcoal for approximately 8 minutes per side.

While the meat is grilling, place green peppers and onions in a grill basket or in a cast-iron pan on top of the grill with a very small amount of oil and cook. When the steak is done, remove it to a cutting board and slice thinly across the grain. Place spoonfuls of the steak on steam-softened, store-bought tortillas (or fresh cooked if you have the talent and time) and dress with the green peppers, onions, sour cream, and guacamole, according to preference. Roll and bite into a mouthful of delicious delight!

Note: I use Adams Fajita seasoning, which contains an excellent tenderizer. However, if this brand is not available, do not substitute another fajita seasoning.

YIELDS 8 SERVINGS.

MARGARITAS
★★★★★

Fort Brown was severely undermanned, and as a result, Sarah was eventually issued a musket when Santa Anna's forces attacked. While dodging cannon and musket fire, she actively participated in the fighting and never missed striking a target or preparing a meal. When breveted to Colonel by General Taylor, Sarah became the first woman to hold this rank in the U.S. Army.

After the war, Sarah opened a hotel in El Paso, which became a favorite of the 49ers heading for the California gold fields. Later, she moved to Yuma, Arizona, and ran a saloon there until her death in 1866. Col. Borginis was buried at Fort Yuma with full military honors.

2	6-OUNCE CANS FROZEN LIMEADE	¼	CUP PINEAPPLE JUICE
12	OUNCES TEQUILA		ICE
6	OUNCES TRIPLE SEC		

In a blender combine the above ingredients. Add 3 to 4 cups of ice and blend until smooth. Salt the rims of 4 margarita glasses and serve immediately.

YIELDS 4 SERVINGS.

"In January orders arrived from Washington to form the first regiment of the United States Infantry at Ringgold Barracks, Texas, on the lower Rio Grande. . . . The departure for Texas was delayed until the month of April, when we sailed in the steamship Ohio bound for New Orleans via Havana. . . . After a sail of three days we stopped at Galveston, Texas, one of the principal ports of the state. [It was at a small fort on Galveston Island that Jane Long, the Mother of Texas, endured an isolated winter after soldiers abandoned the Fort.] We stopped for twenty-four hours at Galveston and . . . we arrived . . . at the hotel just in time for dinner. . . . We left Galveston with a glimpse of its melancholy beauties impressed on the pages of our memory. . . . About three miles before we came to Fort Brown. . . . It was here that General Taylor achieved his second victory." [Teresa Vielè, 1851]

A Day on Fish Lake

★　★　★　★　★

If one goes to fish lake just for sport, . . . flies should be used always, but if one gets up there when the shadows are long and one's dinner depends on the fish caught . . . begin at once with grasshoppers. . . . I cast one over before the boat had fairly settled into position. It was siezed the instant it touched the water, and down, down went the trout, its white sides glistening through the clear water. . . .

One of the enlisted men prepared dinner for us, and fried trout in olive oil, the most perfect way of cooking mountain trout in camp. They were delicious—so fresh from the icy water that none of their delicate flavor had been lost, and were crisp and hot. . . . A flat boulder made a grand table for us, and of course each one had his camp stool to sit upon. Altogether the dinner was a success, the best part being, perhaps, the exhilarating mountain air that gave us such fine appetites. . . . We had more fish for our breakfast, that time fried with tiny strips of bacon.

MOUNTAIN TROUT

MOUNTAIN TROUT
★★★★★

6	MOUNTAIN TROUT	1	TABLESPOON SALT
8	STRIPS BACON, COARSELY CHOPPED	2	TEASPOONS BLACK PEPPER
¼	CUP ALL-PURPOSE FLOUR	¼	TEASPOON CAYENNE PEPPER
1	CUP CORNMEAL		LEMON WEDGES, OPTIONAL

Wash the trout and pat dry. Sprinkle the trout cavities with salt and pepper to taste. In a large frying pan over medium heat, cook the bacon until crisp. Remove the bacon from the pan, reserving the drippings in the pan. On a piece of waxed paper combine the flour, cornmeal, salt, pepper, and cayenne. Coat the trout on both sides with the mixture. Arrange half of the trout in the pan. Cook, turning once, until the fish is lightly browned and flakes readily when prodded in the thickest portion with a fork. For each 1 inch thickness of fish (measured in the thickest portion), allow 10 minutes total—5 minutes on each side. Repeat the frying process until all fish is fried. Cook the remaining fish in reserved drippings or vegetable oil as needed. Place on a paper-towel lined plate to drain and keep warm. Prior to serving, place chopped bacon in the cavity of each fish. Garnish with chopped parsley and lemon wedges if desired.

YIELDS 6 SERVINGS.

THE MILITARY WIVES' COOKBOOK

"The strain of that winter on my husband and his Staff, the long days and evenings of feverish planning, the unrest and uncertainty that were felt by everyone, began to tell. George felt something should be done to relieve the tension. We had been at Fort Myer for nearly a year and had no time to think of receiving the Army. Few of the officers had ever been in the chief of Staff's house, many did not know him by sight. When spring came, we decided to give a garden party on May 1st. There were twelve hundred invitations mailed, we prepared for fifteen hundred people, two thousand came. Knowing Washington receptions, my husband had trucks of provisions stand by to take care of the situation in the event of shortages. We had often remarked about the tendency of people to congregate in one room . . . while they talk[ed] to friends, utterly unconscious of newly arriving guests. To relieve this situation, George devised a plan: Mrs. Stimson [wife of the secretary of war] was to receive with me . . . in the drawing room. . . . George woud be on the side lawn."

As the guests arrived, they would ask about the general and were told by Mrs. Marshall, "'He is waiting to see you out on the lawn.' They would look relieved and those two-thousand people passed through the house steadily with no signs of congestion anywhere.

"The same refreshments were served out of doors as in the dining room. Outside there were tables and gay-colored chairs so that the guests could form groups and sit comfortably, while the band played on the terrace below. At five-thirty when the sun-set gun went off, Mrs. Stimson and I joined General Marshall just before the flag was lowered and the band played the Star-Spangled Banner. This was a solemn moment to that gay crowd. There was a long pause before the guests moved; they stood silently as the flag was folded. It was a dramatic moment, for each one present knew that war was growing daily nearer." [Katherine Tupper Marshall]

SIGNIFICANCE OF THE FLAG FOLDING CEREMONY

In the Armed Forces of the United States, at the ceremony of retreat the flag is lowered, folded in a triangle fold, and kept under watch throughout the night as a tribute to our nation's honored dead. The next morning it is brought out and, at the ceremony of reveille, run aloft as a symbol of our belief in the resurrection of the body.

- The first fold of our flag is a symbol of life.
- The second fold is a symbol of our belief in eternal life.
- The third fold is made in honor and remembrance of the veteran departing our ranks who gave a portion of life for the defense of our country to attain a peace througout the world.
- The fourth fold represents our weaker nature, for as American citizens trusting in God, it is to Him we turn in times of peace as well as in times of war for His divine guidance.
- The fifth fold is a tribute to our country, for in the words of Stephen Decatur, "Our country, in dealing with other countries, may she always be right; but it is still our country, right or wrong."
- The sixth fold is for where our hearts lie. It is with our heart that we pledge allegiance to the flag of the United States of America, and to the republic for which it stands, one nation, under God, indivisible, with liberty and justice for all.
- The seventh fold is a tribute to our Armed Forces, for it is through the Armed Forces that we protect our country and our flag against all her enemies, whether they be found within or without the boundaries of our republic.
- The eighth fold is a tribute to the one who entered into the valley of the shadow of death, that we might see the light of day, and to honor mother, for whom it flies on mother's day.
- The ninth fold is a tribute to womanhood; for it has been through their faith, love, loyalty and devotion that the character of the men and women who have made this country great have been molded.
- The tenth fold is a tribute to father, for he, too, has given his sons and daughters for the defense of our country since they were first born.

- The eleventh fold, in the eyes of a Hebrew citizen, represents the lower portion of the seal of King David and King Solomon, and glorifies, in their eyes, the God of Abraham, Isaac, and Jacob.
- The twelfth fold, in the eyes of a Christian citizen, represents an emblem of eternity and glorifies, in their eyes, God the Father, the Son, and Holy Ghost.

When the flag is completely folded, the stars are uppermost, reminding us of our national motto, "In God We Trust."

After the flag is completely folded and tucked in, it takes on the appearance of a cocked hat, ever reminding us of the soldiers who served under Captain John Paul Jones who were followed by their comrades and shipmates in the Armed Forces of the United States, preserving for us the rights, privileges, and freedoms we enjoy today.

U.S. Air Force Protocol Office

Ft Logan, WWI

LORETTO HEIGHTS SERVICE CAMP

Lisa De Los Santos:
HELPING OTHERS STAY FIT AND BE HEALTHY

Lisa De Los Santos, a military wife and a former military member herself, is a certified personal trainer. Lisa originally became interested in fitness during college, but it wasn't until she became a mother that the field became her passion and a career. In fact, for two years, Lisa had a gym membership that she rarely used. Then, during her first pregnancy, she gained a significant amount of weight. "Everything hurt," Lisa says. "I felt miserable." Even before the birth of her son, she determined to lose the weight. So after a PCS move to San Antonio, Texas, Lisa and her husband, an Ironman tri-athlete, immediately joined a gym and began to work out. Four months later, Lisa had lost more than forty pounds of "baby weight." Less than a year later—right according to plan—Lisa became pregnant with their second child. A healthier diet and a more active lifestyle contributed to a more manageable pregnancy weight. A few months after delivering their daughter, the family moved to the Sultanate of Oman, where she had more free time. Lisa used this opportunity to work out more frequently and focus on getting fit.

Lisa had long planned to return to school and earn a master's degree before her G.I. Bill benefits expired in 2005, but fate intervened. When Lisa's husband received an unaccompanied assignment to the United Arab Emirates in 2004, they agreed to delay Lisa's continuing education so that she could return to Texas and care for their children during that year. Back in San Antonio, Lisa learned that she could apply her G.I. Bill benefits toward a personal training certification that she could earn while studying at home. Lisa completed her certification and soon accepted a part-time training position at the local gym, where she was already a member. Suddenly, Lisa's longstanding desire to help others combined with her newfound interest in health and fitness seemed to be pointing to a career as a personal trainer.

Her husband's next assignment took the family to Montgomery, Alabama, where Lisa continued her career as a personal trainer, training clients as much as forty-five hours a week. During this time, Lisa also trained and competed in the 2006 Super Natural Bodybuilding & Fitness Capital Classic competition. Her hard work culminated in her winning the Women's Novice and Overall Bodybuilding titles, as well as the coveted Ms. Montgomery title.

At their next assignment, Vandenberg AFB in central California, Lisa's husband assumed a squadron command position and Lisa became active as a commander's spouse. In addition to leading the squadron's spouses group, she also volunteered to lead the Vandenberg Spouses' Club Diet and Fitness Group. This proved very successful as she used teaching, motivation, weigh-ins, and friendly weight-loss challenges to help members achieve their goals. Some members lost as much as forty-five pounds, while others significantly improved their fitness levels, decreased their body fat percentage, gained confidence, and completely changed their lifestyles. As a result of her efforts, Lisa received the spouse's club John A. Sesto Volun-

teer of the Year Award. The following year, she resumed working as an independent personal trainer at the base fitness center. Soon, she was fully booked with clients and a lengthy waiting list.

In addition to her personal training certification, Lisa also has a Bachelor of Science degree in business and management from the University of Maryland. In 2007, she completed a Master Fitness Specialist certification through the Cooper Institute. Since then, she has also completed her first sprint triathlon and three half-marathons. Lisa plans to expand her business by pursuing additional certifications in nutrition and wellness, and hopes to one day become an author and a motivational speaker. She is also developing a business plan to market herself as a Personal Lifestyle Designer, in which she will offer intense three-month one-on-one life-changing programs that will teach clients how to eat and prepare healthy foods, successfully lose and keep weight off, and set and achieve specific fitness goals.

OVER THERE:
AN INTERNATIONAL AFFAIR

"Over there, over there, Send the word, send the word to beware—
That the Yanks are coming, the Yanks are coming. . . ."

"Very few women, even the most ambitious for their husband's future, but would have confessed at the close of war, that the glory came with too great sacrifices, and they would rather gather their husbands, lovers and brothers into the shelter of the humblest home than to endure the suspense and loneliness of war times." [Libbie Custer, *Tenting the Plains*]

In 220 years of American history, more than two million women have served their country at home and abroad. On the front-line and the homefront they were here and "over there," performing jobs they had never done before.

Moroccan Magic

★ ★ ★ ★ ★

With the coming of the Second World War, many imprisoned in Europe turned hopeful eyes toward the freedom America offered. Those seeking American refuge could not always get there directly, so a round-about refugee trail sprang up: Paris to Marseilles, across the Mediterranean to Oran, then by train, or auto, or foot, across the rim of Africa to Casablanca in French Morocco.

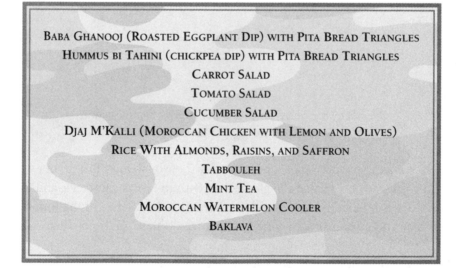

BABA GHANOOJ (ROASTED EGGPLANT DIP) WITH PITA BREAD TRIANGLES

HUMMUS BI TAHINI (CHICKPEA DIP) WITH PITA BREAD TRIANGLES

CARROT SALAD

TOMATO SALAD

CUCUMBER SALAD

DJAJ M'KALLI (MOROCCAN CHICKEN WITH LEMON AND OLIVES)

RICE WITH ALMONDS, RAISINS, AND SAFFRON

TABBOULEH

MINT TEA

MOROCCAN WATERMELON COOLER

BAKLAVA

BABA GHANOOJ
★★★★★

On November 8, 1942, sixty nurses landed with the assault troops in North Africa near the town of Arzew.

2	MEDIUM OR 1 LARGE EGGPLANT		1	TABLESPOON OLIVE OIL
3	CLOVES GARLIC, PRESSED		½	CUP TAHINI (SESAME SEED PASTE)
1	SMALL ONION, FINELY CHOPPED		1	TEASPOON SALT OR TO TASTE
	JUICE OF ONE LEMON		3	TABLESPOONS PARSLEY, FINELY CHOPPED
¼	TEASPOON CAYENNE PEPPER			

Preheat the oven to 350°F. Rub the eggplant with a small amount of olive oil and place on a tray in the middle of the oven for 45 minutes or until soft. Allow the eggplant to cool. Cut in half, and scoop out the flesh. In a blender or food processor blend the eggplant, garlic, onion, lemon juice, tahini, and olive oil until smooth. Season to taste with cayenne and salt, and stir in half of the parsley. Place in a serving dish and sprinkle the rest of the parsley on top. Serve with pita bread.

YIELDS 6 SERVINGS.

SOLDIER CARRYING FERTILIZER IN NORTH AFRICA

HUMMUS BI TAHINI
★★★★★

Often under sniper fire, nurses of the 48th Hospital set up shop in an abandoned civilian hospital and with limited supplies, electricity, and running water began caring for invasion casualties.

2	15-OUNCE CANS CHICKPEAS, DRAINED (RESERVE LIQUID)	**GARNISH:**	
	JUICE OF TWO LEMONS	¼	CUP CHOPPED PARSLEY
¾	CUP TAHINI		PAPRIKA
4	CLOVES GARLIC, PRESSED	3	TABLESPOONS OLIVE OIL
¾	TEASPOON SALT		

In a food processor combine the chickpeas, lemon juice, tahini, and garlic, and purée until smooth. Add reserved liquid as necessary to thin the mixture to the consistency of a hearty dip. Add salt to taste and more lemon juice if needed. To serve, transfer the hummus to a serving plate, sprinkle with paprika and chopped parsley, and pour olive oil on top. Serve with pita bread.

YIELDS 8 TO 12 SERVINGS.

CARROT SALAD
★★★★★

8	MEDIUM CARROTS, COARSELY GRATED	2	TEASPOONS GROUND CINNAMON
1	CUP FRESH-SQUEEZED ORANGE JUICE	⅛	TEASPOON GRATED NUTMEG
2	TABLESPOONS SUGAR		SALT TO TASTE

In a medium bowl mix all of the ingredients together. Transfer to a serving bowl and chill for at least 1 hour prior to serving.

YIELDS 8 SERVINGS.

TOMATO SALAD
★★★★★

4	MEDIUM TOMATOES, CHOPPED	½	CUP FINELY CHOPPED PARSLEY
¼	CUP FRESH LEMON JUICE		SALT AND WHITE PEPPER TO TASTE
¾	CUP ONION, COARSELY CHOPPED	½	TABLESPOON FINELY CHOPPED CILANTRO
¼	CUP OLIVE OIL		

Place chopped tomatoes in a serving bowl. In a small bowl combine the remaining ingredients. Pour over the tomatoes. Refrigerate for at least 1 hour before serving.

YIELDS 4 TO 6 SERVINGS.

CUCUMBER SALAD
★★★★★

4	MEDIUM CUCUMBERS, PEELED, SEEDED AND COARSELY CHOPPED	1	TABLESPOON FINELY CHOPPED CILANTRO
¾	CUP COARSELY CHOPPED ONION	¼	CUP FRESH LEMON JUICE
½	CUP FINELY CHOPPED PARSLEY	¼	CUP OLIVE OIL
			SALT AND WHITE PEPPER TO TASTE

Place the chopped cucumbers in a serving bowl. In a small bowl combine the remaining ingredients. Pour over the cucumbers and refrigerate for at least 1 hour before serving.

YIELDS 4 TO 6 SERVINGS.

DJAJ M' KALLI

PICKLED LEMONS

★★★★★

On July 5, 1943, Congress signed the bill creating the Women's Army Corps, giving women permanent status. More than forty thousand WACs served and many deployed to North Africa, Europe, and China-Burma-India.

6	LEMONS		SCREW-TOP GLASS JARS
	KOSHER SALT		

Prepare the lemons 2 weeks in advance. Scrub the lemons thoroughly under running water. Transfer to a bowl, cover with water, and allow to soak for 1 hour. Drain the water and pat the lemons dry. Quarter the lemons, leaving one end attached (like an open flower bud). Fill each lemon "bud" with salt and place in a glass or stoneware bowl. Place as many salt-filled "buds" in the bowl as will fit and weigh the lemons down. Allow to stand undisturbed until the juices are exuded and the lemons are covered in liquid (2 to 3 days). Pack the lemons in large glass jars and pour the juices over them to cover completely. If there is not enough liquid, boil some water, allow it to cool to lukewarm, and pour over the lemons. Screw the jar lids on tightly and allow to stand for 2 to 4 weeks. Lemons may be refrigerated for up to six months. Rinse before using.

YIELDS 6 LEMONS.

CHICKEN WITH GARLIC SALT RUB

★★★★★

3	WHOLE CHICKENS (APPROXIMATELY 2 POUNDS EACH)	2	TABLESPOONS KOSHER SALT
7	TO 8 CLOVES GARLIC, CRUSHED		

This dish must be made 24 hours in advance of serving. In a small bowl crush the garlic and salt together until a pasty rub is formed and set aside. Cut chickens into 4 portions or more and remove all visible fat. Rub portions with garlic salt rub. Place the chicken in a large pot with sufficient water to cover and soak for 1 hour. While chickens are soaking, prepare marinade.

MARINADE

¾	CUP OLIVE OIL	¼	TEASPOON GROUND CUMIN
3	CLOVES GARLIC, PEELED AND CRUSHED	1	TEASPOON GROUND BLACK PEPPER
2	TEASPOONS GROUND GINGER	⅛	TEASPOON POWDERED SAFFRON
1 ¼	TEASPOONS SWEET PAPRIKA	1	TEASPOON KOSHER SALT
¾	TEASPOON GROUND TURMERIC		

In a large bowl combine the above ingredients and set aside. Remove the chicken from the pot, discarding the water. Place the chicken in a large, nonreactive bowl, rub with the marinade mixture, and marinate overnight.

STEWING INGREDIENTS

2¼	CUPS GRATED SPANISH ONIONS, DRAINED	1	TEASPOON GROUND CINNAMON
3	TABLESPOONS CHOPPED ITALIAN FLAT-LEAF PARSLEY	1½	CUPS KALAMATA OLIVES
3	TABLESPOONS CHOPPED FRESH CORIANDER	1	PICKLED LEMON
	MEDIUM TOMATOES, PEELED, SEEDED AND CHOPPED		

Place ¼ cup of oil on the bottom of an enameled roasting pan. Place pan over 2 stove burners and heat oil over medium-high heat. Add the chicken and cook until browned. Drain all oil from the marinade and retain the sediment. Add onions, garlic, parsley, coriander, marinade sediment, cinnamon, and 2½ cups of water, and bring to a boil. Reduce the heat to low, cover, and simmer for 1 to 1½ hours or until very tender with the meat falling easily from the bone.

Remove the chicken to a serving platter, cover with foil, and keep warm. Skim any remaining fat from the sauce. Add the olives and rinsed pickled lemon to the sauce, simmer uncovered for 5 to 10 minutes. Cook the sauce down until fairly thick. To serve, arrange the chicken pieces in a serving dish. Cover with sauce, and garnish the top with lemon.

YIELDS 8 SERVINGS.

TABBOULEH

★★★★★

Army Nurse Hilda Nevin received the Bronze Star for service in Russia, Teheran, Tripoli, Algiers, and Casablanca.

1	CUP BULGUR WHEAT	¼	CUP OLIVE OIL
1½	CUPS BOILING WATER	¼	CUP LEMON JUICE
¼	CUP FRESH CHOPPED MINT OR 2 TABLESPOONS DRY MINT	1	TEASPOON SALT
¼	CUP CHOPPED GREEN ONIONS	¼	TEASPOON GARLIC POWDER
2	TABLESPOONS CHOPPED FRESH PARSLEY	½	TEASPOON DRIED OREGANO LEAVES
2	LARGE TOMATOES, CHOPPED	⅛	TEASPOON CAYENNE PEPPER

In a large bowl pour the boiling water over the bulgur wheat, and allow it to stand for 1 to 1½ hours until light and fluffy. Drain well. Add the mint, onion, parsley, and tomato, and toss lightly. In a jar mix together the olive oil, lemon juice, salt, garlic powder, oregano, and cayenne pepper, and shake well. Pour the oil mixture over the bulgur and stir well. Refrigerate for several hours prior to serving.

Use romaine lettuce leaves as scoops for the tabbouleh, holding a filled lettuce leaf crimped between the first 3 fingers.

YIELDS 6 SERVINGS.

MINT TEA
★★★★★

In Morocco, this tea is prepared in a special teapot. After it has brewed for a bit, it is poured back and forth between the serving glass and the teapot. This technique is said to improve the brewing process. Finally, when brewed to perfection, the tea is poured into serving glasses from a height of 1 to 2 feet.

1	TABLESPOON PLUS 1 TEASPOON CHINESE GREEN TEA		ADDITIONAL SPRIGS FOR GARNISH
2	MEDIUM BUNCHES OF FRESH MINT, STEMS DISCARDED	10	SUGAR CUBES

Bring a kettle of water to a boil. In a large teapot cover the green tea with 1 cup of boiling water to rinse the tea and warm the pot. Quickly drain off the water without discarding the tea. Return the remaining water to a rolling boil.

Pack the mint leaves and sugar cubes into the teapot. Add approximately 4 cups of the boiling water. Cover and steep for about 5 minutes.

Pour the tea into glasses or cups garnished with mint sprigs and serve warm or cold.

YIELDS 6 SERVINGS.

MOROCCAN WATERMELON COOLER
★★★★★

4	CUPS WATERMELON JUICE	2	TABLESPOONS LIGHTLY PACKED FRESH MINT LEAVES, RINSED
½	TEASPOON ORANGE-FLOWER WATER		

Obtain the juice from a watermelon by cutting the fruit from the rind; cut into 1-inch chunks, removing the seeds, and process in the blender in batches until smooth. Pour through a fine strainer into a pitcher. Return the juice to the blender. Add the orange water and mint leaves, and process until the mint is minced. Pour into tall, ice-filled glasses and garnish with fresh mint leaves.

YIELDS 4 SERVINGS.

RICE WITH ALMONDS, RAISINS, AND SAFFRON
★★★★★

4	CUPS LONG GRAIN RICE	¾	CUP FINELY CHOPPED ONION
2¼	CUPS CHICKEN BROTH	¼	TEASPOON SAFFRON
1	TABLESPOON OLIVE OIL	¼	TEASPOON TURMERIC
1¼	TEASPOONS SALT	½	CUP PLUS 2 TABLESPOONS SLICED ALMONDS, TOASTED
1¼	TEASPOONS WHITE PEPPER		
2	TABLESPOONS SNIPPED FRESH CHIVES	½	CUP PLUS 2 TABLESPOONS PARBOILED YELLOW RAISINS

In a medium saucepan over high heat bring the broth to a boil. When the water boils, remove the pan from the burner and stir in rice and seasonings. Cover and bake in a pre-heated 350°F oven for 15 minutes.

Remove from the oven; allow to rest for 5 minutes, but do not uncover. Prior to serving, fluff the rice, add the almonds and raisins, and sprinkle with snipped chives.

YIELDS 6 TO 8 SERVINGS.

THE MILITARY WIVES' COOKBOOK

BAKLAVA
★★★★★

More than two thousand women served in North Africa alone. From North Africa, these women were sent to Italy to serve with the 5th Army.

FOR THE SYRUP:

3	CUPS SUGAR
2	CUPS WATER
1	TABLESPOON LEMON JUICE
1	TABLESPOON ROSE WATER

FOR THE PASTRY:

3	POUNDS PISTACHIO MEATS, COARSELY GROUND
½	CUP SUGAR
2	TABLESPOONS ROSE WATER
2	POUNDS UNSALTED BUTTER, MELTED
2	POUNDS PHYLLO DOUGH SHEETS

To make the syrup, in a small saucepan over medium-high heat combine the sugar and water; bring to a boil and continue to boil for 10 minutes. Add the lemon juice, remove the pan from the heat, and allow to cool. Add the rose water and refrigerate for at least 1 hour. The mixture should be very cold prior to use.

In a medium bowl mix the pistachios with the sugar and rose water; set aside. Grease a large baking sheet with butter. Place the phyllo sheets in the pan, one layer at a time. Brush each with melted butter before adding the next. Continue this process until 1 pound of the phyllo has been used. Fold in the nut mixture and spread evenly over the phyllo. Repeat the phyllo dough procedure until all the leaves have been used. Using a very sharp knife, cut the baklava into diamonds. Bake in a preheated 350°F oven for 1½ to 2 hours. Remove from the oven and immediately spoon syrup evenly over the baklava.

YIELDS 8 TO 10 SERVINGS.

"WINDS OF WAR"

"Then came December 7th and 8th, '41, and a succession of days and events which changed the world. . . . The very day war was declared was the day on which Bruce was advanced from the rank of aviation cadet to that of second lieutenant. We did not want ours to be a 'war marriage' in one sense of the word— good only for the duration. . . . We wanted it to be an enduring thing, built on the strong foundation of experiences shared together. Experiences based on our combined efforts to build a home and raise a family. Our forefathers faced a future more uncertain than ours with courage. They continued to marry and build families which are now part of the foundation of our country. If they hadn't faith in the future, how much more the Revolution, Civil War, and World War I would have slowed down our progress! Those who lose that faith lose the very thing for which wars were fought. Facing the future together, whatever is to come was the decision we finally made. . . . And we have never regretted our choice."

Betty Utley St. John

On the homefront, wives, especially those following soldiers who were part of the new Army Air Corps, faced all the challenges of pioneering a new frontier. . . . Like Martha, Libbie, and all those who went before them, they chose to share their lives with men committed to serving and protecting their country.

Dear People:
Yesterday mark[ed] the end of our first week together. . . . Have been busy as a bee lately trying to become a model housewife. . . . The Army, however, calls for much more versatility and resourcefulness than civilian life, and I've much to learn before I can be considered a successful Army wife. . . . I have to be a manager, buyer, dietitian, cook, financier, hostess, . . . interior decorator, good-will ambassador, mind reader, . . . professional entertainer, experienced packer and modern gypsy. . . . It is a big order. Wish me luck with it.

Loving you all
Betty

Often following their husbands to desolate training locations without established base housing, they confronted shortages in suitable housing and other requirements for creating comfortable homes for themselves and their spouses. Families sometimes doubled up. Never complaining, they relied on their own ingenuity to create homes in the most desolate of places.

Dear People:
In Army terms, Blythe is a splinter "town," . . . a post of hastily constructed barracks and not much else. . . . The Army quarters for an officer usually consists of a six or seven room "post" house, which is usually partially furnished with G.I. [government issued] desks, chairs, tables and dining, kitchen,

and bedroom sets. . . . Splinter towns, lacking all the above-mentioned features, make it necessary for the officers to find homes off the base."

Missing You
Betty

Darlings:—
Believe it or not we have found TWO places in which to live! . . . The tourist court bungalow consists of one bedroom, a combination bedroom–living room, a small kitchen and a bath. It is a bit cramped for two couples and the rent is enough to make your hair stand on end, but it is a good stopping place until we can move to the ranch. It has two large bedrooms, a den, big closets and a screened porch. But it is old and ram-shacklely, dirty, . . . and boasts of neither running water, electricity, telephone, nor any other modern conveniences. [The deserted ranch belongs to a large-scale rancher] who has offered it to us "rent free" in exchange for fixing it up. Today pioneers Marshall* and St. John practically bought out the town's supply of odds and ends. . . . Tomorrow we are going to work—ascrubbing and acleaning."

Our love to you all
Betty

* No relation to Katherine Tupper Marshall.

Dear Folks:—
Dick arrived from Kelly Field yesterday to find three anxious people and a new Captaincy awaiting him. 'Twas very exciting to be at the base and see the planes buzz the field, peel off, and land . . . Last evening we took him down to the ranch to show off our house, our work, our plans, our shady house. . . .

Gertie and I are quite disappointed . . . However, our better judgment tells us that Bruce and Dick are right. The ranch is too far . . . from the field for the boys, and too primitive for all of us. In a couple of weeks the novelty of fancying ourselves pioneers would have worn off and there we'd be—stranded in a house with no water. No electricity. No phone. No gas. No anything, except bees and a whitewashed outhouse!

An Idyllic Italian Afternoon

★ ★ ★ ★ ★

In Italy, female soldiers handled communications. While serving with the Fifth Army they moved all over Italy, gaining the respect of their fellow soldiers as they trudged through mud, lived in tents, and dove for the cover of foxholes during the Anzio air raids.

SPAGHETTI ALLE VONGOLE

ITALIAN GARDEN SALAD

ITALIAN BREAD

ITALIAN CRÈME CAKE

SPAGHETTI ALLE VONGOLE
(SPAGHETTI WITH CLAM SAUCE)
★★★★★

Army nurses waded ashore at Anzio within five days of the invasion. During the Anzio air campaign, six Army nurses lost their lives during the bombing and strafing of the tented hospital area. Four of those nurses who survived were awarded Silver Stars for extraordinary courage under fire.

⅓	CUP VIRGIN OLIVE OIL	1	POUND SPAGHETTI
3	TO 4 CLOVES GARLIC, CRUSHED	½	CUP DRY WHITE WINE
1	LARGE ONION, CHOPPED	¼	TEASPOON CRUSHED RED PEPPER (OPTIONAL)
4	7-OUNCE CANS MINCED CLAMS, DRAINED	⅓	CUP MINCED FRESH PARSLEY
¼	CUP BOTTLE CLAM JUICE		

In a large saucepan heat the oil over medium-high heat. Add the onion and garlic, reduce the heat to medium, and stir continuously until the onion is transparent. Add the clam juice. Reduce the heat to low and continue to cook for an additional 20 minutes. While the sauce is simmering, cook the pasta to al dente. One minute prior to the end of the sauce's cooking time, add the clams, wine, red pepper, and parsley; stir well.

Note: Although fresh is best, if you find yourself on the "frontier" far from fresh seafood, this is a great recipe.

YIELDS 6 SERVINGS.

ITALIAN GARDEN SALAD
★★★★★

On August 5, 1943, the Women Airforce Service Pilot (WASP) was formed. They ferried military aircraft, flight-tested planes, towed targets, and transported cargo and personnel. More than 1,070 women served; 38 were killed in plane crashes while serving.

1	CLOVE GARLIC, CRUSHED	5	PLUM TOMATOES, SLICED
8	CUPS MIXED SALAD GREENS (CURLY ENDIVE, ROMAINE, RADICCHIO, ETC., ABOUT 5 OUNCES)	1	SMALL BERMUDA ONION, SLICED THIN
		1	TABLESPOON LEMON JUICE
2	TABLESPOONS CHOPPED FRESH BASIL	¼	CUP OLIVE OIL

Rub a serving bowl with the crushed garlic. Add the salad greens, tomatoes, and onion. In a separate container combine the olive oil and lemon juice; mix well and dress the salad. Gently toss and evenly distribute the ingredients. Cover the bowl and refrigerate.

YIELDS 6 SERVINGS.

"Then in 1942, bang! The war started. . . . My sister and I were together for a few days, getting ready to send our husbands off to war and wondering how to do it. Mother had already sent father [General George S. Patton] off, and as I looked at all the young anxious faces of our friends, I said to my sister, "Where is all the Old Army? Do you remember how it was when we were kids?" (All the older wives helped the younger wives, had such good advice, and knew how to cope with every situation.) My sister said, 'I guess we're the Old Army now; it's up to us.'" [Mrs. Ruth Ellen Patton Totten, widow of Major General James W. Totten]

Dear Family:—
Since my marriage and, shall we say, my induction into the Army, I have had all sorts of hints and suggestions handed to me regarding what and how to do this 'n' that. . . . The fact that our country is at war now makes obsolete many of the old Army customs, hereto "musts" in post etiquette. . . .

One custom that is still in the lead, however, is that of newlyweds making a formal call on the Post C.O. and his wife. . . . Last night we finally pulled ourselves together and warmed up our feet enough to get us over to the post C.O.'s house. 'Twas quite a problem deciding which one of us would knock on the door, but we managed to come to a decision without any casualties.

Colonel and Mrs. Lee were both very gracious and put us completely at ease. . . . Save for the faux pas of having left no [calling] cards, we feel that our first Army social call went quite well.

No other news
Betty

PICNICKING IN THE PARK.

Betty's problems with formal calls and official Army protocol were minor compared to those experienced by Katherine Tupper Marshall. Listen as she recounts her experiences, especially those experienced in prewar Washington, D.C.

"The Army had its code—a very rigid one. . . . Sunday afternoon was the favorite time for the Army to call." Traditional Army courtesy calls require a new officer arriving to the post to call on each of his colleagues and leave his card. Within ten days, these officers were required to reciprocate the call, leaving their own card. Calls involving only the wives occurred during an "At Home" day. Just as in the days of Abigail Adams, this type of call was not expected to last more than fifteen minutes. The Senior wife established a day when she would be at home and would open her house to receive callers. The calls next described by Mrs. Marshall were joint calls involving the military member and their spouse. Again, these calls were not expected to exceed fifteen minutes. *"After two months of receiving capacity houses, we needed recreation and fresh air, so each Sunday we would make for the park with a picnic lunch. Coming back late, invariably we would find at the front door a snowdrift of [calling] cards. I had heard army wives on Posts count how many calls they had gotten off their list on Sundays when they knew the officers would be out, so this was not as unsociable as it sounds. The Code was kept, they had made their gesture and we enjoyed a few hours of peace in the park.*

"Of course I had heard stories of hostesses who, through ignorance of established customs, had made blunders embarrassing to them and amusing to the rest of official Washington. . . . At that time I knew as little about the demands of official life in Washington as I had of Army traditions and customs when I arrived at Fort Benning. . . . Protocol was not so perplexing for it was a cut and dried code, but there were many unwritten rules and customs, even more hide-bound. In official [Washington] your first duty was to leave your card at the White House. The wives of cabinet members each had her day At Home, and you were expected to call at least once during the season—on those days only and the call must be no longer than fifteen minutes. That winter while George was concerned with great affairs I had my hands full with the smaller ones. By Christmas I had made all my official calls and had received hundreds of Army callers at home."

Saludos from Spain

★ ★ ★ ★ ★

PAELLA VALENCIANA
SALAD (SEE INDEX FOR CHOICES)
CRUSTY BREAD
TIRAMISU

PAELLA VALENCIANA
★★★★★

⅔	CUP OLIVE OIL, DIVIDED	2	LOBSTERS, CUT UP IN SHELL
1	1½- TO 2-POUND CHICKEN, SECTIONED	12	FRESH STEAMING CLAMS
½	POUND PORK TENDERLOIN, CUBED (1 INCH)	18	SHRIMP, SHELLED
1 ½	CUPS CHORIZO, SLICED (1 INCH)	6	ARTICHOKE HEARTS (CANNED)
¼	CUP CHOPPED ONION	1	CUP FROZEN PEAS, THAWED AND DRAINED
4	CLOVES GARLIC, MINCED	1	TEASPOON PAPRIKA
4	LARGE TOMATOES, SEEDED AND CHOPPED	2	CUPS RICE
3	RED PEPPERS, PEELED AND SEEDED	4	CUPS CHICKEN BROTH
½	CUP DICED PIMIENTO	1	BOUILLON CUBE
½	POUND SQUID, CLEANED AND SLICED INTO RINGS (OPTIONAL)	¾	TEASPOON SAFFRON, CRUSHED
			SALT AND PEPPER

In a large saucepan heat ½ cup of olive oil. Add the chicken, pork, and sausage, and fry for 10 minutes. Add the onion and garlic, stir and cook an additional 2 minutes. Add the tomatoes and red peppers; stir and add the squid, lobster, clams in their shells, and shrimp. Simmer an additional 5 minutes. In a paella pan heat the remaining olive oil over medium-high heat and sauté the rice, stirring constantly and taking care that it does not burn. When the rice is light brown, add the meat and fish mixture. Measure any liquid remaining in the pan and add a sufficient amount of chicken broth to make 4 cups. Add the remaining ingredients and bring to a boil. Reduce the heat to medium and cook uncovered for 20 minutes. When the cooking is complete, remove the pan from the heat and allow to stand for 20 minutes prior to serving. Garnish with slices of lemon.

YIELDS 8 TO 10 SERVINGS.

KEEPING THE PEACE

"From Christmas 1940 it became apparent to me that my number one great objective must be to keep my quarters Number 1 at Fort Myer a place of peace and quiet, a sanctuary for my husband where he could rest and relax and gather strength from the time he entered his home in the evening until he had to face the demands of the next day. There were few callers received and we accepted practically no social invitations. . . . From the time he got up in the morning until we retired at 9:00 in the evening, as far as home was concerned, there was to be no confusion, no household irritations. This I say was my objective—whether I reached it or not was another matter. . . .

"When the telephone rang each day at luncheon time and word was received that the General had left his office, it was as though an electric switch had made contact through the house, each member of the staff hurrying to get his part done. When George came through the door all was serene and luncheon was immediately served to however many he had brought with him,—just as if the number of guests had been known for weeks. This of course was the work of his secretary [who] would let us know the number of probable guests. . . . 'There will be three,' then, later, 'No four,' or 'Luncheon for two,' or 'General Marshall will be detained at the White House.' . . . . This is maddening to the average housekeeper but after you get used to uncertainty it ceases to be uncertain; you expect it and know exactly what to do. . . .

"So much for the domestic side of the picture in 1941. As for the official side, it was a case of preparing the country for war. It was necessary now that he have the funds and the authority to train an ever-expanding Army." [Katherine Tupper Marshall]

"Maneuvers began Monday. . . . And just what are maneuvers? Well, frankly I don't know much about them myself except that there are realistic war games held as part of the desert training here. . . . The principal thing about maneuvers, as far as the wives are concerned, is that there is no longer any schedule possible for any day. . . . Lunches and dinners are uncertain affairs. Any gal who starts her cooking before seeing the whites of her husband's eyes is doomed to serve a burned meal. I know, because I tried it. Now Pam and I just wait at the window with pots and pans in one hand, food in the other, and matches in our teeth.

Loving you all
Betty"

"Dearest Mom and Dad, George and Granny;—
The people for whom I feel sorry are not ourselves. They are the tank corps men, who have been thicker than flies hereabout since the start of maneuvers. They live and work all day under adverse conditions and then on nights and weekends . . . they have no homes to which they can go.
. . . Actually I feel more strongly each day that Bruce and I are lucky merely to be together. Despite every difficulty and inconvenience of this desert life, I still wouldn't trade anything for the chance to be with my honey!

Best love and luck, more soon
Betty"

SERVING TOGETHER.

Postcards from France: Remember Rouen

★ ★ ★ ★ ★

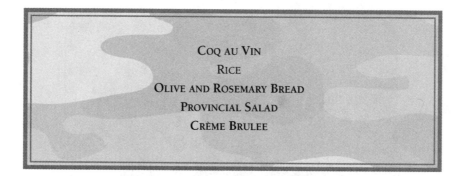

COQ AU VIN

RICE

OLIVE AND ROSEMARY BREAD

PROVINCIAL SALAD

CRÈME BRULEE

COQ AU VIN
★★★★★

While serving in France, "No mail, low morale" was the motto of the 6888th Central Postal Directory Battalion. Commanded by Major Charity Adams Earley, the women of the 6888th were the only black WACs to serve overseas during World War II.

1	3-POUND CHICKEN (CUT INTO SERVING PIECES)	1	BAY LEAF
½	CUP ALL-PURPOSE FLOUR	½	TEASPOON DRIED THYME
½	TEASPOON GROUND NUTMEG	½	TEASPOON DRIED ROSEMARY, CRUSHED
1	TEASPOON SALT	1	TABLESPOON ALL-PURPOSE FLOUR
¼	CUP BACON DRIPPINGS	1	CUP CHOPPED HAM
2	TABLESPOONS BUTTER	1½	CUPS DRY RED WINE, PREFERABLY BURGUNDY
1	CUP DICED ONIONS	½	CUP CHICKEN BROTH
5	SLICES BACON, DICED	18	SMALL WHITE ONIONS, FRESH OR FROZEN (PEELED)
3	CLOVES GARLIC, MINCED	1½	CUPS BABY CARROTS, FRESH OR FROZEN
¼	CUP WARM COGNAC	18	MUSHROOM CAPS

Wash the chicken thoroughly under cold running water and set aside in a colander to drain. In a shallow bowl combine the flour, nutmeg, and salt. Use this mixture to dredge the chicken, shaking off the excess flour. Repeat the process until all chicken pieces are coated. In a large casserole pan, brown the chicken in bacon drippings and butter until the chicken is golden on all sides. Remove the chicken from the pan. Add the onion, bacon, and garlic and sauté over medium heat until transparent. Return the chicken to the casserole, cover with cognac, and set aflame. Sprinkle with flour. Add the bay leaf, thyme, rosemary, and ham, stir, and add the wine and chicken broth. Cover and simmer gently for 45 minutes or until the chicken is fork-tender.

Add the carrots during the last 15 minutes of cooking time. Shortly before serving, add the onions and mushrooms. At this point the gravy should be sufficiently thick to coat the back of a spoon. However, if necessary, thicken gravy by combining ¼ cup of flour with ¼ cup of chicken broth. Slowly stir the mixture into the sauce and continue to cook until thickened to taste. Serve hot over rice.

YIELDS 4 TO 6 SERVINGS.

OLIVE OIL AND ROSEMARY BREAD
★ ★ ★ ★ ★

Arriving in England in 1945 during the latter part of January, the 6888th Central Postal Directory moved to Rouen, France, in May 1945.

1½	CUPS WARM WATER	3	TABLESPOONS OLIVE OIL
2	ENVELOPES DRY YEAST	1	TABLESPOON DRIED ROSEMARY, CRUSHED
1	TABLESPOON SUGAR	1½	TEASPOONS SALT
5	CUPS BREAD FLOUR		

In a large bowl mix together the water, yeast and sugar. Add 1¼ cups of the flour. Mix and allow to stand for 1 hour at room temperature.

Add the olive oil, rosemary, and salt to the yeast mixture and mix well. Add enough of the remaining flour to form a soft dough. Turn out onto a floured surface and knead until the dough is smooth and elastic, approximately 8 minutes. Add more flour if the dough is sticky. However, be careful not to knead too much or the dough will be tough. Place the dough in a large oiled bowl and turn the dough to coat. Cover the bowl and allow it to rise in a warm, draft-free area until doubled, approximately 1 hour.

Punch down the dough and knead until smooth. Divide and form each half into a smooth ball. Place the balls on a lightly floured baking sheet with sufficient space to allow for rising. Flatten each ball slightly to form a flat bottom on the bread. Cover each round of bread with a dry tea towel. Allow the bread to rise in a draft-free area until almost doubled in volume, approximately 1 hour.

Place the bread in a preheated 400°F oven and bake for approximately 35 to 40 minutes or until brown and the loaves sound hollow when tapped on the bottom. Set aside on racks to cool. Serve with flavored or plain olive oil.

Note: The fragrance of this bread will drive arriving guests to distraction. If at all possible, keep them from the kitchen or there will be none left for dinner.

YIELDS 2 LOAVES.

"*Sunday, December 7, 1941*

Sunday we had a late breakfast . . . in my room, George eating on a tray beside my bed. . . . [An] urgent telephone call came from the War Department. George bathed hurriedly and left for the War Department. That was the morning of December 7, 1941. . . . The Japanese attack on Pearl harbor had galvanized and welded a Nation. War had been declared by Germany and Italy. As the winter advanced there was no time for riding or any other outdoor exercise during the day, so when George

PROVINCIAL SALAD
★ ★ ★ ★ ★

They moved to Paris in October 1945. Rotating eight-hour shifts, seven days a week, the overwhelming duty of the 6888th Central Postal Directory was to censor the mail and get it to the front-lines, posthaste. The women broke all previous records!

8	CUPS MIXED SALAD GREENS (CURLY ENDIVE, ROMAINE, RADICCHIO, ETC., ABOUT 5 OUNCES)
2	CLOVES GARLIC, CRUSHED
1	CAN ARTICHOKES, DRAINED (RESERVE LIQUID)
1	CAN HEARTS OF PALM, DRAINED (RESERVE LIQUID)
1	6-OUNCE CAN PITTED BLACK OLIVES, DRAINED (RESERVE LIQUID)
15	CHERRY TOMATOES, HALVED
3	GREEN ONIONS, SLICED THIN
¾	CUP FETA CHEESE, DIVIDED
2	TABLESPOONS LEMON JUICE
⅓	CUP OLIVE OIL

Rub a serving bowl with crushed garlic. Add the salad greens. Cut the artichoke hearts in half, cut the hearts of palm into ½-inch slices, and halve the olives before adding to the bowl. Add the tomatoes, green onion, and half of the feta. Gently toss and evenly distribute the ingredients. Cover the bowl and refrigerate. Combine ¼ cup of reserved artichoke liquid, ¼ cup of the reserved hearts of palm juice, and ¼ cup of the reserved olive juice with the lemon juice and olive oil. Shake well. Dress the salad just prior to serving. Garnish with the remaining feta.

YIELDS 6 TO 8 SERVINGS.

---

came home in his car at twilight I would have my hat on in readiness and we would . . . take a brisk walk before dinner.

"On these daily walks I would talk little, for I was listening to a man steeling himself to carry a burden so tremendous in magnitude . . . that it was difficult to comprehend how one man could carry it alone.

"Early in August my youngest son, Allen was about to leave for Africa as a tank officer replacement in the 1st Armored Division. He and Madge, his wife, arrived from Fire Island where they had spent Allen's leave. . . . We went in for dinner in high spirits. For that dinner, I had provided all the things Allen liked most. The meal was topped off by a bottle of fine Champagne, which had been given to my husband in Africa. Originally it had been taken from the French by the Germans, then captured from the Germans by the British, and finally presented to the Chief of Staff of the American Army. It was an excellent vintage year and George made a truly wonderful toast for Allen's success. . . . The next day he flew off to England on his way to the front." [Katherine Tupper Marshall]

CRÈME BRULEE
★★★★★

"Our preparation was intense . . . gas mask drills, obstacle course drills . . . and close order drill. I stressed the necessity for our unit to be the best WAC unit ever sent into a foreign theater." [Major Charity Adams Early]

2	CUPS HEAVY CREAM	1½	TABLESPOONS VANILLA EXTRACT
6	SMALL EGG YOLKS	½	CUP PACKED BROWN SUGAR
½	CUP SUGAR		RASPBERRIES AND OR FRESH MINT SPRIGS FOR GARNISH

Preheat the oven to 275°F. In a large bowl, combine the first four ingredients and whisk together until sugar dissolves and mixture reaches a smooth consistency. Pour the mixture into five 5 x 1-inch ovenproof custard ramekins. Prepare a water bath for the custard-filled ramekins. Begin by setting the filled ramekins into an ovenproof baking pan. Carefully fill pan with water only to the custard line, making sure not to get water into the custard. Bake 45 to 50 minutes or until the custard is almost set. (Allow 15 or 20 minutes more cooking time for 4 x 2-inch custard ramekins.)

When the custard is almost set, remove the pan from the oven; remove the ramekins from the water bath and refrigerate overnight. Sprinkle evenly with 1½ tablespoons of brown sugar. Return to a water bath and broil not more than 5-inches from heat source (keep oven door open and watch carefully to prevent burning) until sugar melts. Remove from the oven and allow the sugar to harden before serving.

YIELDS 5 SERVINGS.

Guten Tag from Germany

★ ★ ★ ★ ★

More than eight thousand WACs served in the Eastern Theatre Operations, including England, Scotland, Wales, and Germany.

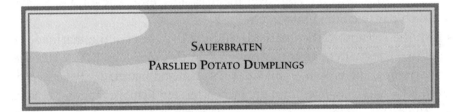

SAUERBRATEN
PARSLIED POTATO DUMPLINGS

SAUERBRATEN
★ ★ ★ ★ ★

1	4- TO 5-POUND EYE OF ROUND ROAST	2	TABLESPOONS DARK BROWN SUGAR
FOR THE MARINADE:		2	TEASPOONS PICKLING SPICE
1	TABLESPOON DRY MUSTARD	2	CUPS WATER
1	BAY LEAF	1	BEEF BOUILLON CUBE
1	TEASPOON WHOLE BLACK PEPPER	2	CUPS RED WINE VINEGAR
1 ½	TEASPOONS SALT		
1 ½	TEASPOONS POULTRY SEASONING	2	TABLESPOONS SHORTENING
½	TEASPOON TARRAGON LEAVES		FLOUR
½	TEASPOON MINCED GARLIC	½	CUP SOUR CREAM
¼	CUP MINCED ONIONS		

Wash the meat under cold running water and pat dry. Place in a nonreactive bowl and set aside. In a large saucepan combine the mustard, water, bay leaf, pepper, salt, poultry seasoning, tarrragon, garlic, minced onion, brown sugar, pickling spice, 2 cups of water, bouillon cube, and vinegar to make a marinade; heat the marinade over medium-high heat but do not bring to a boil. Pour over the roast and refrigerate for 3 to 4 days. Turn at least once each day to ensure uniform coverage.

Remove the roast from the marinade and pat dry; reserve the marinade. Place the shortening in a Dutch oven. Heat to rippling over medium-high heat. Place the roast in the hot shortening and brown on all sides. Pour in the marinade. Bake in a preheated 350°F oven for 3 to 3½ hours or until the meat is tender. Remove the roast to a warm platter. Strain the gravy and thicken with flour; blending in 1⅓ tablespoons of flour for each cup of pan juices. Stir in sour cream if desired and serve with roast and potato dumplings.

YIELDS 6 TO 8 SERVINGS.

PARSLIED POTATO DUMPLINGS
★★★★★

Toward the end of the war, more than eight thousand women were serving in the European Theater. WACs could be found stationed in cities like Berlin, Frankfurt, Wiesbaden, and Heidelberg.

7	MEDIUM BAKING POTATOES, BOILED	2	TABLESPOONS MINCED PARSLEY
2	SLICES WHITE BREAD, CRUSTS REMOVED	½	TEASPOON GROUND NUTMEG
2½	TABLESPOONS BUTTER	⅔	CUPS ALL-PURPOSE FLOUR, SIFTED
1	LARGE EGG, WELL BEATEN	¼	CUP CORNSTARCH
2	TEASPOONS SALT		

Remove the skins from the baked potatoes and mash. Refrigerate uncovered for a minimum of 5 to 6 hours or overnight.

Cut the bread into ½-inch squares. In a skillet melt the butter and sauté the bread until golden; remove from the saucepan and place on a paper towel-lined plate to drain. Stir the egg, salt, parsley, and nutmeg into potatoes; add the flour and cornstarch. Shape the potato mixture into 2-inch balls. Press a bread cube into the center of each dumpling. Bring 2 quarts of salted water to a boil; drop several dumplings into the boiling water, taking care not to crowd. Continue to boil uncovered for 5 additional minutes. Remove the dumplings from the pot with a slotted spoon and drain well before serving.

YIELDS 6 TO 8 SERVINGS.

"That Christmas my grandson James Winn, or Jimmy as we call him, was old enough to know that Santa Claus was coming. He would call up the chimney constantly and was in a great state of excitement. . . . Inside the house lights were all ablaze and the fires crackling. . . . We were so busy with Christmas inside the house that we did not hear what was going on outside until the door was flung open and Molly and her husband walked in. My son-in-law had been given a few weeks leave to spend Christmas at home." [Katherine Tupper Marshall]

Rising Sun Breakfast in Japan

✯ ✯ ✯ ✯ ✯

MISO SOUP

SUSHI RICE

MAKI-SUSHI

AMAZU SHOGA

GRILLED SALMON

PICKLED VEGETABLES

LAVER SPINACH

MISO SOUP (MISO-SHIRU)
★★★★★

"As the war escalated in the Pacific, the women were sent 'over there' as well." [*Ensign Jane Kendeigh, USNR, was the first Navy flight nurse to reach Iwo Jima 9 March 1945*]

1½ OUNCES NIBOSHI, AVAILABLE AT MOST ASIAN FOOD STORES	1 CUP DICED TOFU
5 CUPS WATER	½ CUP LOOSELY PACKED SPINACH, TORN
½ CUP SOYBEAN PASTE (MISO), AVAILABLE AT ASIAN FOOD STORES	½ CUP GREEN ONIONS, SLICED THIN (INCLUDE TOPS)
	½ TEASPOON AJI-NO-MOTO, AVAILABLE AT ASIAN FOOD STORES

Niboshi are small sardines which have been boiled, roasted, and dried. Quickly rinse the niboshi under cold water; place in a saucepan with 5 cups of water and bring to a boil. Boil for 10 minutes; remove from the heat and reserve the broth by straining the niboshi through gauze; discard the niboshi. Return the broth to the saucepan and bring to a boil. Add the miso; stir well; add the remaining ingredients and boil an additional minute or two. Remove from the heat and serve immediately.

YIELDS 4 SERVINGS.

CLASSROOM INSTRUCTION, SHEPPARD FIELD, TEXAS, 1943;
AT THE LEFT IS MY FATHER, SMSGT JOHN G. QUICK, USAF.

SUSHI RICE

★★★★★

Japanese-American WACs trained by the Military Intelligence Service served as written language translators, interrogators, and interpreters.

2	CUPS UNCOOKED WHITE RICE (SUCH AS CALROSE OR TAMANISHIKI)	2	TABLESPOONS SAKI
4½	CUPS WATER	3	TABLESPOONS SUGAR
4	TABLESPOONS RICE VINEGAR	1	TABLESPOON SALT

One hour before preparation, wash the rice in cold water. (During packaging, rice is coated with cornstarch.) Place the rice in a pot and swirl it with your hand. The water will become cloudy as the starch separates from the rice. Pour off the cloudy water and repeat process until the water is clear. Transfer the rice to a fine mesh colander and drain before cooking. After the rice has completely drained, place 4½ cups water in a 2-quart saucepan, transfer the rice to the pot, and bring to a boil over high heat. Immediately reduce the heat to low, add the saki, and cover the saucepan. Cook for 17 minutes.

At the end of the cooking period, without removing the lid, increase the heat to high for 30 seconds to "dry" the rice. Remove the saucepan from the heat and cover the pot with a clean tea towel; allow to rest for 10 minutes before placing the rice in a nonreactive bowl. In a separate bowl combine the salt, vinegar, and sugar. Stir through the rice. To achieve the shiny effect of sushi rice, you must mix the rice and vinegar quickly while simultaneously fanning the rice to bring it to room temperature. Set the rice aside for use in making the various types of sushi.

YIELDS 8 SERVINGS.

WE STAND BY YOU.

THE MILITARY WIVES' COOKBOOK

MAKI-SUSHI
(ROLLED SUSHI)
★ ★ ★ ★ ★

Some of these Japanese-American WACs had been held in American internment camps. Despite this, when their country called, they answered and reported for American military duty at General Headquarters, Tokyo.

2	CUPS COOKED SUSHI RICE
	DRIED SEAWEED (NORI)
3	TABLESPOONS LITE KIKKOMAN SOY SAUCE
1	TABLESPOON SUGAR
½	CUP WATER
½	SMALL CUCUMBER, PEELED, SEEDED AND JULIENNED (CUT TO LENGTH OF NORI)
	WASABI (GREEN HORSERADISH PASTE AVAILABLE AT ASIAN FOOD STORES)

⅓ CUP TOASTED SESAME SEEDS

COMBINATION CHOICES:

A. 3 OUNCES SMOKED SALMON (LOX), CUCUMBER, AVOCADO, PICKLED GINGER

B. 8 TO 10 MEDIUM SHRIMP, PEELED AND BOILED, OR IMITATION CRABMEAT, JULIENNED DAIKON RADISH.

C. CUCUMBER, AVOCADO, ¼ CUP MINCED CILANTRO

Take 1 sheet of the dried seaweed (nori) and crisp it over a dry medium-hot saucepan for about 15 seconds, a few seconds on each side (or follow package directions). Lay it on a bamboo mat (if available), approximately ½-inch from the top of the mat. Spoon the rice over the surface, about ⅛-inch thick, all the way around to the shortest edges, leaving about ½ inch free of rice at the top. Sprinkle approximately 1 tablespoon of toasted sesame evenly across surface of rice. Place a layer of smoked salmon (or choice of other filling) about 1½ inches wide down the length of rice. Dab a very small amount of wasabi on the salmon (optional), then add a cucumber strip, and a line of avocado, followed by a line of pickled ginger (optional, may skip in favor of using as a garnish at time sushi is served). Starting at the bottom of the mat, roll up jelly-roll fashion in the bamboo mat (if available) and roll gently with both hands. Do not roll too tightly or the rice will become an unappetizing paste. Remove the maki-sushi from the mat and slice into 6 pieces for regular rolls or 4 pieces for large rolls. For ease in cutting, dip the knife in the vinegar-water. Continue in this fashion, making a variety of rolled sushi using the combinations listed above, or combinations of your own design.

YIELDS 4 TO 6 SERVINGS.

AMAZU SHOGA
(PICKLED GINGER)
★ ★ ★ ★ ★

2	CUPS WATER	⅓	CUP RICE VINEGAR
⅓	CUP FRESH GINGER, SCRAPED AND SHAVED PAPER THIN	¼	CUP SUGAR
		¼	TEASPOON SALT

In a small saucepan bring the water to a boil. Immerse the ginger and blanche for 30 seconds. Drain the ginger, set aside, and allow to cool. In a small airtight container combine the rice vinegar, sugar, and salt. Add the cooled ginger and refrigerate. Pickled ginger is ready for use within 24 hours and can be kept refrigerated for several weeks.

MAKES ABOUT 1 CUP.

LETTERS HOME

"On March 26th I received the following radio from my son Clifton in Italy: 'My love and greetings on Mother's Day.' From Allen a letter was received: 'My men and I have permission to be relieved after 28 days on the front. I have permission to visit Clifton. We are only seven miles apart. . . .'

"My Easter letter from Allen said: 'Dearest Mum: I had the greatest surprise—a box was delivered to me and when I opened it up I had never seen so many good things to eat and read. I am trying to get a ride to Clifton to give him his share.' His letter ended: 'God did make beautiful things when he made mothers.'

"The morning before Decoration Day, we received letters from our two sons. They had enjoyed three wonderful days together after the fighting at Cassio and before Allen left with the first Armored Division for Anzio Beachhead. Clifton had just returned from the beachhead and they had met in passing and celebrated together. The cry was now, 'On to Rome.' Clifton said, 'The war looks good from here, both in Germany and Japan.'

"When George left for his office that morning there was a song in my heart. An hour later as I stood at the window in my room, I turned to see my husband in the doorway. He came in, closing the door behind him, and told me Allen had given his life that morning in a tank battle on the road to Rome. . . . I had only one thought—that I must get to Madge, Allen's wife." [Katherine Tupper Marshall]

Classic Korean Barbecue

★ ★ ★ ★ ★

When the Korean Communists crossed the 38th parallel, President Truman ordered American troops into South Korea for what was termed a "limited war" and within a few days the Army Nurse Corps was also "over there."

YAKI MANDU
BULKOKI
STICKY RICE
SOOK CHOO NA MOOL

YAKI MANDU
(KOREAN EGG ROLLS)
★★★★★

During the Korean War more than 120,000 women served on active duty, caring for the wounded, planning strategy, and flying air evacuation, among other things.

1	POUND GROUND BEEF		1	TEASPOON GARLIC POWDER
½	CUP CHOPPED ONION		1	EGG
¼	CUP THINLY SLICED GREEN ONIONS		1	PACKAGE WONTON WRAPPERS (ROUND)
2	TABLESPOONS GRATED CARROT			WATER
⅛	TEASPOON SESAME OIL			VEGETABLE OIL

In a large bowl combine the ground beef, onions, carrot, seasonings, and egg; mix well. Place 1 tablespoon of the meat mixture on half of each wonton wrapper. Use your finger to wet the outer edge of each wonton wrapper; fold over; and seal by pressing the edges together. In a large skillet heat 1½ inches of oil to a temperature of 300°F to 325°F and fry until browned. Remove the fried yaki mandu to a paper-lined plate to drain.

MAKES 4 TO 6 SERVINGS.

THEY SERVED AT HOME AS WELL.

THE MILITARY WIVES' COOKBOOK

BULKOKI
(KOREAN BARBECUE)
★ ★ ★ ★ ★

Among them was Captain Lillian Kinkela Keil, quite possibly the most decorated woman in the U.S. military. A member of the Air Force Nurses Corps and World War II veteran, she had more than two hundred air evacuation missions to her credit as well as twenty-five transatlantic flights.

4	POUNDS SIRLOIN	3	TABLESPOONS GINGER ROOT, GRATED
¼	CUP RICE WINE	1	LARGE ONION, GRATED
1½	CUPS SOY SAUCE	¼	CUP THINLY SLICED GREEN ONION
¼	CUP FIRMLY PACKED BROWN SUGAR		PINCH CHINESE 5 SPICE SEASONING
2	TABLESPOONS SESAME OIL		PINCH CAYENNE
5	CLOVES GARLIC, CRUSHED	¼	CUP SESAME SEEDS, LIGHTLY TOASTED AND DIVIDED

This recipe may be cooked on the grill, which is delicious, or pan-fried. If you are grilling the meat, you may leave the sirloin whole and cut the meat in thin slices after it is cooked. However, if you pan-fry the meat, cut it across the grain into thin slices prior to cooking. Wash the meat under cold running water and prepare it according to the cooking method you will use. Place the meat with all remaining ingredients, including half of the sesame seeds, into a sealed plastic bag. Marinate it for 24 to 48 hours.

Cook to well done, sprinkle with the remaining sesame seeds, and serve with sticky rice and Korean bean sprout salad.

MAKES 4 TO 6 SERVINGS.

SOOK CHOO NA-MOOL
(BEAN SPROUT SALAD)
★★★★★

When the Korean conflict erupted, Captain Lillian Kinkela Keil returned to active duty and flew several hundred more missions as a flight nurse in Korea. Her decorations include the European Theater of Operations with Four Battle Stars, the Air Medal with Three Oak Leaf Clusters, the Presidential Unit Citation with One Oak Leaf Cluster, the Korean Service Medal with Seven Battle Stars, the American Campaign Medal, the United Defense Medal, and Presidential Citation, Republic of Korea.

3	CUPS FRESH BEAN SPROUTS	3	TABLESPOONS SOY SAUCE
¼	CUP THINLY SLICED GREEN ONION, INCLUDE TOPS	1	TEASPOON SESAME OIL
2	CLOVES GARLIC, MINCED	1	TABLESPOON RICE VINEGAR
1	TABLESPOON SESAME SEEDS	⅛	TEASPOON CAYENNE PEPPER

Blanche the bean sprouts in boiling water until slightly soft. Drain and immediately plunge in cold water to stop the cooking process. Set aside to drain. In a mixing bowl combine the remaining ingredients. Add the sprouts, toss lightly, and serve well chilled.

MAKES 4 TO 6 SERVINGS.

"THE CITY EXPLODED INTO A SINGING, DANCING PARTY. . . . A GLORIOUS CELEBRATION," AGNES ROTHMAN HERSEY, WAVE, DESCRIBING V-J DAY AND "THE OVERWHELMING JOY OF KNOWING THE WAR WAS OVER."

THE MILITARY WIVES' COOKBOOK

Annabelle Robertson:
INPSIRING OTHERS THROUGH HUMOR

My friend Annabelle Robertson is the author of *The Southern Girl's Guide to Surviving the Newlywed Years: How to Stay Sane Once You've Caught Your Man* and winner of the 2006 USA Best Books Award for humor. We met at Vandenberg Air Force Base like most military spouses meet—during a period of transition. One day after church services, Annabelle and I discovered that we had much in common. Both of us are relatively new Junior League members, lawyers, French-speaking, published authors, and attend the same authors' book fairs. She attended the Cordon Bleu; I was a cookbook author who dreamed of doing the same. Where else but in the military service could two such birds of a feather flock together?

A military spouse who has adapted admirably to the mobile military lifestyle, Annabelle is also the recipient of multiple journalism awards from the Georgia Press Association. She is a full-time freelance journalist and author, writing for a wide variety of publications, including WebMD, the *Atlanta Journal-Constitution*, *Muscle and Fitness Hers* magazine, and Crosswalk.com. Annabelle speaks fluent French and Spanish and holds an undergraduate degree in philosophy and foreign languages from the Académie de Grenoble, a JD from the University of Geneva, and a master of divinity from Regent College in Vancouver. She practiced international corporate law for several years before becoming a writer.

The wife of a U.S. Air Force chaplain and the mother of two, Annabelle is an avid volunteer who has trained hundreds of church and chapel leaders throughout North America. She sits on the executive boards of the Vandenberg Spouse's Club and the Protestant Women of the Chapel at Vandenberg Air Force Base and is a member of the Santa Barbara Junior League. Annabelle is a popular speaker at military bases, chapels, clubs, and nonprofit organizations around the country, where she uses her talent for stand-up comedy to inspire people of all backgrounds.

HOME FOR THE HOLIDAYS
AND OTHER CELEBRATIONS

"I'll be home for Christmas, if only in my dreams."

"When George left America in December, my sister Allene, my daughter Molly and I settled at Leesburg with the children. This was to be our first Christmas in our own home and we women had decided to make it a gay one, at least for the babies. . . . On the door hung a lovely wreath . . . cross the wreath was a set of sleigh-bells tied with a big red bow. Then on Christmas Eve a wonderful thing happened—my husband flew in from the Pacific. When there is lead in your heart and it suddenly disappears, joy rushes in with such a force that it is almost unbearable. So I felt that Christmas Eve." [Katherine Tupper Marshall]

A Colonial Thanksgiving

⭐ ⭐ ⭐ ⭐ ⭐

Excerpted from a letter written by Juliana Smith to her cousin Betsey in 1779, this menu appears to be typical of early New England Thanksgivings.

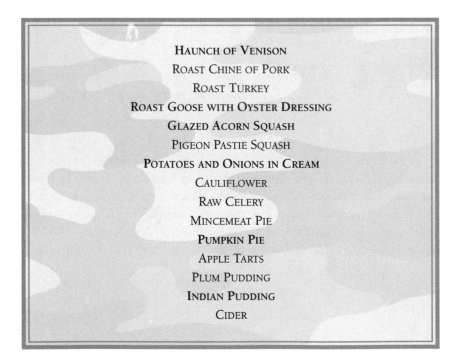

HAUNCH OF VENISON

ROAST CHINE OF PORK

ROAST TURKEY

ROAST GOOSE WITH OYSTER DRESSING

GLAZED ACORN SQUASH

PIGEON PASTIE SQUASH

POTATOES AND ONIONS IN CREAM

CAULIFLOWER

RAW CELERY

MINCEMEAT PIE

PUMPKIN PIE

APPLE TARTS

PLUM PUDDING

INDIAN PUDDING

CIDER

HAUNCH OF VENISON
★★★★★

"None of us have tasted Beef this three years back as it must all go to the Army, and too little they get poor fellows. But, Nayquittymaw's Hunters were able to get a fine red deer. So that we had a good haunch of Venison on each Table."

1	5- TO 6-POUND RUMP ROAST OF VENISON	¼	TEASPOON DRY MUSTARD
3	CUPS TARRAGON VINEGAR	¼	TEASPOON CHILI POWDER
1	TABLESPOON GARLIC POWDER	4	TABLESPOONS FLOUR
1	TABLESPOON ONION POWDER	8	TABLESPOONS BACON GREASE
2	TEASPOONS OREGANO	3	LARGE ONIONS, SLICED
1	TEASPOON MARJORAM	2	BAY LEAVES
½	TEASPOON THYME	1	PACKAGE DRY ONION SOUP MIX
½	TEASPOON BASIL	2½	CUPS BOILING WATER

Wipe the roast with a damp cloth and place in a large nonreactive bowl. Cover with tarragon vinegar and allow to marinade for 3 hours, turning often. While the roast is marinating, combine the remaining dry ingredients as a rub and set aside. Drain the venison, pat dry, and rub seasoning into meat. Rub with bacon grease. Place in an open roaster, cover with onion slices and bay leaf. Mix the onion soup with water and pour into the bottom of the roaster. Roast at 325°F 5 to 6 hours; baste every 15 to 20 minutes.

If the water boils away add an additional cup, but no more than that at one time. Cook until well done.

Remove to a warm platter and make a gravy from pan drippings by stirring in flour until desired consistency is reached.

YIELDS 8 TO 10 SERVINGS.

ROAST GOOSE WITH OYSTER DRESSING AND SAUCE
★ ★ ★ ★ ★

"There were forty people at the [Thanksgiving] dinner [and] Uncle Simeon was in his best mood. . . . He kept both tables in a roar of laughter with his droll stories." Roast goose has become an increasingly popular part of the holiday meal. Today's commercially produced geese have a thin layer of fat between the skin and the meat. This built-in baster keeps the dark meat moist throughout the roasting.

1	8- TO 10-POUND GOOSE	½	TEASPOON ONION POWDER
½	LEMON	½	TEASPOON GROUND BLACK PEPPER
1½	TEASPOONS SALT	3	16-OUNCE CANS OF CHICKEN BROTH
⅛	TEASPOON GARLIC POWDER		SHERRY FOR BASTING (OPTIONAL)

Preheat the oven to 425°F. Remove any excess fat from the inside of the goose. Wash the goose inside and out under running water. Dry the goose and rub the inside with the juice of a lemon. Combine the remaining dry ingredients and season the goose inside and out. Refrigerate the goose while preparing the oyster dressing (see recipe on the next page).

Once the dressing is prepared, remove the goose from the refrigerator. Spoon 1 cup of dressing into the neck cavity. Secure the neck flap with 2 or 3 poultry pins. Spoon the remaining dressing into the body cavity. Insert 5 poultry pins and use kitchen twine to lace the cavity closed, bootlace fashion. Bend the wing tips under the body and twine the legs together. Heat the broth and place in the bottom of the roasting pan. Place the goose in the pan with the broth, breast side down. Roast uncovered for 50 minutes. Pour off the liquid from the pan and reserve for future use. Turn the goose breast side up. Place a rack beneath the goose, and reduce the heat to 350°F. Roast uncovered for 20 minutes. With a fork, carefully prick the skin all over to release the fat. Continue cooking for 2½ hours. Prick twice more during the cooking period. Place the goose on a warm serving platter and allow to stand at least 20 minutes before attempting to carve. Pour off the drippings and degrease. Reserve the drippings for making gravy and sauces.

YIELDS 10 TO 14 SERVINGS.

OYSTER DRESSING
★★★★★

1	LOAF FIRM WHITE BREAD	¼	TEASPOON GROUND BLACK PEPPER
⅓	CUP BACON DRIPPINGS	1	PINT OYSTERS AND THEIR LIQUOR
2	MEDIUM ONIONS, CHOPPED	2	TABLESPOONS CHOPPED GREEN SCALLIONS, INCLUDING TOPS
2	STALKS CELERY, CHOPPED		
2	TEASPOONS SALT	4	STRIPS OF BACON COOKED CRISPY AND CRUMBLED

Remove the crusts from the bread, cube, and set aside. In a large skillet fry the bacon until crispy; then remove to a paper towel to drain. Add additional bacon drippings or oil as necessary to make ¼ cup. Sauté the onions and celery in drippings until the onions become soft. Stir in the breadcrumbs, then add seasonings. Transfer to a bowl. Drain the liquor from the oysters and reserve. Cut the oysters in half. Bring the reserved liquor to a boil. Reduce the heat to low; add the oysters and poach until the edges begin to curl. Drain and stir into the dressing. Add the remaining ingredients, mix well, and use to stuff the goose.

YIELDS STUFFING FOR 1 GOOSE.

OYSTER SAUCE
★★★★★

2	TABLESPOONS OIL	2	TABLESPOONS HEAVY CREAM
⅓	CUP DEGREASED GOOSE DRIPPINGS	1	TEASPOON WORCESTERSHIRE SAUCE
2	TABLESPOONS MINCED ONION	1	CUP FINELY CHOPPED OYSTERS IN THEIR LIQUOR
2	TABLESPOONS ALL-PURPOSE FLOUR		SALT AND GROUND WHITE PEPPER
1	CUP MILK		

In a skillet heat the oil and sauté the onions over medium heat. Stir in the flour, then add the drippings and whisk until smooth. Add the milk, stirring constantly. Once the sauce begins to simmer, add the cream and Worcestershire sauce. Add additional drippings or water to thin, if necessary. Add the oysters, and season with salt and pepper to taste. Serve with roast goose and oyster dressing.

YIELDS ABOUT 2½ CUPS.

POTATOES AND ONIONS IN CREAM
★★★★★

18	MEDIUM POTATOES, HALVED	4	TABLESPOONS PARSLEY
1	TEASPOON SALT	1	CUP HEAVY WHIPPING CREAM
½	CUP SLICED GREEN ONIONS, INCLUDING TOPS	1	TABLESPOON FLOUR
4	TABLESPOONS BUTTER, DIVIDED		SALT AND PEPPER TO TASTE

Place the potatoes in a large saucepan with water to cover by 1 inch. Add the salt and bring to a boil; cook until fork-tender, approximately 15 minutes. Take care not to over-cook. While the potatoes are boiling, place the green onions and 2 tablespoons of butter in a saucepan; sauté the onions over medium heat until tender but not wilted. Add the parsley; cook an additional minute and remove from heat. When the potatoes have completed cooking, place in a colander; rinse with hot water and drain. Place the cream and flour in a saucepan and whisk until the flour disappears. Bring to a boil; reduce the heat to low and add the remaining butter and potatoes. Simmer for 5 to 10 minutes, warming the potatoes through. Add the green onion mixture to the potatoes and season with salt and pepper to taste. Remove the potatoes to a warmed serving dish. Serve immediately.

YIELDS 10 TO 12 SERVINGS.

GLAZED ACORN SQUASH
★★★★★

Despite war-time conditions, there were vegetables, including "one which I do not believe you have seen. Uncle Simeon had imported the Seede from England just before the War began and only this Year was there enough for Table use. It is called Sellery and you eat it without Cooking."

1	SMALL ACORN SQUASH	**GLAZE**	
2	LARGE APPLES	6	TABLESPOONS MELTED BUTTER
2	CUPS BOILING APPLE JUICE	¼	CUP DARK BROWN SUGAR
1	TABLESPOON LEMON JUICE	¼	TEASPOON GROUND CINNAMON
½	TEASPOON GROUND CINNAMON		PINCH OF GROUND ALLSPICE
⅓	CUP UNSALTED BUTTER		PINCH OF GROUND NUTMEG
¼	CUP HONEY		
½	CUP FIRMLY PACKED BROWN SUGAR		

Preheat the oven to 375°F. Quarter the squash lengthwise; remove the seeds and fibrous material from the squash and discard. Pierce each squash piece with a fork several times. Pare, core, and slice the apples. Place the apples and squash pieces in a large baking dish. In a small bowl mix the apple juice with the lemon juice, cinnamon, butter, and honey; pour over the squash. Sprinkle evenly with brown sugar. Cover the pan tightly with aluminum foil and bake until very tender, approximately 20 to 25 minutes.

In a small bowl combine all of the glaze ingredients and use to baste the squash quarters.

Transfer the squash to a large cookie sheet. Prepare the glaze (see recipe below) and brush over squash. Bake the squash, uncovered, until it reaches a deep golden brown color, approximately 15 minutes. Baste occasionally with glaze. Transfer the squash to a platter or individual serving plates.

YIELDS 6 TO 8 SERVINGS.

PUMPKIN PIE
★ ★ ★ ★ ★

"All of the baking of pies and cakes was done at our house and we had the big oven heated and filled twice each day for three days before it was done. The Pumpkin Pies, Apple Tarts and big Indian Puddings lacked for nothing save appetite by the time we got around to them."

4	EGGS	½	TEASPOON GRATED NUTMEG
2	16-OUNCE CANS PUMPKIN FILLING	¼	TEASPOON GROUND ALLSPICE
1	CUP SUGAR	2	13-OUNCE CANS EVAPORATED MILK
½	TEASPOON SALT	2	UNBAKED PIE CRUSTS
2	TEASPOONS GROUND CINNAMON		

Preheat the oven to 350°F. In a large bowl combine the filling ingredients and mix well. Divide between the pie crusts. Bake at 350°F for 30 minutes or until a knife inserted in the center comes out clean,.

YIELDS 2 PIES.

" *M*any generations later, during a war which would put to the test a fledgling nation, Abraham Lincoln would proclaim the last day in November to be a National Day of Thanksgiving. 'In the trenches at Petersburg, Union cooks served up 120,000 turkey and chicken dinners to the men of Grant's great army. Dug in only yards away, the Confederates had no feast, but held their fire all day out of respect for the Union holiday.'" [*The Civil War*, Geoffrey C. Ward with Rick Burns and Ken Burns]

INDIAN PUDDING
★ ★ ★ ★ ★

"And it was GOOD, though we did have to do without some things that ought to be used . . . happily Uncle Simeon still had some spices in store."

3	CUPS MILK	½	TEASPOON GROUND NUTMEG
½	CUP YELLOW CORNMEAL	¾	TEASPOON GROUND GINGER
1	TABLESPOON BUTTER	⅛	TEASPOON BAKING SODA
2½	TABLESPOONS SUGAR	1	EGG
¼	CUP MOLASSES		MAPLE SYRUP
1	TEASPOON GROUND CINNAMON		

Preheat the oven to 300°F. Coat an ovenproof serving dish with butter and set aside. In a medium saucepan bring the milk to a boil and rapidly whisk in the cornmeal. Whisk continuously while the meal cooks for 15 minutes. Remove the pan from the heat. Add the butter, spices, sugar, and molasses. Remove approximately half of the cornmeal from the pot and mix in the egg. Return this mixture to the pot and whisk well. Pour into a baking dish and bake for 1 hour or until the center is set. Serve with heated syrup and butter.

YIELDS 6 TO 8 SERVINGS.

Christmas in the Confederate White House

✴ ✴ ✴ ✴ ✴

"For as Christmas season was ushered in under the darkest clouds, everyone felt the cataclysm . . . but the rosy expectant faces of our little children were a constant reminder that self-sacrifice must be the personal offering of each member of the family. At last quiet settled on the household and the oldest members of the family began to stuff stockings with molasses candy, red apples, and an orange.

For the President there were a pair of chamois-skin riding gauntlets exquisitely embroidered on the back with his monogram in red and white silk, made as the writer wrote, under the guns of Fortress Monroe late at night for fear of discovery." [*Excerpts from an article written by Mrs. Jefferson Davis for the* New York World, *Sunday, December 13, 1896]*

VARINA DAVIS

ROAST TURKEY WITH FRUIT GLAZE
ROAST BEEF
CONFEDERATE PLUM PUDDING
MINCE PIE
GINGER SNAP COOKIES
SPICED CIDER
EGG NOG

ROAST TURKEY WITH FRUIT GLAZE
★★★★★

"Our chef did wonders with the turkey and roast beef . . ." [Varina Davis]

1	18- TO 24-POUND TURKEY		1	GREEN PEPPER, SEEDED AND QUARTERED
4	TABLESPOONS SEASONED SALT		1	NAVEL ORANGE, QUARTERED
2	TABLESPOONS POULTRY SEASONING		1	APPLE, SEEDED AND QUARTERED
4	TEASPOONS GROUND THYME		2	CELERY STALKS WITH LEAVES, HALVED
3	TEASPOONS MEAT TENDERIZER		1	CUP ORANGE JUICE
3	TEASPOONS GARLIC POWDER			FOR THE GLAZE:
3	TEASPOONS ONION POWDER		1	16-OUNCE CAN CRANBERRY SAUCE
3	TEASPOONS GROUND PEPPER		½	CUP SEEDLESS RASPBERRY PRESERVES
2	TEASPOONS GROUND SAGE		1	TABLESPOON DIJON MUSTARD
½	TEASPOON GROUND PAPRIKA		½	CUP PORT WINE
1	LARGE ONION, QUARTERED		⅛	TEASPOON SAGE

Preheat the oven to 325°F. Remove the turkey from its packaging. Remove the giblets and neck; set aside for the giblet gravy. Rinse the bird under cold running water, pat dry, and then place it breast side up in a roasting pan. In a small bowl mix together the seasoning ingredients and thoroughly season the bird inside and out with the mixture. Don't forget the neck cavity and the back. Fill the neck and body cavity with the cut-up vegetables, fruit, and orange juice. Fold the wings under the body and tie the legs together. Cover the breast with an aluminum foil tent and roast approximately 15 minutes per pound.

Baste approximately every 30 minutes, and remove the foil after 1 hour to allow the turkey to brown. Check it often. Should it begin to brown too quickly, replace the foil and continue to cook.

To make the glaze, in a medium saucepan over medium heat combine the glaze ingredients and heat until liquid. During the last 30 minutes of cooking brush the entire turkey with glaze, and watch closely as the sugar will burn. Transfer to a platter for carving and allow to rest for 15 minutes. Save the pan drippings for gravy. If your turkey does not brown evenly, or is otherwise less than attractive, combine one can of chunky cranberry sauce with equal parts of pan drippings and sherry (not cooking) and use the mixture to dress the turkey and hide the flaws. Beautifully delicious!

YIELDS 8 TO 10 SERVINGS.

ROAST BEEF

★★★★★

". . . and drove the children quite out of their propriety by a spun sugar hen, life size on a nest full of blanc mange eggs." [Varina Davis]

2	CUPS BURGUNDY WINE		¼	CUP WORCESTERSHIRE SAUCE
½	CUP COGNAC		½	CUP VEGETABLE OIL
1	LARGE YELLOW ONION, COARSELY CHOPPED		1	4- TO 5-POUND BEEF TENDERLOIN
4	CLOVES GARLIC, MINCED		½	POUND FRESH MUSHROOM BUTTONS
¼	TEASPOON OREGANO		¼	CUP VEGETABLE OIL PLUS 4 TABLESPOONS UNSALTED BUTTER FOR SAUTÉING BEEF
½	TEASPOON ROSEMARY			
½	TEASPOON THYME		2	BEEF BOUILLON CUBES
1	TABLESPOON FRESH PARSLEY, MINCED		2	TABLESPOONS TOMATO PASTE
			½	CUP HOT WATER

In a nonreactive roasting pan combine first the burgundy, cognac, onion, garlic, oregano, rosemary, thyme, parsley, Worcestershire sauce, and oil. Wash the beef and pat it dry, place in the marinade and refrigerate overnight or up to 2 days. Turn often.

In a large saucepan over medium heat the oil and butter, taking care not to burn butter. Remove the roast from the roasting pan, reserve the marinade, and place the roast in the saucepan with butter and oil and brown.

Dissolve the bouillon cubes in hot water and mix in the tomato paste. Add the mixture to the marinade in the roasting pan and mix well. Return the beef to the roasting pan. Roast at 350°F for 30 minutes. Add the mushroom buttons. Roast for an additional 30 minutes or until a meat thermometer registers 140°F for rare roast or 160°F for a medium-rare roast.

YIELDS 6 TO 8 SERVINGS.

"Also in the Chief of Staff's heart there was happiness in the knowledge that his plan for the soldiers' Christmas would be carried through again. . . . Each soldier was to receive his Christmas turkey dinner with all its 'trimmings.' . . . A turkey dinner means home to an American soldier." [Katherine Tupper Marshall]

CONFEDERATE PLUM PUDDING
★★★★★

"The mince pie and plum pudding made them feel, as one of the gentlemen laughingly remarked, 'like their jackets were buttoned.'" [Varina Davis]

2	POUNDS GRATED OR SOAKED BREAD		1	CUP LIGHT CREAM
1	CUP BRANDY		½	TEASPOON BAKING SODA
6	EGGS, BEATEN		1	TEASPOON SALT
1	POUND CURRANTS		1	TEASPOON GRATED NUTMEG
1	POUND STONED RAISINS		1	TEASPOON GINGER
2¼	CUPS SUGAR			SPRAY OF HOLLY FOR GARNISH
1	POUND SUET, CHOPPED FINE			

In a large bowl combine the breadcrumbs, brandy, and eggs; add the remaining ingredients. If not sufficiently moist, add as much milk as necessary. Place the pudding in a "closed tin form" or greased, covered casserole. Cover and place it into a pot of boiling water. Boil 5 hours, adding more hot boiled water as the water boils away. Keep a kettle of boiling water on the stove for this purpose. Do not move the pot or the pudding will fall. When done remove from the heat and lift the casserole dish gently from the boiling water, remove the cover, place a round plate over the top of the dish and turn out the pudding onto it. Decorate with a small sprig of holly. Serve with hard sauce.

YIELDS 8 TO 10 SERVINGS.

HARD SAUCE

⅓	CUP BUTTER, SOFTENED AT ROOM TEMPERATURE		1	TEASPOON RUM EXTRACT
1	CUP CONFECTIONERS' SUGAR			

In a small bowl cream the butter until it is very soft, then stir in the confectioners' sugar and rum extract. Place in a cool place until required for use. Place on individual servings of plum pudding.

MINCE PIE
★★★★★

"There were no currants, raisins or other ingredients to fill the old Virginia recipe for mince pie. Apple trees grew and bore in spite of the war's alarms, so the foundation of the mixture was assured." [Varina Davis]

	PASTRY FOR A TWO-CRUST PIE	1½	CUPS PREPARED MINCEMEAT
2	SMALL APPLES, PEELED AND CORED	¼	CUP APPLE CIDER
¼	CUP SUGAR	1	TABLESPOON LEMON JUICE
1	TABLESPOON ALL-PURPOSE FLOUR	2	TABLESPOONS BUTTER, SOFTENED
¼	TEASPOON SALT	1	CUP FINELY GRATED CHEDDAR CHEESE
¹⁄₁₆	TEASPOON CURRY POWDER		

Preheat the oven to 425°F. Line a 9-inch pan with pastry. Set the remaining pastry aside for the top. In a medium bowl combine the remaining ingredients, and place in the pie shell. Adjust the top crust, cut vents, and flute the edges. Cover the pie edges with a 2- to 3-inch strip of aluminum foil to protect the edges from burning. Remove the foil during the last 15 minutes of baking. Bake in the preheated oven until the pastry is golden. Allow to partially cool on a rack and garnish with cheese before serving.

YIELDS 6 TO 8 SERVINGS.

GINGER SNAP COOKIES
★★★★★

"Crisp home-made gingersnaps and snowy lady cake completed the refreshments of Christmas Eve." [Varina Davis]

¾	CUP BUTTER	2	TEASPOONS BAKING SODA
¾	CUP SHORTENING	⅛	TEASPOON GROUND ALLSPICE
2¾	CUPS SUGAR	2½	TEASPOONS GROUND CINNAMON
2	EGGS	2	TEASPOONS GROUND CLOVES
½	CUP MOLASSES	2	TEASPOONS GROUND GINGER
4	CUPS SIFTED ALL-PURPOSE FLOUR		

Preheat the oven to 350°F. In a large bowl cream the butter and shortening until light and fluffy. Gradually add 2 cups of the sugar while continuing to cream the mixture. Add the eggs and molasses. Beat thoroughly. In a separate bowl sift together the dry ingredients. Gradually add the dry ingredients to the creamed mixture. Roll soft dough into balls 1 inch in diameter. Roll the balls in sugar and place on a baking sheet approximately 3 inches apart. Bake for 12 to 15 minutes. Remove the cookies from oven and allow to stand for a minute before cooling on a wire rack.

YIELDS APPROXIMATELY 100 COOKIES.

SPICED CIDER
★★★★★

"Cider seemed a blessed certainty, but the eggnog . . . [where] were the eggs and liquors to be procured?"
[Varina Davis]

2	TABLESPOONS WHOLE CLOVES		½	CUP FIRMLY PACKED BROWN SUGAR
2	TABLESPOONS WHOLE ALLSPICE		½	CUP SUGAR
6	CINNAMON STICKS		36	OUNCES APPLE JUICE
4	CUPS WATER			

Place the first 3 ingredients in a muslin or gauze "spice" bag. In a large pot simmer the water, sugars, and spice bag for 10 or 15 minutes. Add the juice and simmer an additional 15 minutes.

YIELDS 8 TO 10 SERVINGS.

"Christmas of 1944 was quite different from those of 1942 and 1943. In thousands of homes that Christmas, in spite of the empty places at dinner tables—many never to be filled again—there was thankfulness for the successes of our fighting forces and a prayer that our soldiers and sailors would soon be home." [Katherine Tupper Marshall]

EGG NOG
★★★★★

"After redoubled efforts, the liquor and other ingredients were secured in admirable quantities. Then the coveted egg nog was passed around in tiny glass cups and pronounced good." [Varina Davis]

12	EGG YOLKS, LIGHTLY BEATEN, WHITES RESERVED (SEE NOTE, BELOW)	2	TEASPOONS GRATED NUTMEG
2	CUPS SUPERFINE SUGAR	2	TABLESPOONS VANILLA EXTRACT
26	OUNCES BRANDY	2	QUARTS HEAVY WHIPPING CREAM
2	CUPS DARK JAMAICA RUM	12	EGG WHITES
2	CUPS WHOLE MILK	1	TABLESPOON FRESHLY GROUND NUTMEG

In a large bowl beat the eggs and sugar together until thickened. With a wooden spoon, beat in the whiskey, rum, and milk; mix well. Cover the bowl with foil or plastic wrap and refrigerate the mixture overnight. Just before serving, whip the cream until stiff peaks form. In a separate bowl, with a clean beater, beat the egg whites until stiff peaks form. Fold the whites gently but thoroughly into the whipped cream with a rubber spatula. Pour the eggnog into a chilled punch bowl; add the egg whites mixture and fold together until the egg whites disappear into the egg yolk mixture. Sprinkle with nutmeg just prior to serving.

Note: If you are concerned with using raw eggs, omit the eggs and substitute a gallon of vanilla or egg nog-flavored ice cream.

"The night closed with a 'starvation' party, where there were no refreshments, at a neighboring house. The rooms were lighted as well as practicable, someone willing to play dance music on the piano and plenty of young men and girls comprised the entertainment. The officers who rode into town with their long cavalry boots pulled well up over their knees, but splashed up to their waists, put up their horses and rushed to the places their dress uniforms had been left for safe keeping. They very soon emerged and entered into the pleasures of their dance with the bright-eyed girls, who many of them were fragile as fairies, but worked like peasants for their home and country. . . . The lessons of self-denial, industry and frugality . . . have made them the most dignified, self reliant and tender women I have ever known. All honor to them." [Varina Davis]

Kwanzaa

★ ★ ★ ★ ★

CHICKEN KEDJENOU (SEE THE RECIPE ON PAGE 93)

CUBAN YELLOW RICE (SEE THE RECIPE ON PAGE 95)

MOROCCAN TAGINE BUSROQUE

MOROCCAN BREAD

BRAZILIAN BLACK BEANS

SOUTHERN YAMS

MOROCCAN TOMATO AND HOT PEPPER SALAD

EGYPTIAN TOMATO SALAD

PECAN AND RAISIN PIE

HONEYED SWEET POTATO MUFFINS (SEE THE RECIPE ON PAGE 96)

MOROCCAN TAGINE BUSROQUE

★ ★ ★ ★ ★

Tagines, richly flavored, slowly simmered stews, derive their name from the tagine slaoui (an earthenware dish with a loose fitting conical top) in which they are traditionally cooked over a charcoal brazier. Charmoula is a wonderfully green-hued fish sauce, the primary component of which is a flat leaf parsley.

5	POUNDS FRESH MUSSELS, SCRUBBED AND DEBEARDED	¾	TEASPOON SWEET PAPRIKA
4	LARGE CLOVES GARLIC	½	TEASPOON CAYENNE PEPPER
¾	TEASPOON KOSHER SALT	½	TABLESPOON TOMATO PASTE
⅓	CUP CORIANDER LEAVES, COARSELY CHOPPED	¼	CUP OLIVE OIL
½	CUP FLAT LEAF PARSLEY, COARSELY CHOPPED	2	TEASPOONS CIDER VINEGAR
¾	TEASPOON GROUND CUMIN	2	TABLESPOONS LEMON JUICE

In a large, heavy saucepan steam the mussels over high heat, just until the shells open. Discard any mussels that do not open. Remove the mussels from their shells and set aside. To make the charmoula, mash the garlic and salt together by using the flat blade of a knife. In a blender or processor combine the coriander, parsley, garlic and salt mixture, and ⅓ cup of water. Blend until smooth, approximately 1 minute; pour into a medium-sized, nonreactive saucepan. Stir in the spices, tomato paste, oil, vinegar, lemon juice, and an additional ½ cup of water. Partially cover the pot and cook over medium heat an additional 5 minutes. Reduce the heat to low; simmer an additional 20 minutes.

Add the mussels; cover the pan tightly; remove from the heat and allow to stand for 30 additional minutes so the mussels can absorb the flavor. Just before serving gently reheat and adjust the seasoning, if necessary.

Serve with Moroccan flat bread and a dry rosè.

YIELDS 6 TO 8 SERVINGS.

BRAZILIAN BLACK BEANS
★★★★★

1	POUND DRIED BLACK BEANS	2	BAY LEAVES
¼	CUP BACON DRIPPINGS	1½	CUPS SMOKED HAM, DICED
1	LARGE ONION, MINCED	1	TABLESPOON VINEGAR
4	CLOVES GARLIC, MINCED		

Pick over the beans and soak overnight according to the package directions.

Prior to cooking, melt the bacon drippings in a large cooking pot and sauté the onion and garlic until the onion is soft. Drain the beans and rinse, then add to the pot with the onion and garlic. Add the bay leaves and sufficient water to cover by 2 inches. Bring to a quick boil and add the remaining ingredients. Stir and reduce the heat to low. Cover and allow the beans to simmer for 2 to 2½ hours or until the beans are tender. Check often and add additional water as needed to prevent sticking. Remove from heat and stir in the vinegar just prior to serving.

YIELDS 4 TO 6 SERVINGS.

SOUTHERN YAMS
★★★★★

8	SWEET POTATOES, PEELED AND QUARTERED	2	TABLESPOONS LEMON JUICE
1	TABLESPOON PLUS 1 TEASPOON LEMON JUICE	⅛	TEASPOON CINNAMON
¼	CUP BUTTER	½	TEASPOON GRATED NUTMEG
⅔	CUP SUGAR		

Place the potatoes in sufficient water to cover and boil until tender. When fork-tender, remove the potatoes from the pot and drain. In the same pot, melt the butter and add the sugar, lemon juice, and spices. Continue to cook over medium heat until the sugar begins to melt and bubble. Stir constantly to prevent scorching. When the mixture begins to thicken, remove the pot from the heat. Return the drained potatoes to the pot, coating with the glaze mixture. Serve immediately or transfer to a buttered glass baking dish and place in a warm oven until ready to serve.

YIELDS 6 TO 8 SERVINGS.

MOROCCAN TOMATO AND HOT PEPPER SALAD
★★★★★

2	GREEN BELL PEPPERS	3	CLOVES GARLIC, FINELY MINCED
2	YELLOW BELL PEPPERS	¼	TEASPOON GROUND CUMIN
2	CUCUMBERS, SEEDED AND DICED		SALT AND PEPPER TO TASTE
2	TABLESPOONS DICED ONIONS	¼	CUP OLIVE OIL
1	SMALL JALAPEÑO PEPPER, SEEDED AND MINCED	¼	CUP CHOPPED CILANTRO
¼	CUP FRESH LEMON JUICE		

Char the peppers under a broiler. Periodically turn the peppers until they are charred on all sides. Quickly place the peppers in a plastic bag and then tightly seal the bag. Allow the peppers to cool. The steam created in the bag will facilitate removal of the charred skin. Once the peppers have cooled, remove them from the bag; remove the charred skin; rinse the peppers, pat dry, and dice.

In a large bowl toss the vegetables together and add salt and pepper to taste. In a separate bowl combine the lemon juice, garlic, cumin, and olive oil and toss. Add the dressing to the vegetables. Refrigerate. Just before serving, add the cilantro and toss well.

YIELDS 6 TO 8 SERVINGS.

EGYPTIAN TOMATO SALAD
★★★★★

6	TO 8 TOMATOES, CUT INTO WEDGES	¼	CUP FINELY MINCED CILANTRO
⅓	CUP FRESH LEMON JUICE	⅓	CUP OLIVE OIL
1	JALAPEÑO PEPPER, FINELY MINCED	⅛	TEASPOON CAYENNE PEPPER
1	SMALL CLOVE GARLIC, FINELY MINCED		SALT AND PEPPER TO TASTE

Place the tomato wedges on an attractive serving platter. Combine the remaining ingredients and drizzle over the tomatoes. Serve at once or refrigerate until ready to serve.

YIELDS 6 TO 8 SERVINGS.

PECAN RAISIN PIE
★ ★ ★ ★ ★

1	CUP WHITE KARO SYRUP		½	TEASPOON VINEGAR
½	CUP SUGAR		2	TEASPOONS VANILLA EXTRACT
3	EGGS, SLIGHTLY BEATEN		1	TEASPOON GROUND CINNAMON
¼	CUP MELTED BUTTER		1	TEASPOON GROUND ALLSPICE
½	CUP COARSELY CHOPPED PECANS		½	TEASPOON GROUND CLOVES
½	CUP RAISINS		1	UNBAKED 9-INCH PIE SHELL

Preheat the oven to 350°F. In a medium mixing bowl combine all of the ingredients except the pastry; mix well and pour into the shell. Bake approximately 50 to 60 minutes until firm.

YIELDS 6 TO 8 SERVINGS.

GWENDOLYN HORISTON AND BEAU

A New Year's Day Buffet

★ ★ ★ ★ ★

"In one respect there never was a life such as ours; it was eminently one of partings." But in between, *"there were promotions to celebrate, an occasional son and heir to toast. Birthdays to celebrate so often"* and a New Year to be brought in! [Libbie Custer, Tenting the Plains]

GLAZED COUNTRY HAM

BAKED CHICKEN

SWEET POTATO CASSEROLE

COLLARD GREENS

BLACK EYED PEAS À LA CAROLYN

RICE

CORNBREAD STICKS

RED VELVET CAKE

SWEET POTATO PIE

PECAN PIE

CHAMPAGNE PUNCH

GLAZED COUNTRY HAM
☆☆☆☆☆

"We found our new quarters admirable for the garrison gayety. During the early part of the winter while the eggs we had brought from St. Paul lasted, Mary used to give us cake, frozen custard or some luxury of which these formed a part." [Libbie Custer]

1	WHOLE VIRGINIA OR SMITHFIELD COUNTRY HAM		WHOLE CLOVES SUFFICIENT TO GARNISH HAM
	WHOLE CLOVES	¼	CUP MOLASSES
10	WHOLE ALLSPICE	¾	CUP HONEY
5	WHOLE PEPPERCORNS	1	CUP CORNMEAL
1	CINNAMON STICK	¼	CUP FIRMLY PACKED BROWN SUGAR
2	WHOLE APPLES, PEELED AND QUARTERED	3	TABLESPOONS DRY MUSTARD
2	BAY LEAVES	½	TEASPOON GROUND ALLSPICE
¼	CUP FIRMLY PACKED BROWN SUGAR	¼	TEASPOON GROUND CLOVES
½	NAVEL ORANGE	⅛	TEASPOON GROUND CINNAMON
1	QUART APPLE CIDER		

In a large pot cover the ham with cold water and soak 24 to 36 hours before cooking. Drain the water from the ham. Using a stiff brush, scrub away any mold from the ham surface.

In a large kettle add the cloves, allspice, peppercorns, cinnamon stick, apples, bay leaves, brown sugar, and cold water to cover. Slowly simmer for 20 to 25 minutes per pound, or until the ham reaches an internal temperature of 150°F. Add the apple cider and orange for the last 30 minutes of cooking.

When the cooking time is complete, drain the liquid from the ham. Remove the skin while the ham is still warm, leaving the fat intact. Trim the excess fat and score the surface into diamond shapes. Place a whole clove in the middle of each visible diamond. In a small bowl combine the honey and molasses; brush all over the scored ham. In a separate bowl combine the cornmeal, brown sugar, mustard, allspice, cloves, and cinnamon; mix well and dust the ham with this cornmeal and spice mixture. Place the ham in a preheated 425°F oven long enough to glaze. Slice very thin. May be served warm or cold.

YIELDS 10 TO 12 SERVINGS.

SWEET POTATO CASSEROLE
★★★★★

"We thought no more of borrowing for any company or unusual festivity that we had, than if we had been making demands on our mothers or sisters living near. We lent our houses and everything in them for months at a time." [Libbie Custer]

5	CUPS COARSELY MASHED SWEET POTATOES	¾	TEASPOON GRATED NUTMEG
½	CUP FIRMLY PACKED BROWN SUGAR	3	TEASPOONS GROUND CINNAMON
½	CUP SUGAR	¾	TEASPOON GROUND ALLSPICE
1	CUP MELTED BUTTER	1	CUP PECAN HALVES
1	TABLESPOON VANILLA EXTRACT	½	CUP RAISINS
1¾	CUPS CRUSHED PINEAPPLE, DRAINED	2½	CUPS MINIATURE MARSHMALLOWS, DIVIDED (RESERVE 1 CUP FOR TOPPING)

In a large bowl mix together all of the ingredients except for 1 cup of the marshmallows reserved for the topping. Place the mixture in a well greased 11 x 7-inch baking dish. Bake at 250°F to 300°F for 30 minutes. Remove the casserole from the oven and sprinkle the remaining marshmallows on top. Place under a broiler to brown.

YIELDS 6 TO 8 SERVINGS.

COLLARD GREENS

★★★★★

"We had no locks on our doors, nor was ever a key turned in a trunk or on a closet, if we happened ever to have the latter luxury." [Libbie Custer]

¼	CUP BACON DRIPPINGS OR 4 TO 5 STRIPS OF BACON	1	POUND SMOKED HAM HOCKS OR SMOKED TURKEY WINGS
1	SMALL ONION, CHOPPED	4	POUNDS FRESH COLLARD GREENS, CLEANED

In a large pot heat the drippings or fry the bacon until drippings are rendered. If using bacon, remove it from the pot and reserve. Sauté the onion until soft; add the meat and sufficient water to cover. Reduce the heat to medium-low. Cover the pot and simmer for 1 hour.

Remove the stems from the collard leaves. Stack 7 or 8 leaves and tightly roll, cigar fashion. Cut into 1-inch strips and add to the pot with the seasoning meat. Cook an additional 45 minutes and check often, adding additional water as necessary to prevent scorching.

YIELDS 6 TO 8 SERVINGS.

"The servants knew that everyone was welcome to our things, so they did not even ask us; and if I recognized anything at a friend's house when the refreshments were served in the evening, there was a significant smile from the hostess as I ate with my own spoon and used a napkin with a big C in the corner."

CUSTERS' QUARTERS, WINTER

One of the pleasurable excitements of garrison or camp life was promotion. The lucky man . . . was instantly surrounded by his comrades, who after congratulating him, immediately proceeded to besiege him for a 'spread!' They daringly suggested how he should celebrate, and news went flying about as if they were a parcel of school boys. . . . At these celebrations we all made merry till the host despaired of getting rid of us . . . and though there was so little in that meagre life to celebrate with, that made little difference; it was only one more occasion of the many we rejoiced in for all to come together; and if by chance no one had a pair of shoulder straps to emphasize the accession to greatness . . . the host was decorated with the insignia of the rank cut out of white cotton and sewed on his fatigue jacket." [Libbie Custer, Following the Guidon]

Pomp and Circumstance: A Military Dining-Out
★ ★ ★ ★ ★

The dining-out has served the Air Force well as an occasion for military members to meet socially at a formal military function. It enhances the esprit de corps of units, lightens the load of demanding day-to-day work, gives the commander an opportunity to meet socially with their subordinates and enables military members of all ranks to create bonds of friendship and better working relations through an atmosphere of good fellowship.

The dining-out represents the most formal aspects of Air Force social life.

"We toast our faithful comrades
Now fallen from the sky
And caught by God's own hand
To be with him on high"

[Air Force Academy Protocol Office]

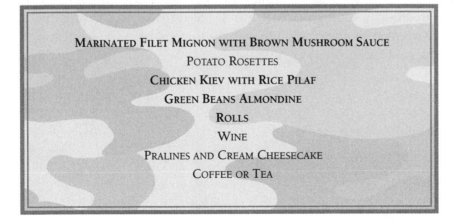

MARINATED FILET MIGNON WITH BROWN MUSHROOM SAUCE
POTATO ROSETTES
CHICKEN KIEV WITH RICE PILAF
GREEN BEANS ALMONDINE
ROLLS
WINE
PRALINES AND CREAM CHEESECAKE
COFFEE OR TEA

MARINATED FILET MIGNON WITH MUSHROOM SAUCE
★★★★★

The military dining-out evolved from the ancient tradition of the dining-in, the origins of which are unclear. However, it is clear that these formal dinners are rooted in tradition.

4	8-OUNCE FILETS, 2 INCHES THICK		4	TABLESPOONS BUTTER
2	TABLESPOONS DIJON MUSTARD		1	BOUILLON CUBE
¼	CUP RASPBERRY VINEGAR		1	CUP FRESH MUSHROOMS, SLICED (RESERVE 4 WHOLE CAPS)
2	CUPS SHERRY, DIVIDED			
½	CUP WORCESTERSHIRE SAUCE		1	TABLESPOON ALL-PURPOSE FLOUR
3	CLOVES GARLIC, FINELY MINCED AND DIVIDED		3	TABLESPOONS WATER
4	TABLESPOONS SHALLOTS, DIVIDED		1	TABLESPOON MINCED PARSLEY

Wash the filets under cold running water; pat dry and set aside. In a medium nonreactive bowl whisk together the mustard, vinegar, 1 cup of the sherry, Worcestershire, and half of the garlic and shallots. Place the meat and marinade in a large, sealed plastic bag and refrigerate overnight; turn often at regular intervals.

The next day, in a 9-inch skillet, melt 2 tablespoons of butter over medium-high heat. Remove the filets from the marinade and sauté for 2 to 3 minutes on each side for rare to medium meat; approximately 2 minutes longer for well done. Remove the filets to a hot warming plate while preparing the brown sauce. Add the remaining garlic and shallots; and quickly sauté. Deglaze the pan by adding the remaining sherry; mix well before adding the bouillon cube and mushrooms. In a cup combine the flour and water, mix well and slowly add to the pan while constantly stirring until thickened. Score the tops of the whole mushroom caps in a star shape. Return the filets to the pan to warm through before removing to warmed serving plates; top with mushroom sauce and garnish with minced parsley and scored mushrooms.

YIELDS 4 SERVINGS.

PINE RIDGE AGENCY, SOUTH DAKOTA, GENERAL MILES AND STAFF AT MESS.

CHICKEN KIEV
★★★★★

From ancient Roman legions to second-century Viking warlords to King Arthur's knights in the sixth century, feasts to honor individual and unit achievements, as well as military victories, have become custom.

4	LARGE CHICKEN BREASTS, SKINNED AND DEBONED	⅛	TEASPOON GARLIC POWDER
¼	POUND UNSALTED BUTTER	¼	TEASPOON WHITE PEPPER
2	TABLESPOONS CHOPPED CHIVES		FLOUR
2	TABLESPOONS CHOPPED PARSLEY		EGG
1	CLOVE GARLIC, MINCED		SEASONED BREADCRUMBS
¾	TEASPOON SALT		SHORTENING FOR FRYING
¼	TEASPOON ONION POWDER		

Place a breast between 2 pieces of waxed paper. With a mallet, pound to a thickness of ½ inch. Repeat the process with the remaining 3 breasts. Cut the butter in half lengthwise and crosswise to form four "logs" and set aside. Combine the chopped herbs with seasonings and roll each butter log in the mixture until thoroughly coated. Place 1 log in the center of each breast. Divide any of the remaining seasoning mixture among the 4 breasts and fold/roll the breasts envelope style (fold sides in first) so that the butter "log" is completely enclosed. Secure with a wooden pick, if necessary, but be sure to remove it prior to serving. Dust with flour, brush with egg, and roll in seasoned, dry breadcrumbs. Fry in 1½ inches of fat heated to 360°F until golden. Drain well on paper toweling prior to serving.

YIELDS 4 SERVINGS.

RICE PILAF
★★★★★

Some trace the origins of the dining-in to the old English monasteries. The custom was taken up by the early universities and eventually adopted by the military with the advent of the officers' mess.

1	CUP CHOPPED ONION	1⅓	CUPS CHICKEN BROTH
½	BAY LEAF	½	CUP WATER
2	TABLESPOONS BUTTER	2	TABLESPOONS CHOPPED FRESH PARSLEY
¾	CUP LONG GRAIN RICE		FRESHLY GROUND PEPPER TO TASTE
¼	CUP VERMOUTH	⅛	TEASPOON GARLIC POWDER

In a medium saucepan sauté the onions and bay leaf in butter until the onions are softened. Add the rice and continue to cook over medium heat, stirring constantly, until the rice is golden. Add the vermouth, broth, water, parsley, pepper, and garlic powder. Bring to a boil. Reduce the heat, cover, and simmer for 25 minutes or until the liquid is absorbed, or place in a covered casserole dish and bake for about 40 minutes.

YIELDS 4 SERVINGS.

GREEN BEANS ALMONDINE
★★★★★

British soldiers brought the dining-in custom to colonial America, where it was eventually adopted by George Washington's Continental Army. The U.S. Air Force dining-in tradition probably began in the late 1930s with "Hap" Arnold's "Wing-Dings."

1½	CUPS FRENCH-CUT FROZEN GREEN BEANS,		SALT AND PEPPER TO TASTE
2	TABLESPOONS BUTTER	½	CUP SLIVERED ALMONDS, TOASTED
½	TEASPOON FRESH LEMON JUICE		

Cook the green beans until crisp tender according to the package directions. Drain and remove to ice water to stop the cooking process. When the green beans are cold, drain again and refrigerate until ready to use. In a 9-inch skillet melt the butter and sauté the green beans to warm over medium heat. Season with lemon juice, salt, and pepper to taste. Garnish with almonds and serve immediately.

YIELDS 4 SERVINGS.

$\mathscr{E}$ven before the advent of the dining-out, there was no lack of celebration on the frontier, as evidenced by these two vignettes from frontier wives:

"Our little party was a grand success, but I am wondering how it came about that Mrs. Barker and I gave it together, for although we are all in the same company and next-door neighbors, we have seen very little of each other. . . . It was an easy matter to arrange things so the two houses could, in a way be connected, as they are under the same long roof, and the porches divided by a railing only, that was removed for the one evening. The dancing was in our house, and the supper was served at the Barkers'. And that supper was a marvel of culinary art, I assure you, even if it was a fraud in one or two things. We were complimented quite graciously by some of the older housekeepers, who pride themselves upon knowing how to make more delicious little dishes out of nothing than anyone else. . . . The chicken salad—and it was delicious—was made of tender veal, but the celery in it was the genuine article, for we sent to Kansas City for that and a few other things. The turkey galantine was perfect . . . and was composed almost entirely of wild goose! There was no April fool about the delicate Maryland biscuits, however, and the other nice things that were set forth." [Frances Roe, Fort Lyon, Colorado Territory, January 1872]

"The companies each gave a ball in turn during the winter, and the preparations were begun long in advance. There was no place to buy anything save the sutler's store and the shops in the little town of Bismarck, but they were ransacked for materials for the supper. The bunks where the soldiers slept were removed from the barracks, and flags were festooned around the room. Arms were stacked and guidons arranged in groups. A few pictures of distinguished men were wreathed in imitation laurel leaves cut out of green paper. Chandeliers and side brackets carved out of cracker-box boards into fantastic shapes were filled with candles at either end of the room, and we danced several times. One of the men whose voice was clear and loud sang the calls. . . . 'Oh swing those girls, those pretty little girls, those girls you left behind you!' . . . We were escorted out to the supper in the company room. . . . The general delighted the hearts of the sergeant and ball-managers by sitting down a bowl of potato-salad. It was always well-flavored with the onion, as rare out there and more appreciated than pomegranates are in New York. We ladies took cake, of course, but sparingly, for it also was a great luxury." [Libbie Custer]

ROLLS
★ ★ ★ ★ ★

The close bonds of friendship enjoyed by the Air Corps officers and their British colleagues of the Royal Air Force during World War II surely added to the dining-in custom. Later these events included family and friends and came to be known as dining-outs.

1	CUP WHOLE MILK, SCALDED		1	TABLESPOON HONEY
1	CAKE COMPRESSED YEAST		½	TEASPOON SALT
¼	CUP BUTTER		2	EGGS, WELL BEATEN
¼	CUP SOLID VEGETABLE SHORTENING		1½	CUPS ENRICHED FLOUR, SIFTED
½	CUP SUGAR			

Preheat the oven to 420°F. In a medium saucepan scald the milk and cool to lukewarm. Add the yeast and stir until dissolved. In a large bowl cream the butter with the shortening and gradually add the sugar, honey, and salt. Add the eggs one at a time, and beat well. Sift the flour and remeasure. Gradually add the flour, alternating with the milk mixture and mix well after each addition. Beat for 2 to 3 minutes after the final addition. Place in a greased bowl, cover with a tea towel, and allow to rise in a warm place for 1 hour or until doubled in bulk.

Cover lightly with plastic wrap and refrigerate until chilled.

Turn out onto a floured board; roll to a thickness of ½-inch and cut out the rolls with a biscuit cutter. Place in a greased baking pan, brush with melted butter, and allow to rise until doubled in size. Bake for 10 to 15 minutes or until golden.

YIELDS 6 TO 8 ROLLS.

MS. RUTH YEAGER, COLONEL BLACK, MILDRED SINGLEY,
AND BEVERLY WITHERSPOON.

The most common social occasion, still practiced in military service, is known as the hail and farewell, which welcomes arriving officers and spouses and bids farewell to those officers being reassigned to a permanent change of station (PCS):

"Last evening we gave a delightful little dance in the hall in honor of the officers and their wives who are to go, and the officers who have come. . . . There are two very pretty girls from the East visiting in the garrison . . . the mingling of the pretty faces and bright colored dresses with the dark blue and gold of the uniform made a beautiful scene. It is not in the least surprising that the girls become so silly over the brass buttons." [Frances Roe, Camp Supply, Indian Territory, 1873]

No, it is not surprising, in the least, that they would fall in love, marry, follow their husbands, and share in his love of country and commitment to service life—and yes, on sad occasion, become the girl they left behind.

THE MILITARY WIVES' COOKBOOK

A Valentine's Day Dinner for Lovers

★　★　★　★　★

ELEGANT BEEF WELLINGTON WITH MADEIRA SAUCE

WILD RICE WITH ALMOND SLIVERS

TOMATOES WITH HORSERADISH CREAM

BOW-TIE ASPARAGUS BUNDLES

CROISSANTS

BLACK FOREST CAKE

COFFEE

BRANDY AND CHOCOLATES

ELEGANT BEEF WELLINGTON WITH MADEIRA SAUCE
★★★★★

"Sarah my love for you . . . seems to bind me with mighty cables that nothing but Omnipotence could break, and yet my love of Country comes over me like a strong wind and bears me unresistably on with all of the chains to the battle field." [Sullivan Ballou, 1861]

4½ POUNDS BEEF FILET (12 INCHES LONG)	1 EGG
SALT AND PEPPER TO TASTE	SESAME SEEDS
BUTTER PASTRY (RECIPE FOLLOWS)	MADEIRA SAUCE (RECIPE FOLLOWS)
DUXELLES (RECIPE FOLLOWS)	

Preheat the oven to 425°F. Salt and pepper the beef to taste. If necessary, tie the small end under so that the filet is only 12 inches long. Place the filet on a rack in a shallow baking pan. Bake at 425°F for 30 minutes. Reduce oven temperature to 375°F and remove the roast from the oven. Allow to stand until cool. Trim away all excess fat. Roll the pastry to a rectangle large enough to wrap around the beef. The pastry rectangle should be about 9 x 14 inches, large enough to enclose the beef. Spread the pastry with duxelles, leaving a 1-inch border uncovered. Place meat in the center, topside down, and fold pastry over the meat. Dip fingers in water and run along the seams; press in place to seal. Trim the excess pastry from the ends, so that a single layer covers the ends of the roast. Place the roast seam side down in a shallow, buttered baking pan. Roll out the excess pastry and cut from it several leaves. Shape the remaining pastry into berries and vines. Use these designs to decorate the roast. Using a sharp knife, cut several slits around the designs and prick the sides with a fork to allow steam to escape. In a small bowl combine the egg with 1 table-spoon of water. Using a pastry brush, apply the egg mixture to the pastry. Sprinkle with sesame seeds. Sixty-five minutes before serving, place roast in a preheated 475°F oven and bake for 15 minutes. Reduce the heat to 375°F and roast an additional 30 minutes or until the pastry is golden brown.

Allow to stand for 15 to 20 minutes before serving. Using 2 spatulas, carefully transfer the roast to a heated serving platter. While the roast is cooling, reheat the Madeira sauce. After the roast has cooled, slice into 1½-inch servings. Spoon the Madeira sauce evenly onto the serving plates and top each with a portion of the tenderloin.

YIELDS 8 SERVINGS.

BUTTER PASTRY

3¾ CUPS SIFTED FLOUR

1 TEASPOON SALT

1 CUP COLD BUTTER, DIVIDED

2 TABLESPOONS SHORTENING

¾ CUP ICE WATER

In a large bowl combine the flour and salt; cut in the chilled butter and shortening. Add the ice water one tablespoon at a time. Gently mix to form a stiff dough; shape and refrigerate until chilled.

DUXELLES

1½ POUNDS MUSHROOMS, CLEANED AND FINELY CHOPPED

7 GREEN ONIONS, TRIMMED AND CHOPPED FINE

¼ CUP BUTTER

¼ TEASPOON SALT

½ TEASPOON MARJORAM

2 TABLESPOONS ALL-PURPOSE FLOUR

DASH FRESHLY GROUND PEPPER

¼ CUP BEEF BROTH

2 TABLESPOONS CHOPPED PARSLEY

½ CUP FINELY CHOPPED BLACK FOREST HAM

Over medium-high heat, sauté the mushrooms and onions in butter until the liquid is absorbed. Stir in the salt, marjoram, flour, pepper and broth. Continue to cook, stirring constantly, until the mixture comes to a boil and thickens. Remove from the heat; stir in the parsley and ham; allow to cool.

MADEIRA SAUCE

1 CLOVE GARLIC, CRUSHED

JUICE FROM ROAST AFTER THE FAT IS SKIMMED FROM IT

½ CUP BEEF STOCK

1 CUP MADEIRA WINE

SALT AND PEPPER TO TASTE

⅛ TEASPOON PAPRIKA

⅛ TEASPOON THYME

4 TABLESPOONS CORNSTARCH

4 TABLESPOONS COLD WATER

Rub a medium-sized saucepan with crushed garlic and discard the clove. Place the remaining ingredients except the cornstarch and water in the pan. Cook down for 5 minutes and season to taste. In a cup dissolve the cornstarch in water; mix well and add to the sauce. Allow to thicken over low heat. Refrigerate and reheat before use.

YIELDS 2 CUPS.

WILD RICE WITH ALMOND SLIVERS
★★★★★

"The memories of the blissful moments I have spent with you come creeping over me, and I feel most grati-fied to God and to you that I have enjoyed them so long." [Sullivan Ballou, 1861]

4	TABLESPOONS BUTTER	1	BAY LEAF
1	CUP THINLY SLICED GREEN ONIONS	2	CUPS WILD RICE
2	CARROTS, FINELY DICED	3½	CUPS BEEF BROTH (BOILING HOT)
1	SMALL CELERY STALK, FINELY DICED	1	CUP SLIVERED ALMONDS TOASTED
	SPRIG OF THYME		

In a saucepan melt the butter and sauté the vegetables in the butter for 10 minutes. Add the herbs, wild rice, and boiling broth. Cover and cook for approximately 30 minutes. Stir occasionally to avoid sticking.

While the rice is cooking, place the almonds on a shallow baking pan and bake at 400°F for approximately 5 minutes, or until golden. Check often to prevent scorching. When the almonds are sufficiently toasted, remove from the oven and set aide.

When the rice is done, drain away any excess water, and test for seasoning. Prior to serving, add the almonds and fluff. While the rice may be made a day in advance, the almonds should not be added to reheated rice until just before serving.

YIELDS 8 SERVINGS.

TOMATOES WITH HORSERADISH CREAM
★ ★ ★ ★ ★

"Never forget how much I love you, and when my last breath escapes me on the battle field, it will whisper your name." [Sullivan Ballou, 1861]

8	SMALL TOMATOES	½	TEASPOON DIJON MUSTARD
½	CUP WHIPPING CREAM		DASH OF SALT
1	TABLESPOON HORSERADISH		PARSLEY FOR GARNISH

Cut the tops from the tomatoes and hollow slightly, scooping out the seeds. Drain the tomatoes upside down.

In a medium bowl whip the cream until stiff. Fold in the horseradish, mustard, and salt. Fill the tomatoes with cream and garnish with a small sprig of parsley just prior to serving.

YIELDS 8 SERVINGS.

BOW-TIE ASPARAGUS BUNDLES
★ ★ ★ ★ ★

"But O Sarah! I shall always be near you: in the gladdest days and in the darkest nights . . . always, always, and if there be a soft breeze upon your cheek, it shall be my breath, . . . as the cool air fans your throbbing temple, it shall be my spirit passing by." [Sullivan Ballou, 1861]

40	FAT ASPARAGUS SPEARS, STALKS PEELED AND TRIMMED	⅓	CUP BUTTER, MELTED
8	THIN GREEN ONIONS	2	TABLESPOONS FRESH LEMON JUICE

Steam the asparagus spears in a vegetable steamer or on a rack over boiling water until tender, 4 to 5 minutes. Rinse underneath cold water to stop the cooking process and preserve the color. Dip the onions into boiling water until flexible enough to bend without breaking. Divide the asparagus into 8 bundles of 5 each. Place one onion beneath each bundle, wrap and secure with a double knot. May be made one day in advance, but do not add dressing. Just prior to serving, combine the butter and lemon juice and use to dress the bundles.

YIELDS 8 SERVINGS.

BLACK FOREST CAKE
★★★★★

"Sarah do not mourn me; think I am gone and wait for thee, for we shall meet again." [Sullivan Ballou, Camp Clark, Washington, July 14, 1861]

6	EGGS	1/8	TEASPOON GRATED NUTMEG
1	CUP SUGAR	1/2	CUP SIFTED COCOA
1/2	CUP SIFTED ALL-PURPOSE FLOUR	1/2	CUP UNSALTED BUTTER, MELTED AND CLARIFIED
1/2	TEASPOON GROUND CINNAMON		

Preheat the oven to 350°F. Grease and lightly flour four 9-inch layer cake pans and set aside. In a medium mixing bowl sift together the flour, cocoa, and spices and set aside. In a large mixing bowl stir the eggs and sugar for 1 minute or until just combined. Set the bowl over a saucepan containing 1/2 inch of hot water. Water should neither touch the bowl nor be allowed to boil. Place the saucepan and bowl over low heat for 5 to 10 minutes or until the eggs are lukewarm. Heating the eggs increases the whipping volume. It is unnecessary to beat the eggs continuously while warming. However, do lightly stir 3 to 4 times to prevent sticking. When the eggs feel lukewarm to your finger and look like a bright yellow syrup, remove the bowl from the heat. Beat at high speed with an electric mixer for 10 to 15 minutes, scraping sides of the bowl with a rubber spatula until the syrup becomes light, fluffy, and cool to the touch. It should triple in volume and look like whipped cream. Sprinkle the flour mixture on top of the whipped eggs a little at a time; fold in gently. Add slightly cooled, clarified butter (see below); mix well. Divide between pans and bake for 50 to 55 minutes or until the cake begins to pull away from the side of the pan and a tester inserted in the center comes out clean. Repeat this process to make 2 more cakes.

To clarify the butter, place it in a small saucepan and melt over high heat and continue cooking until the foam disappears from the top and a light brown sediment appears on the bottom of the pan, about 3 to 5 minutes. When the butter is clear, remove from the heat. Allow the milk solids to settle on the bottom of the pan. Skim the brown crust from the top of the clear butter; pour the clarified butter from the pan, leaving the sediment.

SYRUP

3/4	CUP SUGAR	1/3	CUP KIRSCH LIQUEUR
1	CUP COLD WATER		

In a saucepan combine the sugar and water; bring to a boil over moderate heat, stirring only until the sugar disappears. Boil briskly uncovered for 5 minutes. Remove the pan from the heat. When the syrup has cooled to lukewarm, stir in the Kirsch. Transfer the cakes to a long strip of waxed paper and prick each layer lightly with the tines of a fork. Sprinkle 3 of the layers evenly with the syrup and allow to rest for at least 5 minutes. Do not sprinkle the fourth cake.

FILLING AND TOPPING

4½	CUPS HEAVY CREAM		2	21-OUNCE CANS CHERRY PIE FILLING
¾	CUP CONFECTIONERS' SUGAR			MARASCHINO CHERRIES
¼	CUP KIRSCH LIQUEUR		1	8-OUNCE SEMI-SWEET BAR OF CHOCOLATE

In a large, chilled bowl beat the cream with a wire whisk or electric beater until it slightly thickens. Sift ½ cup of confectioners' sugar over the cream and continue beating until the cream forms stiff peaks on the beater. Add the Kirsch in a thin, steady stream. Beat only until the Kirsch is absorbed. To make chocolate curls for the top of the cake, chocolate should be at room temperature. Hold the chocolate bar over waxed paper and using a sharp vegetable peeler, shave the bar into thin curls. Draw a knife across the broad surface of the bar for wide curls and along its side for thin curls. Handle the curls with care and as little as possible for best results. Freeze or refrigerate the curls, which can be made a day ahead.

To assemble: place one cake layer on a serving plate. With a spatula, spread the cake-top with a ½-inch-thick layer of whipped cream and spread one-third of the cherry filling across the surface. Leave a ½-inch border surrounding the cake free from cherries. Gently build 2 more layers by repeating this process. Spread the sides with the remaining cream. Crumble the fourth layer into fine crumbs. Press the crumbs into the side of the cake all the way around the cake. Gently press chocolate curls into the cream and arrange a few curls and maraschino cherries on the top of the cake.

YIELDS 8 TO 12 SERVINGS.

JUNCTION OF THE MISSISSIPPI

ZOAVE BAND

Memorial Day Catfish Fry

★ ★ ★ ★ ★

"We wear yellow ribbons around our hearts every day;
because we know that every day a military family is separated
by time and distance while that military member stands watch at freedom's door."
From "United in Spirit," Author Unknown

FRIED CATFISH

HUSH PUPPIES

SHREDDED PORK

COLE SLAW

POTATO SALAD

SLICED TOMATOES AND CUCUMBERS

SWEET TEA

FRIED CATFISH
★★★★★

Throughout history, brave men and women have dedicated themselves to the proposition of preserving freedom and, when necessary, have died so that this great nation might live.

5	POUNDS CATFISH FILLLETS	½	TEASPOON CAYENNE PEPPER
2	CUPS CORNMEAL	3	EGGS, SLIGHTLY BEATEN
½	CUP ALL-PURPOSE FLOUR	¼	CUP BACON DRIPPINGS
1	TABLESPOON SALT	¼	CUP VEGETABLE OIL
2	TEASPOONS PEPPER		

Wash the fillets and pat dry. Lightly season with salt and pepper and set aside. In a shallow bowl combine the cornmeal, flour, salt, pepper, and cayenne. Dip the fillets in the beaten eggs, then in the cornmeal mixture. Place the fillets on a waxed paper-covered plate and refrigerate at least 1 hour prior to frying to allow the cornmeal coating to set. In a large cast-iron frying pan heat the bacon drippings and shortening to 370°F. The oil is sufficiently hot when a haze forms above the oil and a drop water can dance across the surface. Fry until golden brown and drain on paper towels. Serve immediately. The fish may also be fried in a deep fryer according to the manufacturer's directions.

YIELDS 6 TO 8 SERVINGS.

In 1913, a fiftieth anniversary reunion was held at Gettysburg. The climax of the event was a reenactment of Pickett's Charge.

At the proper moment, as the former rebels approached northern lines, they gave forth one last defiant rebel cry. At the sound of it, the Yankees surged the dividing stone wall as best they could considering their advanced ages. They then flung themselves at the advancing rebel charge, but not in the heat of battle. Rather, they embraced each other on the field of battle, reunited in brotherly love.

It is likely that at that moment, they turned to face the admiration of their courageous wives who also sacrificed and suffered in this struggle for the survival of our common ideals. And recognized in each other the true partnership that ensured a nation made great by sacrifice would long endure. It is very likely that they remembered also the moment of their first meeting.

HUSH PUPPIES
★★★★★

Therefore, "It is for us, the living, rather to be dedicated to the unfinished work which they have, thus far, so nobly carried on." [Abraham Lincoln, The Gettysburg Address]

¼	CUP CHOPPED ONIONS	½	TEASPOON ONION POWDER
1	CUP CORNMEAL	¼	TEASPOON GARLIC POWDER
1	CUP ALL-PURPOSE FLOUR, SIFTED	⅛	TEASPOON CAYENNE PEPPER
¾	TEASPOON BAKING POWDER	1	EGG SLIGHTLY BEATEN
½	TEASPOON SALT	⅔	CUP BUTTERMILK
1	TEASPOON SUGAR		VEGETABLE OIL FOR FRYING

In a large bowl combine the onions, cornmeal, flour, baking powder, salt, sugar, onion powder, garlic powder, and cayenne, and set aside. In a separate bowl beat together the eggs and buttermilk. Add the egg mixture to the cornmeal mixture and mix well. Drop the batter by heaping teaspoonfuls into hot (375°F) vegetable oil. Cook, turning frequently, about 3 to 5 minutes or until golden brown.

YIELDS 2 DOZEN.

COLE SLAW
★★★★★

"It is rather for us to be here dedicated to the great task remaining before us—that from these honored dead we take increased devotion to that cause for which they here gave the last full measure of devotion." [Abraham Lincoln, The Gettysburg Address]

1	SMALL HEAD OF CABBAGE, SHREDDED	1	TEASPOON SALT
2	MEDIUM CARROTS, SHREDDED	⅛	TEASPOON CELERY SEED
½	TABLESPOON COARSELY GRATED ONION	1	TABLESPOON CIDER VINEGAR
¼	CUP PLUS 2 TABLESPOONS HEAVY CREAM		
⅓	CUP MAYONNAISE		
2	TABLESPOONS SUGAR		

In a large serving bowl combine the cabbage, carrots, and onions. In a separate bowl combine the remaining ingredients, pour over the salad and toss lightly.

YIELDS 12 SERVINGS.

POTATO SALAD
★ ★ ★ ★ ★

". . .that we here highly resolve that these dead shall not have died in vain—that this nation under God shall have a new birth of freedom and that government of the people, by the people, for the people, shall not perish from the earth." [Abraham Lincoln, The Gettysburg Address]

4	LARGE POTATOES	2	CLOVES GARLIC, FINELY MINCED
½	CUP COARSELY CHOPPED BERMUDA ONION	¾	TEASPOON SALT
2	TABLESPOONS FINELY CHOPPED FRESH PARSLEY	¼	GROUND BLACK PEPPER
¼	CUP OLIVE OIL	2	TABLESPOONS SUGAR
3	TABLESPOONS VINEGAR		

Boil the potatoes until soft; drain and allow to cool. Slice into 1/4-inch slices and place in a large serving bowl. Add the chopped onion. In a small bowl combine the oil, vinegar, garlic, minced parsley, sugar, salt, and black pepper. Pour the mixture over the potatoes and onions and toss lightly. Season to taste with additional salt and pepper, and refrigerate. This salad is at its zenith when refrigerated overnight. Garnish with sprigs of parsley prior to serving.

YIELDS 4 TO 6 SERVINGS.

SWEET TEA
★ ★ ★ ★ ★

7	TO 12 TEA BAGS	LEMON WEDGES
3	QUARTS COLD WATER	MINT LEAVES
3½	CUPS SUGAR	

Place the tea bags and sugar in a heat-proof pitcher. Bring the water to a quick boil; pour over the contents of the pitcher and steep 5 minutes. Remove the bags and refrigerate to chill, approximately 1 hour.

Pour the tea over cracked ice into 8 tall glasses. Garnish with lemon wedges and mint leaves.

YIELDS ABOUT 10 SERVINGS.

A June Bride's Anniversary Dinner
★ ★ ★ ★ ★

"General Custer graduated at West Point just in time to take part in the battle of Bull Run. He came to his sister's home in my native town, Monroe, Michigan, during the winter of 1863, and there I first met him." [Libbie Custer]

Libbie's father, a judge, did not approve of the match. He knew the life of an army officer's wife to be arduous and sought to protect his only child from its hardships. However, he eventually relented and Elizabeth Clift Bacon and George Armstrong Custer were married in the Presbyterian Church in Monroe.

GARLIC SHRIMP APPETIZER
STUFFED FILET MIGNON WITH BROWN SAUCE
ROASTED POTATO FANS
GARDEN SALAD
STRAWBERRIES AND CREAM WITH MACAROONS

GARLIC SHRIMP APPETIZER
★★★★★

Delicate and refined, nothing in her background or experience could prepare Libbie for the hardships of frontier life, which she gladly endured to "follow" her husband and his regiment. Celebrations often occurred while the regiment was on the move.

1	POUND LARGE SHRIMP	¼	TEASPOON CURRY POWDER
1	CUP OLIVE OIL	⅓	CUP CHOPPED PARSLEY
12	CLOVES GARLIC, CRUSHED	1	TEASPOON MINCED CILANTRO
1	TEASPOON CAYENNE PEPPER		

Shell and devein the shrimp, leaving the tails attached. Wash the shrimp in cold water, pat dry, and place in an oven-proof dish. Mix the remaining ingredients and pour over the shrimp. Place in the refrigerator and allow to marinate for at least 2 hours.

Remove the shrimp from the dish, reserving the oil and seasonings. Place the dish containing the reserved oils and seasonings in a preheated 400°F oven until the oil begins to smoke, but make sure that it does not burn. Quickly remove the garlic, add the shrimp, and return to the oven. Cook until the shrimp are pink and opaque. Remove from the oven and drain.

Serve at once with wedge of lemon.

YIELDS 4 TO 6 SERVINGS.

STUFFED FILET MIGNON WITH BROWN SAUCE
★★★★★

On one such occasion, Mary, the cook who accompanied them, decided to prepare an impromptu celebratory feast on board a train on which the regiment was traveling. "When it stopped Mary went into town. Returning to the car stove which she discovered was filled with a deep bed of coals, she broiled us a steak and baked some potatoes." [Libbie Custer]

2	TABLESPOONS BUTTER, DIVIDED		2	8-OUNCE FILETS, 2 INCHES THICK
2	TABLESPOONS FINELY CHOPPED SHALLOTS, DIVIDED		¼	CUP DRY SHERRY
2	CUPS FINELY CHOPPED MUSHROOMS, (RESERVE 3 TO 4 WHOLE MUSHROOMS FOR LATER USE)		½	CUP DIJON MUSTARD
			¼	CUP BEEF BROTH
	SALT AND PEPPER TO TASTE			

In a small saucepan melt the butter and sauté 1 tablespoon of shallots over medium heat for 1 minute. Add the chopped mushrooms and continue to quickly sauté until nicely browned, approximately 1 to 2 additional minutes. (Recipe may be prepared 1 to 2 days in advance up to this point; tightly cover and refrigerate.) Cut a horizontal pocket into the meat from the side, forcing a pocket with a knife and your fingers. Keep the opening as small as possible. Stuff half of the mushroom mixture into each pocket. Close the opening with 1 or 2 toothpicks.

In a 9-inch skillet melt 1 tablespoon of the butter over medium-high heat and sauté the stuffed filets for 3 minutes on each side for a rare to medium filet. Remove to warm serving plates and remove the toothpicks.

BROWN SAUCE

A board covered with a clean white towel was placed across the couple's lap and served as an impromptu table.

Add 1 tablespoon of shallots to the skillet and sauté one additional minute. Deglaze the pan by adding wine and mustard, mixing to dissolve any caramelized bits. Add the beef broth. Slice the reserved mushroom caps and add to the sauce. Cook until the mixture is reduced to approximately ⅓ cup and spoon over the filets.

ROASTED POTATO FANS
★★★★★

"We did not dare move, and scarcely ventured to giggle, for fear we should overturn the laden board in our laps." [Libbie Custer]

2	LARGE BAKING POTATOES, PEELED	1/8	TEASPOON ONION POWDER
1/4	CUP MELTED UNSALTED BUTTER	1/8	TEASPOON GARLIC POWDER
1/4	TEASPOON SEASONED SALT	1/4	TEASPOON CRUSHED ROSEMARY

Cut the potatoes in half lengthwise. Place the rounded outside of the potato down in baking dish. Score the flat face of the potato diagonally and about halfway through with knife. Repeat the scoring in about ½-inch increments. Pour melted butter over the potatoes. In a small bowl combine the remaining ingredients and use to season the potatoes. Bake in the preheated oven (basting occasionally) for approximately 1 hour or until the potatoes are golden.

YIELDS 4 SERVINGS.

GARDEN SALAD
★★★★★

"We were so hungry that we scarcely realized that we were not the embodiment of picturesque grace. No one could be otherwise than awkward in trying to cut food on such an uncertain base, while Mary had taken the last scrap of dignity away from the general's appearance by enveloping him in a kitchen towel as a substitute for a napkin." [Libbie Custer]

	ARUGULA	4	HEARTS OF PALM, CUT INTO LENGTHWISE STRIPS
	RADICCHIO	1/2	CUP PITTED OLIVES, SLICED IN HALF
	BOSTON LETTUCE		ITALIAN DRESSING
	BIBB LETTUCE	1/2	CUP PARMESAN CHEESE

On a serving plate arrange the lettuce, olives, and heart of palm, and garnish with Parmesan cheese and chives to taste. Combine the olive oil and lemon oil and dress the salad just prior to serving.

YIELDS 4 SERVINGS.

STRAWBERRIES AND CREAM WITH MACAROONS
★★★★★

"For dessert, a large plate of macaroons was brought out as a surprise. Mary told me, with great glee, how she had seen the general prowling in the bakers' shops to buy them, and described the train of small boys who followed him when he came back with his brown paper parcel." [Libbie Custer]

2	CUPS STRAWBERRIES		½	CUP HEAVY CREAM
½	CUP SUGAR		¼	TEASPOON ALMOND EXTRACT
½	CUP COINTREAU		¼	TEASPOON VANILLA EXTRACT
½	PINT VANILLA ICE CREAM		½	CUP MACAROON CRUMBS PLUS 2 WHOLE COOKIES

Hull and wash the strawberries. Pat dry and place in a mixing bowl. Sprinkle the strawberries with sugar and Cointreau. Toss lightly to mix and refrigerate for 1 hour, stirring occasionally. Soften the ice cream at room temperature for 1 hour. Beat the heavy cream until stiff peaks form. Fold in the vanilla and almond extracts. Just prior to serving, divide the crumbs between 2 dessert dishes. Gently fold the whipped cream and softened ice cream into the strawberries, divide between dessert dishes, and garnish with a cookie. Serve immediately.

YIELDS 2 SERVINGS.

FOURTH OF JULY 1890s

Independence Day Pig Roast
★ ★ ★ ★ ★

"I long to hear that you have declared an independancy—and by the way in the new Code of Laws which I suppose it will be necessary for you to make I desire you would Remember the Ladies." [Abigail Adams]

"—I am apt to believe that [Independence Day] will be celebrated by succeeding Generations as the great Anniversary Festival. . . . It ought to be solemnized with Pomp, and Parade, with Shews, Games, Sports, Bells, Bonfires, and Illuminations from one End of this Continent to the other, from this Time forward for evermore." [John Adams, in a 3 July 1776 letter to Abigail Smith Adams]

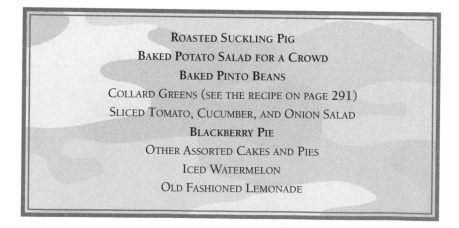

ROASTED SUCKLING PIG

BAKED POTATO SALAD FOR A CROWD

BAKED PINTO BEANS

COLLARD GREENS (SEE THE RECIPE ON PAGE 291)

SLICED TOMATO, CUCUMBER, AND ONION SALAD

BLACKBERRY PIE

OTHER ASSORTED CAKES AND PIES

ICED WATERMELON

OLD FASHIONED LEMONADE

ROASTED SUCKLING PIG
★ ★ ★ ★ ★

"We remembered the Fourth this morning as we rode breakfastless along and sighed for the roast pig and its concomitants with which those at home were celebrating the day." [Eveline M. Alexander]

1	10- TO 15-POUND SUCKLING PIG (1 POUND PER PERSON), SPLIT IN HALF AND PREPARED BY THE BUTCHER FOR ROASTING	1½	TEASPOONS FRESHLY GROUND PEPPER
15	LARGE CLOVES GARLIC	½	TEASPOON GROUND CAYENNE PEPPER
2	TABLESPOONS SALT	½	CUP FRESH LEMON JUICE
1	TABLESPOON ONION POWDER	¼	CUP FRESH LIME JUICE
¼	TEASPOON SAGE	¼	CUP ORANGE JUICE
½	TEASPOON GROUND CLOVES		CHARCOAL
			HICKORY CHIPS

One day prior to cooking, wash the pig inside and out under cold, running water and pat dry with a clean absorbent cloth. Mash the garlic and combine with the salt, onion powder, sage, cloves, and ground peppers to form a paste. Place the pig in a large roasting pan and rub inside and out with the garlic paste. In a small bowl combine the lemon, lime, and orange juices and pour over the pig. Cover with aluminum foil and refrigerate overnight.

About 30 minutes before cooking the pig, soak the hickory chips in water according to the package directions and ignite the coals in an open pit grill. Allow the coals to cook down for 30 minutes. Spread the chips evenly over the coals. Place the grating approximately 12 inches above the burning coals. Wrap the pig's ears and tail in aluminum foil to prevent burning. Place a small ball of aluminum foil in each eye socket to maintain shape. Place the pig, opened flat and skin side down on the grill. Allow 25 minutes cooking time for each pound of meat and turn every 25 minutes for even cooking.

During the last 2 hours of cooking, remove the foil from the ears and tail and baste with homemade barbecue sauce. Test for doneness by checking the pig's inner cavity for any pink spots. When done to an internal temperature of 185°F to 190°F and the juices run clear when the thigh is pierced with a fork, remove the meat to a large platter.

Join the pig halves together and allow to rest for 15 to 20 minutes prior to carving. Place cherries or cranberries in the eye sockets. At intervals, place toothpicks and clusters of grapes around the pig's neck.

YIELDS ABOUT 10 SERVINGS.

BAKED POTATO SALAD FOR A CROWD
★★★★★

"After breakfast we felt more cheerful. The whole command were asleep pretty much all day, which was hot, as the Fourth usually is. About noon, after we had taken a long nap, Andrew and I had a political meeting, or rather a social gathering at which, after describing imaginary surroundings, I called upon Andrew to respond to a toast. . . . 'A day to celebrate . . .' [he] began his address with great elegance. . . ."
[Eveline M. Alexander]

10	TO 12 RUSSET POTATOES, PEELED	3	TEASPOONS SUGAR
12	SLICES BACON, FRIED CRISP AND CRUMBLED	½	TEASPOON SALT
1⅓	CUPS THINLY SLICED GREEN ONIONS	⅓	CUP SWEET RELISH
7	HARD BOILED EGGS, CHOPPED	⅓	CUP DILL RELISH
¾	CUP MAYONNAISE	⅛	TEASPOON PAPRIKA
1	CUP SOUR CREAM	½	CUP FINELY GRATED CHEDDAR CHEESE
3	TABLESPOONS VINEGAR		

Scrub the potatoes under cold running water; place them in a large pot and cover with cold water. Bring to a boil over high heat. Cook until fork-tender, approximately 20 to 30 minutes. When the potatoes are done remove the pot from the heat, drain the potatoes, and set aside to cool. Remove their skins.

While the potatoes cook, prepare the bacon according to the package directions. Place the cooked bacon on a paper towel-lined plate to drain and set aside. Next, cube the potatoes and place in a large mixing bowl. Add all but ⅓ cup of onions, the eggs, mayonnaise, and sour cream. Dissolve the sugar and salt in vinegar and add to the potato mixture. Add the sweet and dill relishes, and gently mix. Add additional salt to taste and transfer to a serving bowl. Just prior to serving mix in the bacon and sprinkle the salad with reserved onions and cheese.

YIELDS 8 TO 10 SERVINGS.

FOURTH OF JULY CELEBRATION

BAKED PINTO BEANS
★ ★ ★ ★ ★

"We dined about seven: had tomato soup, wild turkey, beefsteak, green peas and canned peaches for dessert. On the whole we passed quite a comfortable Fourth and drank to its many returns in a large cup of lemonade." [Eveline M. Alexander]

4	CUPS DRIED PINTO BEANS	1	CUP MOLASSES
2	MEDIUM YELLOW ONIONS, COARSELY CHOPPED	3	TEASPOONS DRY MUSTARD
2	CUPS STEWED TOMATOES, CHOPPED	1	TABLESPOON CHILI POWDER
¼	CUP TOMATO PASTE		

The night before preparing, pick over the beans, removing any foreign objects, and soak overnight in a container with sufficient water to cover the beans by 2 inches.

The next day place beans and remaining ingredients in casserole. Add boiling water to barely cover and top casserole dish with a tightly fitting lid. Bake 6 to 7 hours, or until tender. Add additional water as necessary to keep the beans sufficiently moist. During the final 30 minutes of cooking, uncover the casserole and allow the beans to cook without adding additional water.

BLACKBERRY PIE
★★★★★

"There are blackberries in the fields so our boys and the Yanks made a bargain not to fire at each other, and went out into the field, leaving one man on each post with the arms, and gathered berries together and talked over the fight, and traded tobacco and newspapers." [Confederate Private, 4th of July, The Civil War]

4	CUPS FRESH BLACKBERRIES, DIVIDED	1	3-OUNCE PACKAGE CREAM CHEESE, SOFTENED
1	CUP WATER, DIVIDED	⅓	CUP CONDENSED MILK
1	CUP SUGAR	2	TABLESPOONS CONFECTIONERS' SUGAR
3	TABLESPOONS CORNSTARCH	1	BAKED PASTRY SHELL
2	TABLESPOONS LIME JUICE		

In a saucepan combine ⅔ cup of the blackberries and ⅔ cup of water in a saucepan and bring to a simmer. Allow the berries to simmer for 3 to 4 minutes. Strain the blackberries through a fine mesh strainer, pressing the berries with the back of a spoon. Discard the pulp and seeds and set the strained juice aside. In another saucepan combine the sugar, cornstarch, and remaining water. Stir until smooth; add the blackberry juice and mix well before bringing the mixture to a boil over medium heat. Continue to cook and stir until thickened, approximately 2 to 3 minutes. Remove from the heat and stir in the lime juice. Set aside and allow to cool.

While the mixture is cooling, combine the cream cheese, condensed milk, and confectioners' sugar in a small mixing bowl and beat until smooth. Spread this mixture evenly over the bottom and sides of the pie shell. Fill the shell with the remaining blackberries. Slowly the pour the glaze over the berries and refrigerate at least 1 hour prior to serving.

YIELDS 6 TO 8 SERVINGS.

Welcome Home, June 17, 2002:
BY ELLEN SPOSA-MARIA

It is quite an understatement to say that after September 11, everything changed. And for military families, our lives would be forever changed by the impact of the War on Terror. My husband and I had been married only a short time, so most of our marriage has been spent in a post–September 11 world. Now seven years later, my husband still proudly serves on active duty, and I try to reflect back to the time before September 11. But our reality has been subsequent deployments and now, frequent trips to Iraq and Afghanistan. Ironically, I can't really recall what "normal" life was like before!

My husband's unit, although due to deploy on its normal rotation to the Persian Gulf, was now called to leave early to support Operation Enduring Freedom and the early actions in Afghanistan. Our country was in turmoil, trying to grasp for some understanding of the horrible attacks that had occurred, and trying to identify how this all had happened. But for military spouses, we also had to deal with the fact that our spouses were potentially going into harm's way, and before they had to leave, they had too much to do, in too short a time. We really didn't have a lot of time to say good-bye.

How you deal with a deployment is a very personal decision. You can either move forward with life or dwell in the pain and anxiety of separation and the unknown. Getting into a routine and finding a support system is important for survival. Having a positive outlet for the range of emotions you experience is just as important as well. The treadmill became my best friend! And twenty-four-hour cable news, especially the coverage after September 11, became my enemy, fueling the anxiety heavy in my head and heart.

I found the most difficult time for me was at night. My days were both full and busy, with a career and responsibilities in our unit's spouses group. I have learned that being busy is just a distraction, and it can be a blessing and a curse. It allows you to function and go about your life, but it also suppresses your emotions deep within. I only came to this conclusion when a coworker commented to me halfway through the deployment how wonderfully I was doing, always having a positive demeanor. But I knew the real story. At night, once it was time to go to sleep, the stillness in the house was all consuming. That was the time when my heart hurt the most, when I felt most alone, and when I didn't think I would be strong enough to hold it together. There were moments when I would have given anything just to hear my husband's voice, or to hear the front door open when he came home from work. Night turned into day, and I kept putting one foot in front of the other.

After seven months, my husband's unit returned. As I waited in the designated location, I could see the ships far off the shore. I knew that my husband would be arriving by helicopter. And finally, off in the distance, one lone helicopter circled the field and landed. The unit's Commander stepped off, followed by my husband. We threw our arms around each other and held each other tightly. As the helicopter took off, the dust kicked up around us. There are no words to describe the emotions we felt at that moment.

REFERENCES

Alexander, Eveline, *Cavalry Wife: The Diary of Eveline M. Alexander, 1866–1867.*

Coffey, Thomas M., *HAP.* New York: The Viking Press, 1982.

Custer, Elizabeth Bacon, *Boots and Saddles.* Norman, Okla.: University of Oklahoma Press, 1966.

Custer, Elizabeth Bacon, *Following the Guidon.* Norman, Okla.: University of Oklahoma Press, 1966.

Fougera, Katerine Gibson. *With Custer's Cavalry.* Caldwell, Ida.: Caxton Printers, 1980.

Marshall, Katherine Tupper, *Together, Annals of an Army Wife* Tupper and Love, Inc., 1946.

Roe, Frances, *Army Letters from an Army Officer's Wife.* Bison Book, 1981.

St John, Betty Utley, *Excess Baggage, or Adventures of an Army Wife.* Hastings House 1943.

Totten, Ruth Patton, "The Army Wife's Heritage," *The Cavalry Journal Armor,* November–December, 1973.

PHOTO AND ILLUSTRATION CREDITS

xxiii: U.S. Army Military History Institute, David Charles Collection; xix: Fort Huachuca Museum; xix, 17, 41, 50, 262, 308: Library of Congress; xxxii: Ashley Elizabeth Tillery; 19, 22, 26, 28, 30, 32, 36, 103, 120, 179, 192, 264, 292, 295, 308, 318, 321: Denver Public Library, Western History Collection; 27: Fred Hulstrand, History in Pictures Collection, NDSU, Fargo, ND; 68: Army Military History Institute Collection; 129: Charles Foster Family; 138: Denver Public Library, Western History Collection, D. F. Barry Collection; 141: U.S. Army Military History Institute, Jeanette S. Maxey Collection; 152: Little Bighorn Battlefield National Monument; 158: U.S. Army Military History Institute, Christiancy Pickett Collection; 175, 176: State Archives and Historical Research Library, State Historical Society of North Dakota; 176: Massachusetts Commandery Military Order of the Loyal Legion and U.S. Army Military History Institute; 179, 196, 201, 203, 276: U.S. Army Military History Institute; 191, 229, 247, 287: Private Collection C.Q. Tillery; 198: Little Bighorn Battlefield National Monument; 220, 257, 300: Sheppard Air Force Base Heritage Center; 223, 224: Denver Public Library, Western History Collection, Collection of George Beam; 236: Edwards Air Force Base Historian's Office; 258: private collection of Mrs. Delores Quick

INDEX